ENRICO ALLIATA, THE DUKE OF SALAPARUTA,
(1879–1946) was born in Sicily. He studied music at the Conservatory of
Milan but eventually gave up music to study agriculture and run the family
wine business.

In 1824, Enrico's great-grandfather, Giuseppe Alliata ("Prince of Villafranca, Prince of the Holy Roman Empire, Grandee of Spain, and Duke
of Salaparuta") founded the Corvo wine company to produce gifts for
diplomats, ambassadors, princes, and noble ladies. Enrico later transformed
the family vineyard into a successful international business.

Among many interests, Enrico Alliata was a dedicated student of diet
and health. He wrote against the "dietary orthodoxy" of the day and advocated a vegetarian diet, which he believed could prolong human life to 130
years and which he called "absolutely regenerative."

To Alliata, however, vegetarianism was no impediment to a good meal:
he often hosted six-course vegetarian feasts, which he believed to be—
along with the house wine—a "solution to human happiness."

THE DUKE'S TABLE

THE
DUKE'S TABLE

The Complete Book of VEGETARIAN ITALIAN COOKING

BY Enrico Alliata, THE DUKE OF SALAPARUTA

Introduction by Antony Shugaar • Illustrations by Olimpia Zagnoli

MELVILLE HOUSE PUBLISHING
BROOKLYN · LONDON

THE DUKE'S TABLE

Originally published as *Cucina vegetariana e naturismo crudo: Manuale di gastrosofia naturista*

© 1930 Hoepli Editore, Milano   Introduction © 2013 Antony Shugaar
Translation © Sellerio Editore, Palermo   Illustrations © 2013 Olimpia Zagnoli
This edition © 2013 Melville House Publishing   Book design by Christopher King

First Melville House printing: March 2013

Melville House Publishing   8 Blackstock Mews
145 Plymouth Street   and   Islington
Brooklyn, New York 11201   London N4 2BT

mhpbooks.com

ISBN: 978-1-61219-139-3

Manufactured in the United States of America
1 2 3 4 5 6 7 8 9 10

A catalog record for this title is available
from the Library of Congress.

Contents

Getting

PART 1

Started

Introduction

BY ANTONY SHUGAAR

———

Enrico Alliata, born in 1879, grew up in Bagheria in one of the jewels of Sicilian architecture, the Villa Valguarnera. When the French novelist Stendhal visited the house, he wrote that its view "draws music from the soul, like a bow from a violin."

The Alliatas were a culinary family. Enrico's great-grandfather bottled a wine under the "Duca di Salaparuta" label. Enrico himself eventually took over the family wine business, bringing new production and commercial skills to the operation and expanding it into an international business. Today the family still controls lands in Contrada Corvo and Contrada Traversa and produces wine under the "Alliata" label. The Corvo Wine Company, an offshoot of the family business that was named by Enrico's father, is today the biggest wine producer in Sicily.

A look at the life of Duke Enrico—as Enrico Alliata, Duke of Salaparuta was known during his lifetime—reads like a who's who of twentieth culture and spirituality. Enrico was a fellow Palermitan prince to Giuseppe Tomasi di Lampedusa, author of one of the greatest works of Italian literature, *The Leopard*. He was married to Sonia Maria Amelia de Ortuzar Ovalle de Olivarez, a promising opera singer raised in Paris who studied under Enrico Caruso. His world also intersected with that of Jidda Krishnamurti, the world-famous Indian author and philosopher.

There is an age-old connection between vegetarianism and spiritualism that is hardly limited to the Mediterranean region, but it seems to have been particularly pronounced in Duke Enrico's case. Indeed, you can glimpse a blend of the ancient spirit of alchemy and the burgeoning industrial revolution in Enrico's ambitious fascination with the culinary conjuring trick he repeatedly performs here—proposing a radical new diet for Italy.

Duke Enrico begins his cookbook with the observation that all the food a person needs to live and thrive is a bowl of pasta with butter and some fruit on the side. Such a focus on grain and fruit is hardly surprising. The area surrounding Sicily's capital, Palermo, is known as the Conca d'Oro, literally, the "Golden Bowl," for its amphitheater shape and the profusion of citrus and other fruit trees that dot its slopes.

Red meat, in fact, has never been a major part of the diet of southern Italy. The ancient Greeks who colonized it looked on meat eating as a sign of barbarism. Sicily was also the breadbasket of the Roman Empire, a valuable cornucopia of wheat when bread was the very basis of political power. Nor was meat a major part of the diet of the Arabs who colonized the island in the Middle Ages.

In the tradition of the Kings of the Two Sicilies, who established pasta mills to better the conditions of their subjects, Enrico Alliata created his vegetarian cookbook (originally published in Italy in 1930 as *Vegetarian Cuisine and Natural Raw Food*) to explain to the farmers and peasants of Sicily, and of Italy at large, the economic and physical benefits of a vegetarian diet.

Indeed, according to his family, Enrico lived his life accustomed to the privileges of a world "he had cheerfully come to hold in contempt and detest," in particular the eating of meat. He early identified as a vegetarian, advocating vegetarianism in his writings as a question of ethics, diet, and health. And in this cookbook—the first vegetarian cookbook published in Italy—he implores his contemporaries to stop eating meat altogether.

He wrote from a city that had a culinary tradition that favored high-calorie, inexpensive foods: fried riceballs stuffed with chopped meat, the less-favored cuts and organs of livestock, cheap and savory street food, fritters and cannoli…

But the Moorish occupiers of Sicily had brought irrigation, citrus fruit, and scented infusions such as rose water and orange blossoms, and these resources—along with productive vineyards and an abundance of fresh vegetables—led Enrico to believe that all that meat was unnecessary. And his experimentations as a cook led him to believe that vegetarian substitutions could be used to re-create almost any classic dish.

His case is made herein: In place of meat kebabs, he offers "stuffed let-tuce" kebabs; as a substitution for clams in soup, he suggests a broth made from zucchini flowers, which "vaguely recall the flavor of seafood"; and to replace beef and pork, he offers all manner of techniques to prepare artichokes, cauliflower and other delights for the grill.

Indeed, alchemy and ingenuity hover over every recipe in *The Duke's Table*. The book is not simply a collection of recipes; it is Enrico's elegant demonstration that a vegetarian cornucopia can be made out of the bounty that nature had showered on his sunny, verdant island.

A NOTE ON THE TEXT

The author of this book wrote for readers who were, in the main, confident cooks. And there were many confident cooks in Italy at the time the book was published. Alliata certainly presumed readers were confident adapting recipes on the fly. Note his use of relative quantities, for example "an equal amount of…" or "two parts potatoes, one part peas." He also trusted readers to use his recipes as a starting place for planning meals. He makes wide allowance for substitutions, and contemporary readers are encouraged to continue substituting for what is seasonally available at the grocery or farmer's market.

   The book has been modernized for the present edition, updating measures and oven temperatures for the modern kitchen or where a product called for is no longer available. In essence, however, the book remains as Alliata published it: a radical and unprecedented attempt to set down a vegetarian diet.

Cooking directions

———

1. The times on the chart are for one pound of vegetable unless otherwise noted.
2. The times are in minutes.
3. A range of time is given because cooking times vary due to the age and size of the vegetables. Vegetables are done when they are tender, but still crisp. (They should never be mushy.)
4. Steaming times begin when the water boils and creates steam.
5. Boiling requires covering the bottom of a pan with ½ to 1 inch of water. Use more water for whole, dense vegetables, such as beets, and turnips. Bring water to a boil before adding vegetables.
6. Some cooking methods are not recommended for certain vegetables. This is indicated in the chart by the abbreviation "NR."

VEGETABLE	STEAM	BLANCH	BOIL	OTHER
Artichoke, whole	30 to 60	NR	25 to 40	NR
Artichoke, hearts	10 to 15	8 to 12	10 to 15	Stir-fry 10
Asparagus	8 to 10	2 to 3	5 to 12	Stry-fry pieces 5
Beans, green	5 to 15	4 to 5	10 to 20	Stir-fry 3 to 4
Beets	40 to 60	NR	30 to 60	Bake 60 at 350°F
Broccoli, spears	8 to 15	3 to 4	5 to 10	Blanch, then bake
Broccoli, florets	5 to 6	2 to 3	4 to 5	Stir-fry 3 to 4
Brussels sprouts	6 to 12	4 to 5	5 to 10	Halve; stir-fry 3 to 4
Cabbage, wedges	6 to 9	NR	10 to 15	Blanch leaves, stuff and bake
Cabbage, shredded	5 to 8	NR	5 to 10	Stir-fry 3 to 4
Carrots, whole	10 to 15	4 to 5	15 to 20	Bake 30 to 40 at 350°F
Carrots, sliced	4 to 5	3 to 4	5 to 10	Stir-fry 3 to 4
Cauliflower, whole	15 to 20	4 to 5	10 to 15	Blanch, then bake 20 at 350°F
Cauliflower, florets	6 to 10	3 to 4	5 to 8	Stir-fry 3 to 4
Corn, on cob	6 to 10	3 to 4	4 to 7	Soak 10; bake at 375°F
Corn, cut	4 to 6	2 ½ to 4	3 to 4	Stir-fry 3 to 4
Eggplant, whole	15 to 30	10 to 15	10 to 15	Bake 30 at 400
Eggplant, diced	5 to 6	3 to 4	5 to 10	Bake 10 to 15 at 425°F
Greens, collard/mustard/turnip	NR	8 to 15	30 to 60	Stir-fry mustard greens 4 to 6
Greens, kale/beet	4 to 6	4 to 5	5 to 8	Stir-fry 2 to 3
Mushrooms	4 to 5	NR	3 to 4 in broth or wine	Stir-fry or broil 4 to 5
Onions, whole	20 to 25	NR	20 to 30	Bake 60 at 400°F
Onions, pearl	15 to 20	2 to 3	10 to 20	Braise in broth 15 to 25
Parsnips	8 to 10	3 to 4	5 to 10	Bake 30 at 325°F
Peas	3 to 5	1 to 2	8 to 12	Stir-fry 2 to 3
Peppers, bell	2 to 4	2 to 3	4 to 5	Stir-fry 2 to 3
Potatoes, whole	12 to 30	NR	20 to 30	Bake 40 to 60 at 400°F
Potatoes, cut	10 to 12	NR	15 to 20	Bake 25 to 30 at 400°F
Spinach	5 to 6	2 to 3	2 to 5	Stir-fry 3
Squash, sliced	5 to 10	2 to 3	5 to 10	NR
Squash, halves	15 to 40	NR	5 to 10	Bake 40 to 60 at 375°F
Squash, whole	NR	NR	20 to 30	Bake 40 to 90 at 350°F
Tomatoes	2 to 3	1 to 2	NR	Bake halves 8 to 15 at 400°F
Turnips, whole	20 to 25	NR	15 to 20	Bake 30 to 45 at 350°F
Turnips, cubed	12 to 15	2 to 3	5 to 8	Stir-fry 2 to 3
Zucchini	5 to 10	2 to 3	5 to 10	Broil halves 5

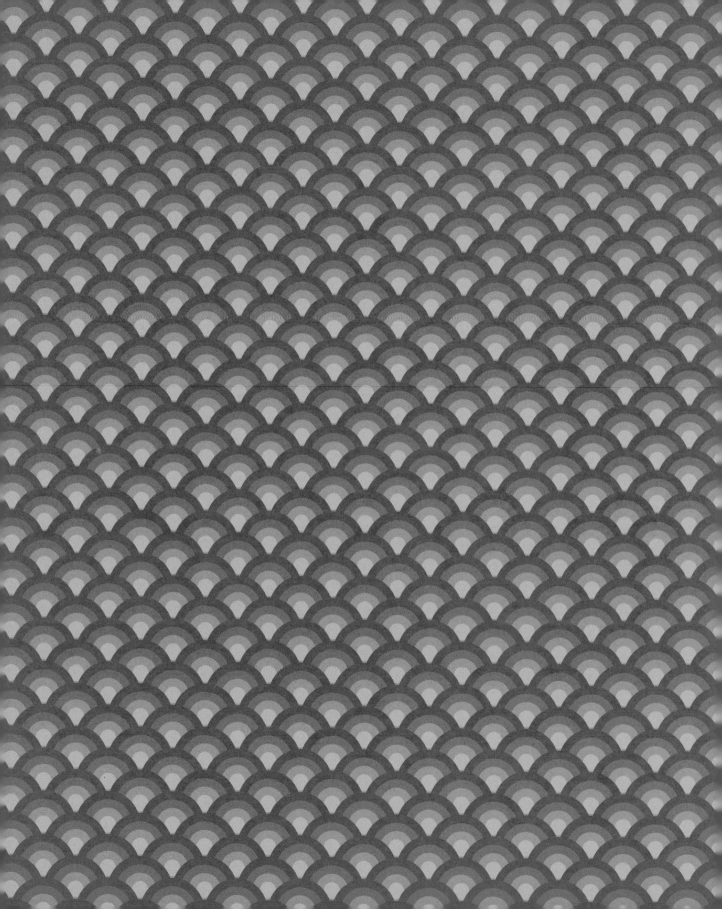

Author's foreword

Let us start by considering the word "vegetarian." First used in English in 1839 to describe a person eating an all-vegetable diet, the term has now come to refer to more than simply one's diet: It is an ethical regime of life in harmony with the laws of nature. It is a lifestyle that allows us to restore our original connection with nature and one that upends centuries of prejudices about food—that meat is required for sustenance, that plants do not contain the proteins necessary for a healthy life. Indeed, "vegetarian" describes a lifestyle concerned with the perfect success of the human body and of the body's harmony with nature.

Historic prejudices about diet have reduced human life expectancy to perhaps half of what it can be, which scientists currently believe to be more than 100 years. It is a mistake to believe that man cannot reverse this and take up a vegetarian regime. Science tells us that only a few basic elements are necessary for human nourishment: proteins, carbohydrates, minerals, fats, cellulose, and various vitamins and enzymes. Nature freely gives us all

of these elements in her golden fields of wheat, her multicolored orchards, her green vegetable gardens and fields of wildflowers from which the cow and the hen happily draw their nourishment, giving us the milk remaining after nourishing their young and the eggs that the hen cannot brood.

Man, abusing his power over animals, has forgotten a life in harmony with living creatures. An ethical life should not allow the destruction of animals by anyone other than nature itself. Man has no right to take away that which he has not given. Even less can he allow his fellow citizens to degrade their sentiments and their instincts in the slaughterhouse or the butcher's shop. Christianity at one time clearly expressed man's responsibility toward animals. In Chap I, v. 26 of Genesis we read: "Then God said: Let us make man in our image and likeness to rule the fish in the sea, the birds of heaven, the cattle, all wild animals on earth, and all reptiles that crawl upon the earth." To "rule" (or to "master," as other translations have it) does not mean to kill in order to satisfy one's appetite. Instead, this edict instructs us to use animals to do useful work in moderation, and to live with animals in a harmonious and productive way.

In origin, many religions have forbidden the eating of meat. In Eastern religions, animals have been the object of worship and respect. And the Old Testament documents the virtues of a vegetarian diet. In Genesis, God says: "I give you all plants that bear seed everywhere on earth, and every tree bearing fruit which yields seed: they shall be yours for food." But these ancient edicts have not led humanity to observe a vegetarian diet. What remains of these traditions are prohibitions such as penitence, fasting, and lent, with promise of spiritual rewards.

It is not just our harmony with nature that has been decimated by a diet consisting chiefly of meat: man has also reduced his natural life span and has burdened himself with serious physical ailments. He has interfered with the overall plan of the Spirit by sacrificing years of life. By following a diet consisting heavily of meat, man has been dragged into a state of degeneration. His goal should be the opposite: to refine life and elevate one's conscience. Let us return to our purest origins! This is the cry that must issue from our lungs for our own happiness and that of our children.

Medical science, too, finds itself paralyzed by outdated notions of a healthy diet, limited to the cure of illnesses already in course. Every day now new spas appear on the scene, sanitariums, and medical centers to treat nutritional problems. Many of these practice vegetarian cures in some form.

However, such delayed intervention can only serve to stop the degenerative process, and what has already been destroyed cannot be restored. Our only recourse is to sound the alarm so that we can recapture a long and healthy life. Man, in his transgression of laws of nature, has willfully sought transitory and senseless pleasures that are in opposition to what is right and healthy.

In taking up a vegetarian or naturalist regime, in addition to pure and healthy foods, one also finds everything needed to satisfy the most refined tastes. A dish of pasta with cheese and butter and a serving of fresh fruit contain all the nourishment needed by the human organism; but that does not mean that it is necessary to give up the pleasures of the table. For pleasure is not intended exclusively as the enjoyment of taste, but as that complex of satisfaction that serves to reconstitute the spirit. To restore the body with a simple meal when it is worn down must coincide with rest after intellectual exertion and with the opportunity to be together with family, friends, and colleagues.

But restoration of the body must not be an end in itself, that is, not a gross physical pleasure, but rather a means of restoring the body's energies so that the spirit may allow life to flow in its fullest, most joyous, and fertile expression. The active vegetative life and the reflective spiritual life are two indivisible expressions of the Spirit.

Religion has always known something like this: we see how the most solemn of sacraments are symbolized by bread, the staple of life, and administered during the supper. From the marriage at Canaan to the modern day wedding, even in the most modest family of peasants, marriage has always been sealed by a feast, as have the most important peace treaties between nations.

Even though man can draw all he needs in the way of nourishment from a mere handful of seeds and fruit, he must not give up, whenever possible, a proper meal. However modest it may be, it represents a moment of relaxation and happiness in life and allows us to reestablish the harmony between our physical being and our emotions. We should not eat our food without enjoying peace and serenity, and we cannot be happy without a healthy diet of pure foods, eaten in moderate quantity and in good company:

Mens sana in corpore sano.

This old Latin phrase—"A sound mind in a sound body"—is the essence of a vegetarian life. Old scientific theories claimed that man could not be healthy without meat. This has been destroyed by experience: It has been proven that man cannot only live, but live better, with only the products of the earth. It is sufficient to observe that the animals whose flesh so many eat are herbivores. If they are capable of carrying out elaborative life process by eating only grasses, we too can accomplish exquisite health exclusively through a vegetarian diet. It has also been demonstrated that humans can transform their diet. And once the body adapts to a vegetarian diet, eating meat will become repugnant, even in others. Thus it is untenable to maintain the utility of resorting to a lazy and degrading carnivorous diet, which is unworthy of the nobility of man, either in terms of ethics or of biological necessity.

The purpose of this book is to transform our diet—and, by doing so, repair our health, our culture, and our world.

—*Enrico Alliata*

Description and value of vegetarian foods

Cereals. This family includes the six grains: wheat, rye, oats, barley, rice, and corn, which represent the most important foods for human nourishment.

Wheat. This is the highest on the list for its content of gluten, vitamins, carbohydrates and minerals. It is also a nourishment of prime importance given its low cost.

Bread, which is the best manipulation of wheat, has been the object of infinite discussions concerning the various recipes and methods of baking. We shall not list the many and varied opinions, almost all of which are extremist, but we shall simply express ours, which falls in a middle ground. Since gluten and vitamins adhere to the outer husk, it is advisable to make whole wheat bread (including the bran) to benefit from the gluten and all the vitamins. However, together with the bran is the inert mass of fine bran that is more or less indigestible. Since a small quantity of inert mass is useful in the digestive process and

a reduced quantity of gluten and vitamins do not greatly decrease the nutritional value, we believe that the best compromise is a bread which is not made entirely of whole wheat flour, nor exclusively of the starchy part of the grain, but a simple brown bread. This is what our peasants made; in their age-old wisdom and taste they have concentrated on the preparation of this food, and have arrived at these proportions.

Pasta (another derivative of wheat). Under this label we include all types of macaroni, spaghetti, lasagna, served and seasoned in the most diverse manners throughout Italy. This excellent and popular food is of prime importance in vegetarian cooking, both for its low cost and its great nutritional value. Given the endless variety of seasonings that can be added to it, pasta can be eaten every day of the year for an entire lifetime without ever becoming monotonous.

Easy to prepare, there is no cook unable to serve up in half an hour's time an excellent dish of pasta with sauce or pasta in soup. A plate of pasta, seasoned with cheese and butter or with a choice of different sauces, is the most complete meal and the most economical. The wheat provides the carbohydrates, gluten, protein and cellulose, while butter provides fat, the taste and flavor; the protein in cheese is complementary to that in the wheat, and furnishes different energetic elements while sharpening the flavor. The manner in which pasta is cooked (especially in the south of Italy), in abundant water, and then drained, makes it much lighter and more easily digestible. Pasta is unjustly and notoriously considered as fattening. If you look at a Sicilian peasant who eats pasta every day, seasoned only with olive oil or cheese or tomato sauce, and no meat or animal fats, he is thin and resistant to the heaviest physical labors, whether under the boiling sun or in the cold of winter.

Sicilian peasants are strangers to obesity, but if we look at the leisured classes who indulge in the luxury of a main meat course, or season their pasta with sausage, beef, clams and animal fats, we see obesity and all the very serious consequences for their organism. Pasta, eaten in appropriate quantities alone or together with raw vegetable dishes, is not at all fattening, being easily assimilated and metabolized.

Rye. It comes immediately after wheat for its nutritional value. Being less rich in starch and having a unique and pleasant favor, it is commonly mixed with wheat to obtain a lighter, more flavorful bread that remains fresh longer.

Barley. This cereal is excellent nourishment. It has long been employed in old wives' remedies and as a laxative since the time of Hippocrates, who prescribed it frequently.

Oats. Both in the form of flour and flakes, which are popular in England and America, it is rich in minerals and phosphorus and is easily digestible. For this reason it is suitable for a child's diet, for the elderly and for those who are engaged in intellectual occupations.

It can be prepared in creams or in soups made with milk.

Rice. It would be a food of great nutritional value, but in industrial shelling and bleaching to make it smooth and white, it is deprived of its most important substances, reducing it to an inert starch. Today whole grain rice can be found which is almost as nourishing as wheat.

Corn. This is of high nutritional value. There are regions where peasants live only on corn made into polenta; in South America it is used in the form of *maizena* (it is first roasted, then ground to a fine powdery flour). This is the best way to use it because it is more digestible and extremely flavorful, especially in the making of cookies and pastries.

Eggs. Having been produced for the formation of a complete animal organism, an egg contains all the elements necessary for the life of that organism. We thus draw a minute quantity of this perfect complex of nutritional substances, both energetic and life-giving. An average egg weighs just above 2 oz; after the shell has been discarded, the yolk constitutes about ½ oz and the white about 1 oz. The white contains mostly proteins; the yolk is rich in fats and vitamins. From one to three yolks a day (the maximum allowed) represent excellent nourishment, and they should always be accompanied by fruit, vegetables and grains.

Legumes. These contain all the constituents of meat along with carbohydrates, minerals, vitamins and other beneficial substances, while the toxic substances of meat are totally absent. Lentils lead the list; then peas, after which beans, chickpeas, broad beans, etc. Unlike cereals, in the outer skins of dried legumes there are minerals that may be difficult to digest or cause flatulence if eaten in quantity. This does not happen with fresh legumes, especially peas, which are very digestible, even for the most delicate stomachs, besides being of excellent flavor. As an aid to the digestion of these insoluble minerals, a pinch of baking soda can be added to the legumes during cooking, and they may be put through a food mill to eliminate the outer skins.

Mushrooms and truffles. These deserve a discussion apart because this particular family of vegetables is unique in all its characteristics and the source of remarkable nutritional values. They contain abundant minerals and cellulose. In limited quantities they are of great utility and of superb flavor. Truffles, however, being very concentrated and expensive, must be used with moderation and only as a flavoring.

Milk. This food, provided by nature in abundance since the cow produces far more than is needed by her calves, is also of prime importance. It contains protein and other vital substances, all in a stable emulsion which is easily digestible. Being rich in calcium, it is a precious substance for children in that it aids bone formation. Fresh milk has the maximum nutritional value, when all its properties are fully efficient. The cow must be in good health and the teats well-cleaned before milking; likewise the hands of the milker. Boiled milk loses its energizing powers and is thus an incomplete food. Boiled milk is also an excellent drink, but it must be supplemented by other foods such as fruit, vegetables, etc.

Butter. Produced from pure cream, in its raw state it is light and digestible because it is derived from milk. In order to profit from its energizing properties and its aromatic quality, it must not only be uncooked, but fresh and made from pure cream.

Cheese. This is derived from curdled milk, and thus allows the extraction of the watery part, leaving, in a condensed mass, all the nitrogenous substances emulsified with the butter. It is thus a pure food, very rich in proteins, fats, minerals, and calcium. Cheeses made of double cream are excellent and nourishing because, before the milk has curdled, additional cream is added from other milk. Whole cheeses are those which contain only their own cream, without extracting or adding any other, and are also excellent. Last in the order of nutrition are low-fat cheeses, which have been made from skimmed milk after the fat has been extracted to make butter.

It is obvious that the double cream cheeses are the most nourishing, that the second are excellent and the last are best employed as a condiment.

Ricotta. This is derived from milk and is a product of great importance; it must be eaten fresh, and it is easy to recognize when it has gone bad because it takes on an acrid odor and acid flavor. It contains the same substances as cheese, but it is more digestible. A variety of dishes can be prepared with ricotta, including excellent light and nourishing sweets.

Oils and fats. Queen of oils is the extra virgin olive oil that is extracted from ripe olives as soon as they are picked; it must not exceed 2% acidity. Oil extracted from olives which have fallen from the tree and dried on the ground, or pressed from the pits, should not be used. Extra virgin oil is extremely light, a first-class fat especially for its vegetable origin. In addition to having a delicate fruity flavor, it is easily emulsified by the liver juices and thus easy to digest and assimilate. It makes it an excellent lubricant for the digestive tract. Oils extracted from peanuts, sesame, cotton seed and others, if refined, are also excellent for cooking. Coconut oil is also excellent for cooking on its own and is edible raw if mixed with butter which gives it flavor. All animal fats, which are heavier than vegetable fats and butter, are more difficult to digest, and they have a more or less nauseating flavor. They contain some of the toxins present in meat and can cause the proliferation of fat cells, thus favoring obesity due to their difficult assimilation.

Leafy and other vegetables. In particular, those which can be eaten raw are of maximum importance in the economy of our organism; in their uncooked state they are rich in vitamins and minerals and are an excellent energizing element, as well as a dissolvent of acids and toxins. The fear of infectious diseases picked up from raw foods is a mere prejudice because if our organism is weakened, it will always find enemies ready to attack whether or not we eat raw vegetables. With a vegetarian regime and a physically and ethically healthy life, the germs that may be present in raw vegetables or in any other food, even on the rim of a glass where a fly has rested, or on a slice of bread touched by a dirty hand, will be attacked and destroyed by our natural defenses when these have not been exhausted and weakened by the laborious digestion of meat products, which are an ideal environment for the cultivation of bacteria.

Salt is contained in our organism and therefore it is believed useful to replace the small quantities eliminated by the body. If used in excessive quantities, it is an irritant for the kidneys and the intestinal lining.

Spices and seasonings. If used only occasionally and in small doses, these are useful not only to flavor food. If used in excessive quantities, they act as irritants, provoking inflammation and serious damage to the urinary and gastric tracts. The most harmful of all is black or white pepper while cayenne and mustard are the strongest, but far less irritating. In any case, it is preferable to use as little as possible.

Sugar. This has a high energy content, concentrated in very small quantities, but also a high caloric content and can be absorbed rapidly without leaving any trace of waste. A small quantity taken after heavy physical exertion is sufficient to provide immediate energy. There is a great difference, which must be kept in mind, between inert sugars, neutralized by industrial refineries, and sugar which is contained in nature's products, such as fruit, roots, milk, honey, etc. This, in active combination with minerals and rich in vitamins, has greater energetic elements and is burned much more easily.

Fresh and dried fruit. Fresh and dried fruit (walnuts, almonds, peanuts, pistachios, pine nuts and nuts, etc.), as we have already said, are the most complete and rational foods for human nourishment. Together they contain every necessary nutritional element: proteins, carbohydrates, fats, minerals, and vitamins. Well-ripened fleshy fruit is both detoxifying and energizing, and is to be prescribed for feverish patients. It is better if fruit is eaten with the skin when this is thin and can be well chewed. Fruit is also useful as a tonic for the brain due to its high content of phosphoric acid and it serves as a dissolvent for uric acid with its high content of potassium and organic acids.

Vitamins. This active principle, of maximum importance for the economy of our organism, was known in Sanskrit as *prana*. Experimental science, in its endless effort to distinguish the true from the false (whereas the occult sciences in the Middle Ages fell into error), has ascertained by experimentation that this active principle is present in foods and that it is indispensable in nutrition, being the essence of life. Scientists have studied the benefits deriving from vitamins and have, at the present time, identified five classes, labeling them with the letters of the alphabet: A, B, C, D, E.

This denomination was given for the first time by Funk in 1911 and their alphabetic classification was determined according to the foods from which they were extracted and their specific characteristics. Thus vitamins of the A class were those identified in the green part of vegetables, in milk, butter and egg yolks. They are unaltered by cooking and their absence in the diet affects growth. Vitamins of the B group are found in the husk of cereals, in fresh and dried vegetables as well as in milk, yeast and bread. Those known by the letter C are to be found in fresh vegetables, fruit, milk, whole eggs and especially in citrus juices. They are sterilized by cooking and if lacking can be the cause of scurvy, Barlow's disease and other unidentified illnesses. While their absence causes serious harm to the organism, their presence stimulates the metabolism and generates vital energy. The vitamin D family is indispensable to avoid demineralization and is a protection against disease. The E vitamins abound in wheat, lettuce, cabbage, etc. and are useful for growth and reproduction.

Drinks. Excluding all alcoholic beverages, we can make a wide variety of drinks with various fruit juices, especially lemons, oranges and other citrus fruits which have great nutritional value. Other, more milky juices can be extracted from almonds, coconut, barley, etc. These are all beneficial to the healthy organism as well as to those who are ill and unable to eat solid foods.

Wine is derived from grapes, one of the best and most useful products of the vegetable kingdom. One of its components, sugar, is transformed (by bacteria) into alcohol. Our palate favors fine aged wines that can be recognized by their delicious natural bouquet. This is produced by the alcohol that is slowly transformed into ether in contact with the acid substances in the wine. A glass of excellent vintage wine aids the digestion and is beneficial to the entire organism.

Vinegar. The alcohol in wine, in contact with another bacteria, is transformed into acid. It can be used, instead, in cooking, because it evaporates at high temperatures. If employed with discretion in cooked dishes, only the aromatic elements remain. In salad dressings it is preferable to use lemon, which contains useful vitamins and adds a flavor of freshness.

PART 2

Appetizers and Salads

ANTIPASTI ED INSALATE

Crostini are small rounds of sliced (and sometimes toasted) bread—usually baguette, sometimes rye, focaccia, or sourdough—spread with a variety of toppings.

1. Crostini with truffles or mushrooms
CROSTINI DI TARTUFI O DI FUNGHI

Cream **3 tbsp butter** together with:

> salt
>
> fresh parsley
>
> a few drops of lemon juice

Slice a **baguette** in ½-inch slices, then spread with the butter and sprinkle with **black truffles** or **chopped fresh mushrooms**. Porcini mushrooms are ideal.

2. Egg crostini
CROSTINI D'UOVO

Slice a **baguette** in ½-inch slices and spread with **butter**. Chop **hard-boiled eggs** on a plate and press the buttered slices into the egg. Salt and pepper to taste.

3. Strong crostini
CROSTINI FORTI

Follow the above recipe, but first spread the bread slices with a **strongly flavored mustard**.

4. Cheese delectables
BOLI DI FORMAGGIO

With a fork, crush **hard-boiled egg yolks** in a bowl. Add **grated Parmesan cheese** and just enough **egg white** to be able to shape the mixture. Form ½-inch balls, and drop these into boiling water for a few seconds, then drain and let cool.

Serve on **cucumber slices** garnished with **mayonnaise** (see recipes 672 to 674).

5. Deviled cheese crostini
CROSTINI DI FORMAGGIO INDIAVOLATI

Slice a baguette in ½-inch slices. Melt **4 tbsp butter** in a skillet, and add:

> 5 tbsp grated Parmesan cheese
>
> a dash of cayenne pepper
>
> mustard (to taste)

Spread on **baguette** slices and enjoy.

6. Tomato crostini
CROSTINI DI POMODORO

In a skillet, melt **1 tbsp of butter**.

 Add:
 1 tbsp of tomato sauce
 2 ½ tbsp of grated Parmesan cheese
 a few drops of lemon juice
 chopped parsley

Slice a **baguette** in ½-inch slices and then spread with the tomato mixture.

7. Toasted butter crostini
CROSTINI TOSTATI AL BURRO

Slice a **baguette** in ½-inch slices and toast under the broiler, then spread with **butter** and salt to taste.

8. English crostini
CROSTINI INGLESI

In boiling water, blanch **4 tomatoes**. Peel, remove the seeds, and chop. Then place the tomatoes in a sauté pan on medium heat with **1 tbsp of butter** and let simmer until the juice has evaporated. Add **three beaten egg yolks**. Cook until the eggs are scrambled, then remove from the flame and add **1 tsp of Worcestershire sauce**. Spread this mixture on buttered **baguette** slices and close to form a sandwich.

9. Garlic crostini
CROSTINI AGLIATI

Toast ½-inch **baguette** slices under the broiler and then, while the bread is still hot, rub each with a peeled **clove of garlic** that has been cut in half. Place on a serving dish and cover each slice with a sauce made of:

 2 tbsp olive oil
 a few drops of lemon juice
 chopped parsley
 salt

A simple fettunta, or "greased slice," is a classic Italian appetizer and was once thought to be a remedy for worms.

10. Stuffed olives
OLIVE RIPIENE

For this dish use **large green olives in brine**. Remove the pits by crushing with a fork, but leave the olives as whole as possible. Soak the olives in fresh (unsalted) water for 6 hours, then stuff with the filling of your choice (for possible fillings, see pages 198 to 200) and sprinkle with finely chopped **parsley** and **oil**.

11. Peppered artichokes
CARCIOFI PEPATI

A simple recipe for 1 to 2 lbs of small artichokes. To begin, prepare the following cold sauce in a bowl by combining:

 3 hard-boiled egg yolks, crushed
 a few drops of lemon juice
 salt
 dash of cayenne pepper
 4 tbsp chopped mint leaves
 crushed capers

1 tsp of finely chopped onion

2 tbsp olive oil

Put the sauce through a sieve. Next, prepare:

6 to 10 soft young artichokes

Shorten the stems to 1½ to 2 inches. In an inch of salted water in a deep, covered pan simmer the artichokes on medium heat.

Remove when they can be pierced easily with a fork but do not come apart—about 15 to 20 minutes—then drain in a colander and let cool. Cut in half lengthwise, place on a platter, and garnish with the sauce.

12. Mayonnaise eggs
UOVA ALLA MAJONESE

A very simple appetizer. Hard boil, then cut **8 eggs** in half and cover with **mayonnaise** (see recipes 672 to 674). Garnish with **capers** and serve the eggs circled with slices of:

fresh tomatoes

cucumbers

green olives

13. Curried rice balls
PALLOTTOLINE AL CURRIE

Prepare **5 oz of white rice.** In a mixing bowl, combine:

2 oz of grated Parmesan cheese

2 tsp of curry powder

salt

finely chopped onion

1 egg

the rice

Mix thoroughly and form balls one inch in diameter.

Roll the rice balls in **flour**, then in **beaten egg** and lastly in **bread crumbs**, and, in a skillet, fry in olive oil. Serve with Worcestershire sauce. These are also excellent cooked in broth.

14. Egg sandwiches
LIBRETTE DI UOVA

Slice a loaf of **bread** into rectangles (1 by 3 inches) or 2-inch triangles and cover one side in melted **butter**. Before the butter solidifies, press the buttered slice into a dish of finely chopped **hard-boiled egg yolks**. Take another buttered slice and spread with **mustard**, then join the two, pressing them together in the palms of your hands.

To prepare ahead of serving, or using day-old bread: Wet a cloth napkin in water, wring it out and wrap the sandwiches after placing them side by side. Leave covered until serving.

15. Tomato sandwiches
LIBRETTE DI POMODORO

Follow the above recipe, substituting the chopped egg yolks for salted, finely chopped, peeled **fresh tomatoes** from which the seeds have been removed.

16. Watercress sandwiches
LIBRETTE DI POMODORO

Follow recipe 14 above, replacing the chopped egg yolks with finely chopped, lightly salted **watercress**.

17. Cheese sandwiches
LIBRETTE DI FORMAGGIO

Follow recipe 14 above substituting thinly sliced **Gruyère** or other fresh cheese of your choice.

18. Parsley sandwiches
LIBRETTE DI PREZZEMOLO

Follow recipe 14 above substituting:
> **finely chopped Italian parsley**
> **salt**
> **mustard**

19. Onion sandwiches
LIBRETTE DI CIPOLLA

As in recipe 14, but with chopped and salted **onions**.

20. Truffle or mushroom sandwiches
LIBRETTE DI TARTUFI O DI FUNGHI

As in the foregoing recipes, but with finely chopped **truffles** or **sliced raw champignons** and salt to taste.

21. Celery sandwiches
LIBRETTE DI SEDANO

As in the foregoing recipes, but with chopped **celery hearts** and salt to taste.

22. Vegetarian foie gras sandwiches
LIBRETTE DI PSEUDO-FEGATO GRASSO

As in the above recipes, but one slice of bread should be spread with a **vegetarian foie gras** (see recipes 545 to 547).

23. Mustard and ricotta sandwiches
LIBRETTE DI SENAPE E RICOTTA

As in the above recipes, but the bread slices should be pressed into a ricotta mixture. To prepare, combine:
> **mustard**
> **ricotta**
> **salt**

Then put the mixture through a food mill.

24. Lemon sandwiches
LIBRETTE DI LIMONE

In a warm bowl (that has been heated over boiling water) prepare a mixture of:
> **butter**

finely chopped parsley

salt

the juice of one lemon

Work the mixture with a knife blade for about 10 minutes. Finish by squeezing the last drops of lemon juice into the mixture and spreading the mixture on the **bread** of your choice.

25. Vermicelli salad
VERMICELLI ALL'INSALATA

Cook **16 oz fine spaghetti** or **vermicelli** (follow cooking instructions in recipe 232). Drain, rinse, and season with:

oil

a few drops of lemon juice

salt

pepper

chopped parsley

minced garlic

oregano

fresh mint

basil

Garnish with **olives**, **capers** or other ingredients of your choice.

26. 'Fidellini' and mayonnaise
FIDELLINI ALLA MAJONESE

Cook and rinse the **pasta** as in the above recipe. Prepare **mayonnaise** (see recipes 672 to 674).

Chop **two small heads of lettuce**—not iceberg—and sprinkle with salt and dry. Then add a **chopped cucumber** or, if you prefer, **boiled or grilled asparagus tips**. Mix with:

1 tbsp of capers

1 tbsp chopped pickles

parsley

mayonnaise

Add the pasta. Serve on a platter garnished with **cucumbers** and **capers**.

27. Homemade cheese
FORMAGGINI GERVAIS O
CREMINI IMPRONTATI

A simple recipe for homemade ricotta. In a medium pot, over medium heat, boil:

4 cups whole milk

2 cups of heavy cream

3 tbsp kosher salt

Stir occasionally as the mixture comes to a boil. Once the milk and cream begin to boil, turn off the heat and add:

3 tbsp white wine vinegar

As soon as you add the vinegar, the milk will begin to curdle and separate into thick parts (curds) and milky parts (whey). Transfer the mixture into a cheesecloth-lined sieve placed over a large bowl, and allow the mixture to drain at room temperature for 20 to 25 minutes, discarding the liquid as it fills the bowl. You can let the cheese drain longer if you prefer a thicker ricotta.

To serve: Spread the mixture over baguette slices. Alternatively, you can roll the ricotta in strips of waxed paper 2 inches wide and place in the refrigerator and serve cold. These rolled ricotta bites make an excellent summer snack, and may be made with sugar for a sweeter cheese, depending on your preference.

28. Tomatoes with mayonnaise
POMIDORI ALLA MAJONESE

Allow **two or more tomatoes per person**, preferably of the smooth round variety. Slice off the tops and scrape out the pulp with a spoon, taking care not to break the shells. Put a pinch of salt in each shell and set aside while preparing **mayonnaise** (recipes 672 to 674). When mayonnaise is ready, drain the tomatoes and fill with the mayonnaise, placing a few **capers** and a pitted **olive** on top of each.

29. The Queen's salad
INSALATA REGINA

In a large pot, in salted water, cook:
> **½ lb white beans (cannellini, navy, or great Northern), which have been soaked overnight**

Stop cooking when beans are soft, or just before they open, about 1 hour. Drain and set aside.

Chop **three or four small heads of garden lettuce**, sprinkle with salt and dry. Set aside.

Then boil together:
> **3 to 4 potatoes**
> **3 to 4 carrots, peeled**
> **2 artichokes hearts**

Drain and chop the above and add:
> **1 sliced cucumber, which has been salted and drained**

You can also add asparagus tips, capers, chopped parsley or other vegetables as you wish (if raw, they must be tender and should be salted and drained to soften).

Mix the above mixture with the beans and lettuce, add **mayonnaise** (recipes 672 to 674) and place on a serving platter, shaping in the form of a cupola. Garnish with **capers** and **sliced pickles**.

30. Russian salad
INSALATA RUSSA

This is a simple potato salad with beets. To prepare: In a large pot of water, boil **2 lbs potatoes.** Once the water is boiling, reduce heat and allow the potatoes to simmer for 10 to 15 minutes or until they can be pierced easily with a knife.

In a separate pot of boiling water, boil **1 lb red beets.** Again, once the water is boiling, reduce heat and allow the beets to simmer for 10 to 15 minutes or until they can be pierced easily with a knife.

Chop the potatoes and beets and, in a large bowl, mix together with enough **mayonnaise** (see recipes 672 to 674) to cover the salad. Chop a **pickle** or **boiled carrots** and add to the mixture. Garnish and salt according to taste.

31. Lettuce and egg salad
INSALATA DI LATTUGA ALL'UOVO

Prepare **3 hard-boiled eggs.** Remove the yolks and set aside the whites. In a bowl, crush the egg yolks and mix with:
> **salt and pepper**
> **a few drops of wine vinegar**
> **olive oil**

Serve this dressing on a **leaf lettuce** salad and garnish with the shredded or sliced hard-boiled egg whites.

32. Mixed vegetable salad
INSALATA MACEDONIA

Combine a variety of vegetables such as green beans, peas, broccoli, potatoes, asparagus tips, artichoke hearts, or beets. Pitted olives, pickles, capers, fresh herbs and chopped hard-boiled egg whites also go well in a simple salad. Use **mashed hard-boiled egg yolks** or **mayonnaise** (recipes 672 to 674) to bind, pouring over the vegetables before serving. Alternatively, you can dress with oil and lemon.

~~~~~~~~~~~~

33. Green beans with lemon
FAGIOLINI AL LIMONE

Cook **green beans** as in recipe 320, but substitute the milk with a small glass of **lemon juice**. Bind with **egg yolks** and **parsley**.

34. Raw cauliflower salad
CAVOLFIORI ALL'INSALATA CRUDI

Remove and discard the stalks from a tender white **head of cauliflower**. In a large bowl, dress the fleshy flowers with **lemon** and **cream** or **oil**. Salt and pepper to taste.

35. Steamed cauliflower salad
CAVOLFIORI COTTI ALL'INSALATA

After having washed and cleaned the **cauliflower**, steam it in a double boiler and then let cool. Chop into small pieces and season with **dressing** of your choice or cream.

36. Simple scones
SCONES

Makes about 16 scones. Heat the oven to 375°F. To prepare the scones, you will need:

> 5 cups (24 oz) flour
> 1/2 cup of frozen butter
> 1 1/2 cups milk
> 3 tsp baking powder
> a pinch of salt

In a large bowl, cut the frozen butter into the flour. Mixing thoroughly after each addition, add the baking powder a spoon at a time and then pour in the milk gradually. Add the salt.

Spread the dough on a pasty board or marble counter and roll out to 1/4 inch thickness, then cut the dough using the floured rim of a glass and place the scones on a greased baking tray. Bake for 10 minutes or just until the scones start to brown. As soon as the scones come out of the oven, break each scone in half, spread with butter and a pinch of salt, replace the top and serve.

37. Peas and potatoes
PATATE CON PISELLI ALLA MAJONESE

After steaming **potatoes** in a double boiler, dice them in 1/2-inch cubes and place in cold water to eliminate the excess starch. Drain and place in a bowl with **peas** that have been blanhced, drained and cooled. Use two parts potatoes to one part peas. Add:

> salt
> white pepper
> chopped parsley

Cover with **mayonnaise** (see recipes 672 to 674).

38. Green bean salad
FAGIOLINI ALL'INSALATA

After cleaning and removing the tips, boil **green beans** in salted water until tender but not over-cooked (they should remain a vivid green). When ready, drain and let cool, then dress with:

- olive oil
- lemon
- salt
- pepper

39. Beet salad
BARBABIETOLE ALL'INSALATA

First boil, then peel and slice **beets**. When they have cooled, dress them with:

- olive oil
- lemon
- salt
- pepper

40. Bean salad
FAGIUOLI ALL'INSALATA

Cook separately an equal quantity of **white beans** and **red beans**, then rinse and drain. When cool dress with:

- olive oil
- lemon juice
- salt
- pepper

Serve on a bed of **leafy green salad**.

41. Mayonnaise bean salad
FAGIUOLI ALLA MAJONESE

Cook **beans** as in the above recipe and season with **mayonnaise** (see recipes 672 to 674).

42. Baked onion salad
CIPOLLE COTTE ALL'INSALATA

Heat oven to 400°F.

Cut **2-3 large onions** into ½-inch slices. Place the onions in a baking pan and drizzle with olive oil. Bake for 30 to 40 minutes, turning occasionally, until onions are light brown. Season with **lemon juice** and serve garnished with **boiled or pickled beets** or **grilled peppers**.

For more salad ideas, see the "Raw Courses" chapter, pages 273 to 280.

Broths and purées

BRODI E PUREE

43. Vegetable broth
BRODO DI VEGETALI

One of the most useful things for a successful cook to have on hand is good broth. Even in the most modest homes, the preparation of broth is a necessary art. Vegetable broth is a nourishing, light base, easy to digest and almost totally lacking in toxins. But it takes at least an hour to make broth, and it is not easy, especially in certain seasons, to find the best ingredients. That said, any kind of homemade broth is preferable in taste to the various vegetarian broth and bouillon products that are sold in groceries. The recipes for broth contained in this chapter are but a small sampling of what is possible and can be modified to your taste, and according to what ingredients are easily available. You can make broth from old or leftover vegetables, and broth keeps in the refrigerator for several weeks and can be frozen (conveniently in ice cube trays) for several months.

44. Broth
BRODO

"Stock" traditionally refers to a broth made from animal bones, so the word is avoided throughout this text. However, many of the vegetarian broth products currently available in groceries are marketed as "stock," and these are often superior to various vegetarian "broths." In general, "vegetarian broth" uses salts, sugars, juices, and vegetable extracts to simulate the flavors of real vegetable broth; "vegetarian stock" is in fact commercially made broth, manufactured using real vegetables, which are often enough listed on the packaging.

45. English vegetarian broth
BRODO VEGETARIANO INGLESE

In a large stock pot, boil 4 quarts of water and:
    1 tbsp rice
When the water begins to boil, add a small quantity of:

lettuce or endive

dried peas

a small cabbage

carrots

celery

parsley

onion

a tomato

The exact quantity of vegetables is not important. Simmer on low heat for 4 hours. Add **1 tbsp salt** and **1 tsp of browned or caramelized sugar** (recipe 889) to give the broth color. Strain through a sieve, keeping only the broth.

46. Superior vegetarian broth
BRODO VEGETARIANO SUPERLATIVO

Ingredients:

5 quarts water

4 oz lentils

4 oz dried beans

4 onions

1 oz butter

parsley

thyme

stock of celery

3 or 4 carrots

6 walnuts

3 cloves

1 small Savoy cabbage

nutmeg

salt to taste

black peper

Chop the vegetables in the above list, and, in a large stock pot, add the chopped onions, parsley, celery and carrots and brown in butter. Add the water and salt, a few grains of pepper, 3 cloves, thyme, nutmeg and finally the lentils and beans and cabbage. When the broth has boiled down to about one-third the original quantity, about 2 hours, filter through a sieve or cheesecloth and color with **browned or caramelized sugar** (see recipe 889). You can make a purée with the leftover legumes (see recipe 73).

47. Italian-style broth
BRODO CONSUMATO ALL'ITALIANA

Slice:

2 or 3 onions

In a large stock pot, fry the onions in 4 tbsp butter and cook until browned. Add:

5 quarts water

6 oz lentils

3 oz beans

6 to 8 carrots

2 or 3 whole onions

a small Savoy cabbage

an herb bouquet (celery, parsley, thyme, etc.)

nutmeg

1 clove

salt and pepper

2 tomatoes or 1 tablespoon of tomato paste

Simmer until the broth has boiled down to one-third the original quantity, about 2 hours, drain and filter through a sieve or cheesecloth. You can make a purée with the leftover legumes (see recipe 73).

48. Cold consommé
CONSUMATO IN GHIACCIO

Any of the above broths can be served cold, though be sure the broth has been carefully filtered.

49. Cereal broth for convalescents
BRODO DI CEREALI PER AMMALATI E CONVALESCENTI

Grains—wheat, rye, barley, oats, rice and corn—belong to a separate family from legumes (such as beans, lentils, chickpeas, etc.).

Cereal broth is no less nourishing than broth made from legumes and is considerably lighter and thus to be preferred for those who are sick or convalescing.

To make the broth, in a large stock pot, mix:

- **6 oz barley (the cereal recommended by Hippocrates)**
- **2 oz each of wheat, rye, oats, corn and rice**

Add:

- **5 quarts of water**
- **3 carrots**
- **a small Savoy cabbage**
- **2 onions**
- **a stalk of celery**
- **parsley**
- **nutmeg**
- **a bay leaf**
- **a pinch of thyme**
- **salt to taste**

Bring to a boil and when it has reduced to a third of the original quantity, about two hours, color with a small quantity of **caramelized sugar** (see recipe 889), strain through a sieve or cheesecloth and dot with butter if serving.

50. Gelatin broth for convalescents
GELEA PER AMMALATI E CAGIONEVOLI

In any of the foregoing broths, dissolve **1 oz of gelatin** for each quart, filter and put in the refrigerator. You may omit the salt and substitute with **1 teaspoon sugar** for each quart. (Note: Few gelatin products are vegetarian. However, groceries often carry Kosher gelatins, which are usually vegetarian. Check the packaging to be sure.)

~~~~~~~~~~

51. Quick broth
BRODETTO IMPRONTATO

In a large stock pot, combine:

- **1 ½ quarts water**
- **4 chopped carrots**
- **1 chopped onion**
- **2 cloves**
- **thyme**
- **a pepper grain**
- **celery**
- **parsley**
- **nutmeg**

Boil for 45 minutes and color with **caramelized sugar** (see recipe 889), filter through a sieve or cheesecloth. Use as a base for pasta, ravioli, etc.

52. 'Monachiglie' in broth
MONACHIGLIE IN BRODO

Make one of the fillings on pages 198 to 200 and knead with:

> bread crumbs
>
> Parmesan cheese
>
> parsley
>
> chopped onion
>
> just enough egg to bind

Roll ½-inch balls and cook in broth (recipes 43–51).

53. 'Agnollotti' in broth
AGNELLOTTI IN BRODO

Agnolloti is a simple ravioli typical of the Piedmont region of Italy. In this variation, it is served in broth. Ingredients:

> 1 ½ cups (5 oz) flour
>
> 6 tbsp grated Parmesan cheese
>
> 4 tbsp butter
>
> ⅓ cup bread crumbs
>
> ⅔ cup walnuts
>
> 5 eggs

To make the filling: In a frying pan with 4 tbsp butter, brown the bread crumbs while stirring continually to avoid burning. When golden brown, remove from flame and mix in a large bowl with: crushed walnuts, half of the Parmesan and 2 egg yolks along with a pinch of salt and pepper, a spoonful of chopped onion and chopped flat leaf parsley. Set aside.

To make the pasta: Make a dough with 1½ cups (5 oz) flour and 3 eggs. Place the flour on a clean work surface. Make a well in the center, and break the eggs into the well. Add a dash of salt. Beat the eggs with a fork and gradually draw the flour in. Once combined, start kneading the dough with both hands. Knead for 3 to 5 minutes, adding a bit of flour if the dough becomes too sticky to handle. Once the dough is elastic, though still slightly sticky, wrap in plastic and let stand for 30 minutes.

Next, roll the dough on a floured board or marble to a thickness of a dime. Place teaspoonfuls of the filling on one half of the rolled dough, then cover with the other half and cut around the mounds of filling with a pasta cutter. Pinch each piece closed with a fork and a few drops of water. Continue until all the dough (or all the filling) has been consumed.

To finish: Boil the agnollotti in broth (recipe 51) for 4–6 minutes. To serve, sprinkle each portion with fresh grated Parmesan.

54. Krapfen in broth
KRAPFEN IN BRODO

This is a savory doughnut, served in broth. Ingredients:

> ⅔ cup finely ground flour
>
> 2 tbsp butter
>
> 1 tbsp yeast
>
> 1 egg
>
> salt to taste

In a large bowl, blend the above ingredients to make a soft dough, then roll on pastry board or marble counter to a thickness of ¼ inch. Cut in rounds about 1 inch in diameter. Allow to rise and when they have puffed up, fry in olive oil.

Serve in any of the above **broths** (recipes 43 to 51) with or without grated Parmesan, according to taste.

55. The Queen's bread
PANATA REGINA

This is a savory adaptation of bread pudding.

To prepare, take **a stale loaf of bread**, remove and discard the crust, and then chop and place in a saucepan with enough water to cover, adding salt and pepper. Cook over a slow flame for one hour and then stir in:

1 tbsp of butter
2 raw egg yolks beaten with 1 tbsp of milk

Leave on the flame just long enough for the eggs to thicken, removing the saucepan from heat before the mixture comes to a boil.

56. Milk squares cooked in broth
LOSANGHETTE DI LATTE PER BRODO

Follow recipe 615, but without placing the dough in egg or bread crumbs, cut into square shapes, toss into boiling **broth** (recipes 43 to 51) and serve immediately.

57. 'Cappelletti' in broth in Romagna style
CAPPELLETTI ROMAGNOLI AL BRODO

To make the filling: Make a pasta filling out of the following ingredients:

½ cup ricotta
½ cup finely chopped walnuts
⅓ cup grated Gruyère cheese
¼ cup Parmesan cheese
1 egg yolk
1 egg
herbs and spices of your choice
salt
parsley

To make the pasta: Make a dough with **1 ½ cups (5 oz) flour** and **3 eggs**. Place the flour on a clean work surface. Make a well in the center, and break the eggs into the well. Add a dash of salt. Beat the eggs with a fork and gradually draw the flour in. Once combined, start kneading the dough with both hands. Knead for 3 to 5 minutes, adding a bit of flour if the dough becomes too sticky to handle. Once the dough is elastic, though still slightly sticky, wrap in plastic and let stand for 30 minutes.

Roll the dough on a floured board or marble to a thickness of a dime. With a floured glass rim, cut out rounds about 2 inches in diameter. Place the filling in the middle and fold the dough in the shape of a half moon. Take the two extremities and pull to attach, thereby forming the "cappelletto" (or little hat).

To make the two ends stick, dampen them with water before pressing closed with your fingers and a fork. Drop them in boiling **broth** (recipe 44) or in the shorter version (recipe 51) and serve with grated cheese.

58. Nun's cous-cous
CÙSCUS DELLE MONACHE

On a pastry board, pour:

2 ½ cups of Durham wheat flour

Make a well in the center, and pour in:

1 whole egg

3 yolks

abundant chopped parsley

a pinch of salt and pepper

Slowly work into the flour until it becomes dry and begins to crumble. Then rub the flour mixture between the palms of your hands until it falls in little pellets of various sizes. Spread these wheat flour pellets on a kitchen towel and let dry. Drop these pieces in boiling broth (recipes 43 to 51) and let boil for a few minutes. Couscous is made by steaming a variety of vegetables and serving them with tomato sauce, sweet pepper and cayenne, all of which go well with this homemade cous-cous.

Purées are a simple Italian dish, served in individual bowls or from a central pot. Any vegetable or legume—including leftovers—can be made into a purée. Use one of the below recipes or take 1 to 2 lbs vegetables in any combination and stew with parley, olive oil, and salt. If you like, purée into a food processor or pass through a food mill.

59. Chickpea purée
PUREA DI CECI PROVINCIALE

Overnight, soak:

1 cup of dried chickpeas

To prepare, drain the chickpeas and place in medium saucepan with enough water to cover. Add one fresh **rosemary sprig** and a **garlic clove**. Bring to a boil and simmer gently for about 2 hours, or until the the chickpeas are tender.

Drain well and return the chickpeas to the saucepan and add salt and pepper to taste. Then add:

1 cup peas

1 tbsp butter or ½ cup cream

Over a low flame, cook for about 5 minutes, or until the peas reach your desired firmness. Spoon the purée into four dishes, drizzle each with olive oil, and serve immediately.

60. Ambassador's purée
PUREA ALL'AMBASCIATRICE

Make a batter of:

rice flour

a pinch of salt

3 pints cold milk

Combine by adding the milk gradually to avoid lumping (if necessary, pass through a sieve). When the batter is smooth, add:

1 cup finely chopped sautéed
   mushrooms

a few spoonfuls of peas and **boiled**
   artichokes

Cook for 30 minutes, stirring continually and add a sprinkling of **chopped truffles or other mushrooms** and **½ cup cream** before serving.

61. Lentil purée with tapioca
PUREA DI LENTI ALLA TAPIOCA

In 2½ quarts salted water, cook:

1 lb lentils

When soft put through a food mill and add water or stock to bring the quantity of purée to 1½ quarts. Put it back on the flame and mix in:

4 tbsp tapioca

Let cook for 10 minutes without stirring and serve with **a pat of butter** or **½ cup milk** beaten in.

62. Indian purée
PUREA INDIANA

In 1 cup of water, dissolve:

1 tbsp rice flour

Place over a low flame and stir continually, adding:

1 tsp curry powder
a pinch of salt

When the purée has thickened, add **a pat of butter** and serve. This can also be made with flour from other grains or legumes.

63. Pea purée
PUREA DI PISELLI

In a large saucepan with 2 qt water, add:

2 lb peas
salt
½ tbsp butter

Cook slowly and when the peas reach your desired firmness, put through a food mill then put back over the flame. When the mixture has thickened adequately (add a pinch of flour if you wish), add another **2 tbsp butter** and serve. The same dish can be made with dried peas by increasing the quantity of water and boiling until the peas disintegrate.

64. Mushroom purée
PUREA DI FUNGHI

Soak in enough water to cover:

1 lb mushrooms
a few drops of fresh lemon juice

Drain and chop. Cook them in a saucepan with some **butter** and **salt** and add:

1 tbsp flour dissolved in a few spoonfuls of water

Cook until thickened. Before serving add:

½ cup cream
croutons

65. Celery purée
PUREA DI SEDANI

Clean and wash:

6 celery hearts

Boil until soft and put through a food mill. Melt some **butter** in a saucepan and add **croutons**; add the celery and a pinch of salt and cook until it reaches the desired thickness. Serve with **cream** or **butter**.

66. Chestnut purée
PUREA DI CASTAGNE

Shell and skin:

1 ½ lb fresh chestnuts

Boil them in 2 quarts water with dash of salt

or sugar, put through a food mill and pour into a saucepan in which you have fried an **onion** in butter. Thin with some **milk** and boil until the purée has thickened. This purée can also be made with chestnut flour which is on sale in most well-furnished grocery stores. Before serving add **½ cup cream** or **2 tbsp butter**.

67. Artichoke purée
PUREA DI CARCIOFI

Ingredients:

 2 lb artichokes

 2 cups milk

 2 cups water

Clean the artichokes, removing all the tough outside leaves, and put them in water with the milk so they do not discolor. Boil them until they fall apart and then put through a food mill. Put the purée back in the saucepan, add:

 salt

 pepper

 1 tbsp butter

Simmer and stir with a wooden spoon, adding a little flour to thicken.

68. Triple purée
PUREA TRIPLA

Take:

 2 tbsp rice flour

 2 tbsp barley flour

 2 tbsp rye flour

Dissolve in **3 pints of water**, adding the liquid little by little to avoid forming lumps. Simmer over a low flame until the purée reaches the desired thickness, then add **salt** and **butter**. Add **½ cup cream** before serving, with or without **croutons**. (This may also be made using milk in place of water.)

69. Bean or lentil purée
PUREA DI FAGIUOLI O DI LENTI

Follow recipe 63 for dried peas.

70. 'Subisso' purée (onion purée)
PUREA AL SUBISSO

In water, blanch:

 4 lb skinned onions

Drain and cut in quarters and place in a saucepan with enough **butter** to sauté. Simmer over a low flame (the onions must not turn brown). When tender, add:

 salt

 1 tbsp flour

 1 qt milk (to thin)

Put the purée through a food mill and serve hot with **fried croutons** and **1 cup cream**.

71. Flour purée
PUREA DI FARINA

In a frying pan, put:

 2 ½ cups flour

Stir continually; when it begins to brown, add **3 pints of water** gradually to avoid lumps, **salt** and **white pepper**. Let simmer until thickened, stirring constantly, then remove from the flame and beat in **2 raw egg yolks**.

72. Brahmin purée
PUREA ALLA BRAMINA

In salted water, boil:

3 ½ lb potatoes, peeled

When soft, put through a food mill one by one, leaving the others in the hot water. When they have all been puréed, add **warm milk** until they reach the desired thickness. Put back on the flame and add peppers of your choice. I suggest **4 sweet** and **2 hot peppers**, which have been cooked in butter. Add **½ cup cream** or **a pat of butter** and serve.

73. Imperial purée
PUREA IMPERIALE

Ingredients:

1 ½ lb dried peas
⅔ cup each of lentils and dried beans (soaked overnight)
⅓ cup butter
carrots, celery, parsley, basil, 2 onions, and a small Savoy cabbage (all chopped)

To start, sauté the carrots, celery, parsley, basil, onions and cabbage in butter and set aside. Next, in a large saucepan, boil:

4 qt water
salt
pepper

When the water comes to boil, add the dried lentils and beans. When cooked, put through a food mill, add **½ cup cream** or **butter**, add the stewed vegetables, and serve with toasted bread. If the legumes are slow in cooking, add hot water as necessary to bring the final quantity to 3 pints.

74. Puréed potatoes
PUREA DI PATATE

Boil in salted water:

4 ½ lb potatoes, peeled

Put through a food mill one by one, letting them fall into **3 pints of milk**. Add:

butter
white pepper
salt

Mix with **Parmesan cheese** and cook until dense, stirring to avoid sticking. You may add cream before serving, or add as much butter as you desire.

75. D. E. A. S. purée (Duke Enrico Alliata of Salaparuta purée)
PUREA D. E. A. S.

Ingredients:

4 lb green peas
2 lb fava beans
⅓ cup butter
½ cup milk

Sauté a **sliced onion** in butter and add the peas with a pinch of salt and water to cover. Remove both outer and inner skins from the fava beans and cook until they have disintegrated in the quantity of water necessary to make a thick purée. Put through a food mill with ⅔ of the cooked peas, salt and pepper. Then reheat and serve (with or without fried croutons), adding the rest of the whole peas and **½ cup cream**.

76. Mountaineer's purée
PUREA ALLA MONTANARA

In **3 pints cold milk**, dissolve:

6 heaping tbsp chickpea flour

Add the milk gradually to avoid lumps. Cook over a low flame with **salt** and **1 chopped onion**. Put through a food mill and reheat with **½ cup cream**.

77. Maizena purée with peas
PUREA DI MAIZENA AI PISELLI

In salted water, boil:

1 lb peas

Put through a food mill. Add water (to bring to a total quantity of 2 quarts) in which you have dissolved **5 tsp of maizena**. Boil for 10 minutes, mixing frequently, remove from the flame and add **a pat of butter** before serving. This purée is also excellent with spinach.

78. Purée with maizena and milk
PUREA DI MAIZENA AL LATTE

In **1 quart cold milk**, dissolve:

6 tbsp maizena (corn starch)

In another pan heat **1 pint of milk** and when it boils, pour in the maizena and milk mixture, stirring continually. Add:

salt

pepper

4 raw egg yolks to bind

a pat of butter

Serve immediately.

79. Maizena purée with tomatoes
PUREA DI MAIZENA AL POMODORO

In a medium saucepan with 5 tbsp butter, sauté over low heat:

1 chopped onion

Once soft, but not brown, add:

4 tsp maizena (corn starch)

2 tsp flour

Remove from the flame and add:

1 pint uncooked tomato sauce

enough water to bring to 2 qt

Boil until it thickens, then pass through a food mill, reheat and serve.

80. Carrot and tomato purée
PUREA DI CAROTE AL POMODORO

Cook in 2 quarts water:

1 lb sliced carrots

1 lb tomatoes

a sprig of parsley

1 chopped onion

2 thick slices of bread fried in butter

salt

pepper

Cook until carrots are tender. Put through a food mill, reheat and serve.

81. Cream of lentils or lentil purée
PUREA O CREMA DI LENTICCHIE

Ingredients:
- 1 ¼ cups lentils
- 3 carrots
- a stalk of celery
- parsley
- 1 large onion
- ⅓ cup butter
- 2 oz flour
- 1 pint milk
- ½ cup cream
- white pepper
- salt
- 1 clove garlic
- nutmeg
- 1 clove

Rinse, then boil the lentils in 2 quart water with the onion, the carrots, the celery, pepper, salt and parsley. Cook until amalgamated and put through a food mill. Melt butter in 1 tbsp flour, and add milk gradually to make a béchamel. Then add the lentil purée and stir over a low flame, adding ½ cup cream before serving.

82. Springtime purée
PUREA DI PRIMAVERA

In ⅓ cup butter, sauté:
- 1 cup chopped onions

Add:
- 1 ¾ cups of lentils, rinsed
- 1 pint water
- salt
- pepper

Simmer until the lentils have come apart. Put through a food mill, and add water to bring to 2 quarts, and add:
- 3 sliced carrots
- 2 leeks
- ½ cup peas
- chopped parsley

Cook for another 30 minutes. Serve with **butter** or **cream**.

83. 'Sagou' purée
PUREA AL SAGOU

Ingredient:
- ½ cup carrots
- 10 oz potatoes
- ⅓ cup butter
- ⅓ cup sagou or tapioca
- 1 qt milk

Chop and cook the carrots and potatoes in 1 quart water with salt and pepper. Put through a food mill, thin with milk, pour in the tapioca and stir continually while simmering for 15 minutes. Add **butter** or **cream** when serving.

84. Mulligataway purée
PUREA MULLIGATAWAY

Ingredients:
- 1 pint vegetable broth
- ¼ cup crushed walnuts
- 3 tbsp butter
- 2 tsp curry
- 6 carrots
- 2 large tart apples
- 2 tbsp flour

juice of one lemon

salt

pepper

2 onions

Sauté the onions in broth (recipes 43 to 51) and chop all the ingredients before adding to the broth. When well cooked, put through a food mill, dissolve flour in a small quantity of cold water, pour it over the vegetable purée, and cook until thickened.

85. Truffle purée
PUREA TARTUFATA

Follow the above recipe, adding a glass of **white wine** in place of the lemon juice and sprinkling **chopped truffles** in the dish.

86. Dried fava bean purée
PUREA DI FAVE SECCHE

This is an excellent remedy for stomach ailments, especially in small children. Cook **3 cups of dried fava beans** with their skins, pinching off only the heads. When well cooked, add a pinch of **celery salt** and put through a food mill. Reheat, then add **¾ cup cream** before serving.

87. Cream of fava beans
PUREA DI FAVE VERDI

Boil in 2 quart water:

7 lb fresh fava beans with shells and skins
   removed

2 carrots

1 onion

garlic

celery

parsley

salt

pepper

When well cooked, put through a food mill, place over the flame, and bind with **3 raw egg yolks** mixed with **½ cup cream**.

88. English style tomato purée
PUREA DI POMODORO ALL'INGLESE

In **3 tbsp butter**, sauté:

3 large onions.

Add:

2 lb sliced ripe tomatoes

3 or 4 stalks of chopped celery

3 carrots

a herb bouquet

Boil for 2 hours, adding:

1 qt vegetable broth (recipes 43 to 51)

salt

pepper

3 slices of bread fried in butter

Put through a food mill, reheat, and add **½ cup cream** before serving.

89. Bisque purée
PUREA "BISQUE"

Ingredients:

2 lb tomatoes

2 onions

3 tbsp butter

3 cups milk

2 tbsp flour

Boil the tomatoes (crush with a fork) with the chopped onion and a pinch of baking soda in ½ cup water for 30 minutes. Put through a food mill and pour into the cold milk. Melt the butter in a separate pan and add the flour, stirring to avoid lumps. When smooth, add the purée and cook until thickened.

90. Almond purée
PUREA ALLE MANDORLE

Ingredients:

- 1 lb potatoes
- 1 qt milk
- ½ cup almonds
- 3 bitter almonds
- 3 tbsp butter or cream

Boil the peeled potatoes in salted water for 30 minutes and when soft, put through a food mill one by one, letting them fall into the milk. Blanch the almonds in hot water and peel, crush and put through a food mill, then mix with the purée, together with salt and white pepper. Boil briefly and bind with **cream** or **butter**. Serve immediately.

91. Peanut purée
PUREA ALLE ARACHIDI

Follow above recipe but use **raw peanuts** in place of almonds.

92. Pepper purée
PUREA DI PEPERONI

Ingredients:

- 1 lb sweet peppers
- 1 cup carrots
- 1 ¼ cups potatoes
- 2 onions
- 1 ¼ cups tomatoes

Chop everything and cook for 1 hour in **2 quarts water** with:

- salt
- pepper
- parsley
- 2 large slices of bread fried in butter

Put through a food mill, boil for 5 minutes more and add **½ cup cream** or **a pat of butter** (and cayenne pepper if desired) before serving.

93. English potato purée
PUREA DI PATATE ALL'INGLESE

Ingredients:

- 1 ½ lb potatoes, chopped
- 2 carrots, chopped
- 2 turnips, chopped
- 1 onion, chopped
- 1 pint milk
- 3 tbsp butter
- 1 pint vegetable broth
- salt
- pepper
- cayenne

Sauté the sliced potatoes and chopped onions in butter, add the broth and all the other ingredients, except milk. Cook for 1 hour, adding hot water as necessary. Put through a food mill, add the milk and broth necessary to bring to 1½ quarts total. Cook for 10 minutes, and add **cream** or **butter** before serving.

94. Creamed barley
PUREA D'ORZO

In a medium sauté pan, place:

3 tbsp butter
1 chopped onion

Sauté. In a bowl, dissolve **3 tbsp white barley flour** in **1 pint milk** and add to the butter and onions together with **1 qt vegetable broth** (recipes 43 to 51). Simmer for 30 minutes and bind with **cream** before serving.

95. Red purée
PUREA ROSSA

Ingredients:

1 ¾ cups red beans
½ cup tomato sauce
1 beet
2 onions
3 tbsp butter
celery
parsley

Soak the beans for 12 hours in 2 qt water and a pinch of baking soda, then boil together in a large stock pot with all the above ingredients, except the tomato sauce and butter. When cooked (approx. 2½ hours), put through a food mill and add the tomato sauce, salt and pepper. When it has come to a boil, remove from flame, add the butter, stir and serve immediately.

96. Rice purée
PUREA DI RISO

Ingredients:

⅔ cup rice
3 pints milk
2 tbsp sugar

Boil the rice in abundant water, strain and rinse in cold water. Heat the milk and sugar (or salt if you prefer) in a medium saucepan and add the rice, cooking until it has become a soft pulp. Add **cream** and serve.

Thick soups and minestre

ZUPPE E MINESTRE

Minestra predates *zuppa* by several centuries. Derived from the Latin *ministrare*, meaning "to administer," minestra was originally served from a central bowl by a figure of authority in the household. Minestra was traditionally the principal—and for the poor, the only—course of the meal.

Today, minestra refers to a first course of vegetables, legumes, pasta or rice cooked in broth. Minestrone is only one of many minestra soups. Regional variations abound, but a minestrone always has a thickening vegetable such as fresh or dried beans or other legumes, potatoes or squash. It also usually includes pasta or rice.

In Italy, soup has even more humble origins. In medieval times, it was made by servants from table scraps. It was served with a slice of bread, thus the Italian word zuppa, which literally means "soaked bread." A number of the soup recipes collected here begin with a bread base, per this tradition.

97. Neapolitan soup
ZUPPA ALLA NAPOLETANA

To make the fried dumplings: Slice **1 loaf dried bread**, removing and discarding the crust, and soak in water for 30 minutes then squeeze to remove excess liquid. Place in a bowl, and add:

¾ cup grated Parmesan cheese
4 hard-boiled egg yolks
chopped parsley
salt
pepper

Then add just enough **raw egg white** to make a semi-solid paste which can be rolled in your hands. Form the mixture into 1 inch balls.

Roll in **flour** and, in a medium sauté pan over medium heat, fry in good olive oil.

To serve: Place in serving dishes and cover with **vegetable broth** (recipes 43 to 51).

98. Portuguese soup
ZUPPA ALLA PORTOGHESE

Take small **bread rolls** and remove the crust, then cut in half horizontally and remove a bit from the inside.

Fill with a stuffing of **mushrooms** and **nuts** (recipe 705). Replace the top, dip in **milk**, then **flour**, then **beaten eggs**, and finally in **bread crumbs**. In a large sauté pan over medium heat, fry in olive oil. Place in soup dishes and cover with **vegetable broth** (recipe 44) to serve.

99. Bread crumb soup
ZUPPA DI PANGRATTATO

To begin, take:

3 pints of a vegetable broth of your
    choice (recipes 43 to 51)

Put half of this in a large saucepan over low heat, and add:

½ cup bread crumbs

Cook until thickened, and add:

1 beaten raw egg
1 handful of grated Parmesean cheese

Allow to thicken, adding the remaining broth to reach the desired consistency. Finish with **butter** or **cream**.

100. Genoese soup
ZUPPA ALLA GENOVESE

Boil:

1 lb spinach

When cooked, drain in a colander, then chop and put in a saucepan with:

1 onion, chopped
herbs

spices
salt
pepper

Cook for 10 to 15 minutes. Allow to cool and add **5 whole eggs** beaten with **3 tbsp grated Parmesan cheese** and place in a steam cooker. When the dish has solidified, remove, cut into squares and serve in a tureen of **vegetable broth** (recipes 43 to 51).

101. 'Cresa' soup
ZUPPA ALLA CRESA

In a stock pot, cook in enough water to cover:

2 lb beets, peeled and quartered
3 large onions, chopped
salt
pepper

When the vegetables are cooked, pass through a food mill. In another saucepan make a velouté sauce by combining:

melted butter
1 tbsp flour
a pinch of salt

Add **1 pint of warm water** gradually to avoid lumps. Pour the beet and onion mixture in, together with **4 beaten eggs**. Stir briefly over a low flame and serve immediately with small slices of buttered, **toasted bread** on top.

102. 'Condé' soup
ZUPPA ALLA CONDÈ

In about four cups of salted water cook:

1 ½ cups red beans
2 or 3 onions

Put through a food mill and lengthen with **vegetable broth** (see recipes 43 to 51) to bring to 3 pints and add a pat of **butter**. Serve with **fried croutons**.

103. 'Aurora' soup
ZUPPA AURORA

Ingredients:
- 1 lb onions
- 8 oz butter
- 1 ¼ cups flour
- 8 cups milk
- 3 raw egg yolks

Finely chop the onions. In a stock pot, sauté the onions in half the butter and stir in the flour. When it begins to take on color, lengthen with warm milk, stirring briskly. Let simmer for 30 minutes, remove from the flame and stir in the three beaten egg yolks. Serve with **toasted bread** cut into cubes.

104. Mock soup 'alla marinara' (sailor style)
PSEUDO-ZUPPA DI TELLINE ALLA MARINARA

Zucchini flowers have a unique flavor that vaguely recalls that of seafood, and especially clams. In a stock pot, sauté in **5 tbsp of olive oil**:
- 2 large sliced onions
- 2 cloves of chopped garlic
- 1 stalk of celery, chopped
- chopped flat-leaf parsley

Add 2 cups of water. Allow to simmer until the celery has softened.

In another pan, in 2 cups salted water, boil:
- 1 lb chopped zucchini flowers
- pinch of saffron

When cooked (this requires no more than 5 to 10 minutes), add to the sautéed onions and bring to a boil. Serve immediately with **fried croutons** or **toasted bread slices**.

105. Almond soup
ZUPPA DI MANDORLE

Ingredients:
- 2 tbsp almonds
- 3 cups milk
- 1 cup cream
- 1 tbsp flour
- 1 onion
- 1 celery stalk, chopped
- 2 tbsp butter

Blanch, skin and chop the almonds. In a stock pot, bring 2 cups of milk to a simmer and add the almonds. Add the chopped onion and the tender part of the celery stalk and cook for one hour. After an hour, remove the onion and celery, stir the flour together with the butter and add to the almond purée together with the rest of the milk, and salt and pepper to taste. Allow to thicken over a low flame, then add the cream and bring to a boil. Serve immediately with croutons.

106. Vegetarian frog soup
ZUPPA DI PSEUDO-RANE

Finely chop:
- 3 onions
- a few carrots
- celery
- parsley

In a large stock pot, sauté the vegetables in **4 oz butter** and an equal quantity of **olive oil**. When the vegetables are soft, add:

> **½ cup white wine**

Then put the mixture through a food mill. Pour this purée into **6 cups salted water** and add:

> **1 oz dried mushrooms** (which have been soaked in warm water for one hour and then finely chopped)
> **another 2 or 3 carrots, chopped**
> **a few tender celery leaves**
> **garlic**
> **spices**

Cook for 30 minutes more and serve.

107. Mock clam soup
ZUPPA DI PSEUDO-VONGOLE

Follow the above recipe for mock frog soup, and add:

> **1 cup chopped zucchini blossoms** (the pollen gives off a seafood flavor)
> **a pinch of powdered saffron**

Serve with **fried croutons.**

108. Celery soup
ZUPPA DI SEDANO

Finely chop:

> **6 celery hearts**
> **2 carrots**
> **2 onions**
> **1 head of Savoy cabbage**

In a large stock pot, sauté the onions in **4 tbsp butter,** then add **8 cups water** and add the other vegetables. Simmer for one hour, adding salt and pepper to taste. Serve with **fried croutons** and **grated cheese.**

109. British soup
ZUPPA BRITANNICA

Ingredients:

> **2 stalks of celery**
> **½ cup butter**
> **4 cups water**
> **salt**
> **white pepper**
> **2 raw egg yolks**
> **5 cups milk**
> **½ cup cream**

In a stock pot, melt the butter and sauté the celery, then pour in the water and simmer until soft. Put through a food mill, then put back in the saucepan and add the milk. Bring to a boil, stirring continually. Beat the egg yolks and cream in a soup tureen and pour over the boiling soup. Serve with or without **buttered croutons.**

110. Mantua style soup
ZUPPA MANTOVANA

In a large saucepan, combine:

> **4 cups vegetable broth** (recipes 43 to 51)
> **a few mushrooms, chopped into ½-inch chunks**
> **2 crumbled black truffles**

Simmer for 30 minutes. Place a slice of **fried bread** sprinkled with **grated Parmesan cheese** in the bottom of each soup dish.

Beat **3 eggs** with:

salt

chopped parsley

herbs

pepper

Allow the soup to cool before adding the beaten egg mixture then put the saucepan back on a low flame and mix until thickened. Serve in the individual soup dishes over the bread.

111. White soup
ZUPPA BIANCA

Ingredients:

8 cups milk

2/3 cup Parmesan cheese

4 eggs

6 to 10 slices of bread

3 large onions, chopped

In a stock pot, sauté the chopped onions in butter until they are golden. Add a soup ladle or two of milk and allow to simmer for 10 minutes, then put through a food mill. Pour back in the saucepan, add the remainder of the milk and bring to a boil with a pinch of salt. Slice the bread and toast under a broiler, then place in layers in a soup tureen, pouring the beaten egg mixture over each layer, and then add the boiling milk. Serve immediately.

112. Dried bread and tomato soup
ZUPPA DI PAN DURO AL POMODORO

Ingredients:

2 lb dried bread

5 lb tomatoes

2 onions

1/2 cup butter

herb bouquet

Place the dried bread in water and when soft, remove the crust. Squeeze out the excess moisture and put through a food mill; then wash the tomatoes and press these through the food mill. In a saucepan, sauté the finely chopped onions in butter and add both the bread and tomato together with the herb bouquet and allow to simmer 15 to 20 minutes, adding water if necessary. Before serving add salt, spices and 1 tbsp butter.

113. Vegetarian bouillabaisse or mushrooms in broth
BOUILLA-BAISSE VEGETARIANA
O BRODETTO DI FUNGHI

Rinse and chop:

1 lb fresh mushrooms

Make a bouquet garni with:

6 onions cut in quarters

2 sliced tomatoes

2 bay leaves

a few pieces of chopped orange rind

4 cloves

Put this in a large saucepan with:

2 cups of dry white wine

salt

pepper

a pinch of powdered saffron

chopped parsley

Add:

1 cup of olive oil

4 cups water (in which 2 tsp potato flour have been dissolved)

Simmer for one hour, then remove bouquet garni and serve the soup over toasted bread slices.

114. Egg and milk soup
ZUPPA DI LATTE ED UOVA

Boil:

6 cups milk

Add a pinch of salt. Bind with six raw egg yolks. When thickened, serve over toasted buttered croutons.

115. Chilean style 'cazzuéla'
CAZZUÈLA ALLA CILENA

Prepare 8 cups quick broth (recipe 51). In a stock pot, add:

6 medium peeled potatoes, quartered

6 medium-sized onions, quartered

6 one-inch cubes of yellow squash (or pumpkin)

3 ears of sweet corn, with the corn removed

6 tbsp rice

salt

pepper

When the vegetables are cooked, serve in individual dishes, distributing the vegetables in each dish with a pat of butter.

116. Bean and celery minestra
MINESTRA DI FAGIUOLI AL SEDANO

Soak 2 ½ cups white beans in water overnight. In a stock pot, combine:

a pinch of baking soda

the beans

Cook over a slow flame. When partly cooked, skim off the skins and add:

a cup of finely chopped celery and carrots

salt

pepper

a spoon or two of good olive oil

Serve.

117. Italian minestrone
MINESTRONE ALL'ITALIANA

Soak 1 cup white beans in water overnight.

In a stock pot, cook the beans and set aside. Chop:

a few carrots

celery

leeks

broccoli

any other vegetables in season

In another saucepan, boil the above in enough water to cover the vegetables. When these are partly cooked, add the beans and:

1 cup rice

salt

pepper

butter or oil

Bring to a boil and simmer, adding water if necessary, until thick and flavorful. This soup can be served hot or at room temperature with a sprinkling of Parmesan cheese.

118. Pasta with lentils (minestra)
PASTA CON LENTI (MINESTRA)

In a stock pot with salted water, cook:

2 cups lentils

Put through a food mill to make a uniform pu-rée. Reheat and add the **pasta** of your choice. (Use one of the small "pastina" made in various shapes intended for cooking in soups). Add:

olive oil

pepper

Serve when ready. This can be seasoned, if you wish, with butter or cream.

119. Pasta and beans (minestra)
PASTA COI FAGIUOLI (MINESTRA)

Follow the above recipe, using **beans** in the place of lentils.

120. Pasta and dried fava beans (minestra)
PASTA COLLE FAVE SECCHE

Follow recipe 118 using **dried fava beans**.

121. Pasta and broccoli (minestra)
PASTA COI BROCCOLI (MINESTRA)

Cut a **small head of broccoli** in small pieces and boil in salted water (calculate 4 cups of water for three or four servings). When it is nearly done, add a handful of **pasta** for each person, along with:

olive oil

salt

pepper

Serve when cooked. (This soup can also be made by putting the broccoli through a food mill for a more uniform consistency and adding butter or cream before serving.)

122. Pasta with fresh fava beans
PASTA COLLE FAVE VERDI

In a large saucepan, boil in salted water:

2 lb fava beans, with shells and
skins removed

When they have become a pulpy mass, add:

1 lb small pasta

Season with:

salt

pepper

oil or **butter**

123. Oriental minestra
MINESTRA ORIENTALE

In a stock pot, prepare **8 cups broth** (recipes 43 to 51) or **cold milk**, and pour:

6 tbsp tapioca or **sago**

Stir continually. Place this over a slow flame for about 20 minutes and continue stirring until cooked. Before serving, add **salt** and **butter**.

124. Springtime minestra
MINESTRA PRIMAVERILE

Ingredients:

- 1 lb (before shelling) green peas
- 1 lb (before shelling) fresh fava beans
- ½ cup rice
- 4 carrots, chopped
- 1 stalk onion, chopped
- a handful of parsley, chopped
- 3 tbsp butter

In a stock pot, sauté the chopped onion in butter and add the peas, fava beans (removing both shells and skins), carrots and 8 cups water. Add salt and pepper and simmer for 30 minutes. Add the rice. When the rice is cooked, serve immediately with or without **grated cheese**.

125. Minestra, Munich style
MINESTRA DI MONACO

Slice a loaf of **Italian bread** in equal shapes and thickness and toast in the broiler, then **butter** and sprinkle with **sugar**. Place these in a serving dish and pour over them:

- 6 cups boiling milk
- a pinch of salt

If you want a thicker soup, add **1 or 2 beaten egg yolks** to the milk before pouring.

126. Vegetarian turtle minestra
PSEUDO-MINESTRA DI TARTARUGA
(MOCK-TURTLE)

In a stock pot, add: **12 cups of broth** (recipes 43 to 51) and a bouquet garni tied in a cheesecloth bag with the following ingredients:

- chopped parsley
- thyme
- sage
- fresh basil
- onion
- 2 cloves
- 2 bay leaves
- peppercorns
- salt
- ground nutmeg

Cook for one hour and then add a few **chopped mushrooms** and a sprinkling of **truffles**. Lengthen with water in which you have dissolved **1 heaping tbsp potato flour**. Add:

- 1 glass of dry white wine
- the juice of ½ lemon
- a pinch of cayenne

Cook for a further 30 minutes and when ready, add **crumbled hard-boiled egg yolks** or **mock eggs** (recipe 466). Take out the bouquet garni before serving and accompany with **fried croutons**.

127. Austrian minestra
MINESTRA AUSTRIACA

Ingredients:

- 1 ¼ cups black beans
- ¼ cup German barley

2 onions

3 cloves

2 whole hot peppers

1 ¼ cups chopped carrots

6 stalks celery

⅓ cup butter

Soak the beans in water for 8 to 12 hours. Chop the onions, celery, hot peppers, and, in a stock pot, sauté in the butter; drain the beans and add to the vegetables, along with the barley and 8 cups of water. Boil for 4 hours, adding more water if necessary. Put through a food mill and season with:

chopped parsley

marjoram

salt

pepper

This may be accompanied by **fried croutons**.

128. Minestra for home
MINESTRA ALLA BUONA MASSAIA

Ingredients:

1 cup of beans

1 Savoy cabbage, chopped

4 oz carrots, chopped

10 oz green beans

8 oz pastina

9 oz potatoes, sliced

1 onion, chopped

2 oz butter and olive oil

parsley

These ingredients serve to make two separate dishes, as follows:

In a stock pot, boil the dried beans in 4 cups water and when cooked, add all the vegetables (except the potatoes and onions), add more water as needed, and salt to taste. When the vegetables are soft, drain them and put aside.

In a separate sauce pan, sauté a chopped onion in the olive oil and butter and add the sliced raw potatoes and sauté until golden brown. Add to the broth and bring to a boil; lastly, add the pastina, parsley. Serve the soup in individual dishes.

The boiled vegetables make a wonderful cold salad. Add **lettuce** or **cucumber** and dress with **mayonnaise**, **capers**, and **pickles**.

129. Minestra with polenta 'al subisso'
MINESTRA DI POLENTA AL SUBISSO

Ingredients:

1 cup polenta

4 cups milk

⅔ cup butter

1 or 2 onions

In a stock pot, sauté the onion in half the butter and when it becomes transparent add the polenta and stir for 3 minutes over a low flame. Then add the milk gradually and water if more liquid is necessary. Season with salt and pepper and stir continually for 30 minutes. Before serving add the remaining butter and **½ cup cream** for a richer dish.

130. Chilean lentils
LENTI ALLA CILENA

Ingredients:
- 3 ½ cups lentils
- ⅓ cup butter
- ¼ cup olive oil
- 1 head of celery, chopped
- cayenne
- 2 onions
- 6 tomatoes

Blanch the tomatoes in hot water to remove the skins and seeds. Chop the onions and tomatoes. In a stock pot, sauté the onions and tomatoes in the butter and olive oil. In a separate saucepan, cook the lentils in water with a pinch of baking soda, adding the chopped celery and cayenne. When cooked, add to the onion and tomato sauté and simmer briefly. This soup can be served with cubes of **toasted bread**.

131. Minestra 'maggiolina'
MINESTRA MAGGIOLINA

Ingredients:
- 1 small Savoy cabbage
- ½ cup chopped carrots
- 8 oz green beans
- 4 oz rice
- 9 oz potatoes
- 8 oz zucchini
- 8 oz shelled peas
- celery
- parsley
- basil
- onion
- butter
- oil

Since all these vegetables require more or less the same cooking time, chop together and place in a stock pot with 3 pints water, salt, pepper, spices and 2 oz each butter and olive oil. Cook over a low flame without stirring and when the rice is done, serve immediately. Salt and pepper to taste.

132. Chilean beans
FAGIUOLI ALLA CILENA

In a stock pot, with 4 qt water with a pinch of baking soda and salt, boil:
- **3 ½ cups white beans (cannellini, navy, or great Northern) that have been soaked overnight**

When nearly soft, drain and throw away the cooking water. Set the beans aside. Sauté **2 onions** in **½ cup olive oil** or **butter** and return the beans to the stock pot. Cook until done, adding small quantities of warm water as necessary. Season with **cayenne** before serving.

133. Minestra 'casata' (with cheese)
MINESTRA CASATA

Follow recipe 131 and before serving, place **6 to 8 cubes of fresh cheese** in each dish, drowning with the hot soup.

134. Minestra with grated bread
MINESTRA PANATA

In a stock pot, make a paste with the following ingredients:

5 oz grated dried bread

4 eggs

3 tbsp grated Parmesan cheese

herbs

Dilute with **warm vegetable broth** (recipes 43 to 51) to the consistency of soup. Cook over a very low flame, scraping the sides of the saucepan as it cooks. When thickened, serve immediately, adding **peas** or other cooked vegetables, as you wish.

135. Sour potato minestra
MINESTRA AGRA DI PATATE

Ingredients:

2 lb potatoes

8 oz butter

3 large onions

1/3 cup flour

2 lemons

herbs

6 walnuts

Peel and dice the potatoes and cover with water. Chop the onions. In stock pot, brown the onions in 4 oz butter, then add the flour and thin with water, stirring constantly to avoid lumps. Drain the potatoes and add to the onions, covering with water. When cooked, add the remaining butter, the juice of 2 lemons and sprinkle with chopped fresh herbs and ground walnuts before serving.

136. Heavenly minestra
MINESTRA DEL PARADISO

Beat **4 egg whites** with a pinch of salt until stiff, then add:

1/2 cup bread crumbs

5 tbsp grated Parmesan cheese

4 oz melted butter

spices

nutmeg

In a stock pot, boil **5 cups quick vegetable broth** (recipe 51) and add the above paste a spoonful at a time, pushing it off the spoon into the boiling broth. After 6 to 10 minutes serve with or without **cheese**.

137. 'Passatelle alla romagnola' in broth
PASSATELLE IN MINESTRA ALLA ROMAGNOLA

Combine the following to form a paste:

3 eggs

4 tbsp grated Parmesan cheese

2 tbsp bread crumbs

2 tbsp ground walnuts

This should be put through a food mill in order to form long worm-like strings and then cooked briefly in saucepan with **3 cups hot broth** (recipes 43 to 51).

138. 'Duxellese' minestra
MINESTRA DUXELLESE

Ingredients:

1 small Savoy cabbage

4 carrots

6 oz butter

4 cups milk

6 leeks

3 onions

2/3 cup flour

pepper
salt

Chop the cabbage, carrots, leeks and onions and place in a stock pot with 1 quart water and half the butter. Bring to a boil and simmer for 30 minutes, then add half the milk and thicken with the flour. Let cook for 10 minutes, stirring constantly, and then remove from the flame and season with salt, pepper, the remaining butter and milk before serving with or without **croutons**.

139. Green minestra
MINESTRA VERDE

In a stock pot with 1 pint water, boil:
> 1 lb shelled peas

After 2 to 3 minutes, add:
> 8 oz chopped spinach
> herbs
> a chopped onion
> a garlic clove
> two slices of bread fried in butter

Simmer for 30 minutes. Remove from the stove, and put the soup through a food mill. Add water, about 1 pint, and bring to a boil. Once the soup is boiling, add **4 tbsp pastina**. When the pasta is cooked, season with salt and pepper and add a pat of butter before serving.

140. Variation on green minestra
MINESTRA VERDE VARIATA

Ingredients:
> 1 bunch of chard
> 1 head of lettuce (not iceberg)
> 1 bunch of spinach
> ¼ head cabbage or 1 small Savoy cabbage
> 2 potatoes
> 1 onion
> 2 or 3 tomatoes

Chop all the ingredients. In a stock pot, sauté the chopped onion in butter and add whatever herbs you like. Add the 2 sliced potatoes with a few chopped (peeled) tomatoes. Add additional water during cooking if necessary along with salt and pepper, then put through a food mill, add water to bring to a total of 2 quarts. Flavor with butter and add **rice** or **pastina** before serving.

141. London style minestra
MINESTRA LONDINESE

Ingredients:
> 1 cabbage
> 5 or 6 carrots
> 4 leeks
> 2 large onions
> 2 stalks celery
> 1 tbsp vinegar
> ⅓ cup butter
> 5 oz rice
> 1 bay leaf
> a pinch of oregano
> thyme
> marjoram
> pepper
> 2 tsp curry (recipe 893)
> ½ cup cream
> 1 lb apples
> 1 tsp lemon juice

Sauté the onion in butter together with the diced apples, then add the chopped vegetables, curry, herbs and rice. When the butter has been absorbed, add 2 qt water and let boil for 2 hours. Serve with cream and lemon juice.

142. Julian soup
ZUPPA GIULIANA

Bring to a boil:

2 qt broth (recipes 43 to 51)

Add:

8 oz peeled, sliced potatoes

6 oz sliced carrots

4 oz turnip cabbage

2 celery hearts

parsley

chopped herbs

When cooked, serve with **croutons** on the side.

143. Macaroni soup, English style
ZUPPA DI MACCHERONI ALL'INGLESE

Ingredients:

6 oz turnips

6 oz carrots

6 oz onions

parsley

1 pint milk

⅓ cup butter

9 oz penne or broken macaroni

Chop the vegetables and boil in 1 quart water with salt and pepper. When almost done, add the milk, pasta and chopped parsley and cook until done, stirring frequently. Add butter before serving.

144. Leek soup
ZUPPA DI PORRI

Ingredients:

1 lb leeks

1 lb potatoes

1 celery heart

2 oz butter

Chop the leeks and peeled potatoes and sauté in butter with salt and pepper. Add 2 quarts water and boil for an hour and a half. Serve with **fried bread cubes**.

145. Egyptian style lentil soup
ZUPPA DI LENTI EGIZIANA

Ingredients:

10 oz Egyptian lentils (or those from Pantelleria)

2 chopped onions

1 pint milk

½ tsp curry

salt

pepper

Soak the lentils in water for a few hours, then cook with the onion, covered with water. When done, put through a food mill. Dissolve **3 tbsp flour** in the milk, add the curry and lentils, allow to thicken over a low flame and serve with **croutons**.

146. Lentil and rice minestra
ZUPPA DI LENTI E RISO

Soak **1 ¼ cups lentils** in water for a few hours and then boil in 2 qt water. When cooked, add:

>   ¼ lb rice
>   2 chopped onions
>   3 chopped carrots
>   parsley
>   salt
>   pepper

Cook until rice is done. Add **½ cup cream** before serving.

147. English milk soup
ZUPPA DI LATTE INGLESE

Ingredients:

>   1 ½ pints vegetable broth (recipes 43 to 51)
>   1 ½ lb potatoes
>   1 onion
>   2 carrots
>   1 stalk of celery

Bring the broth to a boil and add the rinsed and chopped vegetables. When cooked, put through a food mill and replace in a saucepan with the milk. Bring to a boil and serve with **fried bread cubes.**

148. Mushroom soup
ZUPPA DI FUNGHI

Ingredients:

>   1 lb fresh or 5 oz dried mushrooms soaked in warm water for an hour
>   1 ½ pints of vegetable broth (recipes 43 to 51)
>   1 qt milk
>   ¼ lb carrots
>   3 tbsp butter

Slice the mushrooms and cook in the broth until soft. In another pan, gently fry the sliced carrots in butter, then add the mushrooms and milk (in which you have dissolved a spoonful of flour) and serve with **croutons.**

149. Ricotta soup
ZUPPA DI RICOTTA

In **4 tbsp butter**, lightly brown:

>   1 large chopped onion

Add:

>   small glass of dry white wine (let evaporate)
>   ½ lb ricotta, crushed with a wooden spoon
>   1 ½ pints of milk and 1 cup sea water to thin the soup (if not available, substitute salted water)

Cook for 30 minutes and put through a food mill, then reheat and serve immediately with **fried bread cubes.**

150. Winter soup
ZUPPA D'INVERNO

Ingredients:

>   3 lb potatoes
>   1 qt milk
>   ⅔ cup butter
>   abundant parsley
>   10 walnuts
>   4 egg yolks

Peel and boil the potatoes and put them through

a food mill one by one, allowing to drop into a saucepan of warm milk. Bind with 4 egg yolks, add salt and pepper and pour into individual dishes in which you have placed slices of **bread fried in butter**. Sprinkle the crushed walnuts and finely chopped parsley over the soup before serving.

151. Chilean 'puchero'
PUCHERO CILENO

In **3 pints vegetable broth** (recipes 43 to 51), cook:

> 6 chunks of corn on the cob
> 6 pieces of orange squash or pumpkin
> 6 sliced onions
> 1 chopped Savoy cabbage
> 6 peeled and sliced potatoes
> 6 carrots

When cooked, serve the vegetables in individual soup dishes and pour the broth over, adding grated Parmesan cheese.

152. Rumford soup
ZUPPA RUMFORD

Boil in 4 quart water:

> 1 ¼ cups barley
> ¾ cup dried peas

When well cooked, add:

> ½ lb peeled and chopped potatoes
> an herb bouquet
> salt
> pepper
> ½ cup vinegar
> 1 chopped celery stalk
> 1 sliced carrot

> pearl onions
> other vegetables as you wish

Thin with water if necessary and serve with **croutons**.

153. White bean soup
ZUPPA DI FAGIUOLI BIANCHI

Boil in 3 quart water with a pinch of baking soda:

> 1 ¾ cups white beans
> 3 sliced carrots
> 1 chopped onion
> 1 diced celery stalk
> chopped parsley

Add more water during cooking if necessary. Put through a food mill, then put back on a low flame with salt and pepper and bind with a spoonful of flour dissolved in milk. When thickened, add **½ cup cream** and serve over slices of **fried bread**.

154. Green soup
ZUPPA VERDE

Boil in 3 quarts water:

> 4 artichokes
> 1 ½ cups fresh or dried peas
> 2 carrots
> handful of chopped spinach or other leafy
>   green vegetables
> parsley
> onion

Add more water if necessary. When well cooked, put through a food mill, reheat and add **½ cup cream**, serving with **croutons**.

First courses, pasta dishes and timballi

PRIMI, PASTE ASCIUTTE E TIMBALLI

Risotto requires some practice to master, but it is quite simple to prepare. Use Arborio rice—traditional—or your choice of short or medium grain rice. A basic recipe for 4 to 6 servings requires 1 ½ cups of rice and 4 to 6 cups of broth. For vegetable broth, see recipes 43 to 51. To cook, use a medium saucepan over low heat. Start by cooking the rice for 2 to 3 minutes in butter or olive oil, then add enough broth to cover the rice. Stir almost constantly throughout cooking. Once the broth has evaporated, add more, ladleing it in warm so as not to slow cooking. Total cooking time is between 20 and 30 minutes.

155. Risotto 'alla Milanese'
RISOTTO ALLA MILANESE

Ingredients:

1 ½ cups of Arborio or short-grain rice
About six cups of vegetable broth (see recipes 43 to 51)
1 onion
a pinch of saffron
a sprinkling of nutmeg
white pepper
½ cup grated Parmesan cheese
velouté sauce (recipe 650)
2 tbsp butter

In a medium saucepan over low heat, melt the butter and brown a chopped onion. Add the rice, cook for about 2 minutes, and then add enough broth to cover the rice.

As the broth evaporates, add more. Stir continually. When half cooked, add a pinch of saffron, dissolved in hot broth, a sprinkling of nutmeg, white pepper, and ½ cup grated Parmesan cheese. Total cooking time is about 30 minutes. Risotto is done when the rice is tender, though it should still have a slight crunch.

Serve with a **velouté sauce** (recipe 650).

156. Risotto 'al Corvo'
RISOTTO AL CORVO

Follow the above recipe and add **1 cup white wine** to the rice during cooking.

157. Turkish rice
PILÒ O RISO ALLA TURCA

Chop **6 onions** and **1 beet.** In a large saucepan over medium heat, fry lightly in butter with:

> parsley
> garlic
> salt
> pepper
> ground cloves
> ground nutmeg

Stir in:

> **3 cups boiling water**
> **a pinch of saffron**

Allow to simmer for an hour over a low flame, then pass through a food mill. Rinse **1 lb rice,** mix with the above sauce and add **2 tbsp butter** or **½ cup cream.** Cook until rice is done, adding additional water if necessary.

158. Sicilian risotto with peas and artichokes
RISOTTO ALLA SICILIANA CON PISELLI E CARCIOFI

In a large saucepan on medium heat, brown a **chopped onion** in **olive oil** and add:

> **1 lb peas**
> **4 artichokes,** cleaned and cut into
> quarters

Add salt and pepper. When the artichokes are almost soft, pour in **1 lb rice**—about 2 cups—and add hot water until a thick soupy consistency has been reached. Stir continually. When rice is almost cooked, add a **sharp dry cheese** (such as Sicilian caciocavallo, or, if it can't be found, Italian provolone). Total cooking time is between 20 and 30 minutes. Some cooks like to add a few spoonfuls of **tomato sauce** while the risotto is cooking.

159. Risotto 'alla finanziera'
RISOTTO ALLA FINANZIERA

Prepare a **risotto with wine** (see recipe 157), using **1 cup of wine** and **½ cup grated Parmesan cheese.** Place in individual serving dishes with an open well in the center.

To make the filling: Slice **mushrooms,** and in a sauté pan, fry with:

> **2 tbsp butter**
> **chopped parsley**
> **chopped onion**
> **salt**
> **pepper**

Bind with a bit of **white wine,** then add to the risotto and serve. You may also top this off with **chopped truffles.**

160. Rice in tomato shells
RISO IN POMIDORI

Heat oven to 375°F.

Take a **dozen round, ripe tomatoes** and remove the stem and seeds without breaking through the skin. Rinse **1 cup rice** and mix in a bowl with:

> **chopped parsley**
> **chopped onion**
> **salt**
> **pepper**

Fill the tomatoes with this mixture, top off with a dot of butter on each, and bake in a medium oven until the rice is cooked, about 25 minutes.

161. Red risotto
RISOTTO ROSSO

Ingredients:
- 1 lb rice
- 8 oz butter
- ⅓ cup grated Parmesan cheese
- 1 onion, chopped
- 1 can of peeled tomatoes or 1 lb fresh tomatoes, washed and put through a food mill

In a sauce pan over medium heat, sauté the onion in butter until a golden color and add the rice. Pour in hot water and a pinch of salt, stirring continually, and when the rice is half cooked, about 15 minutes, add the tomatoes, continuing to thin with water as necessary. When ready, add the Parmesan and serve immediately. If you wish, additional sauce and cheese may be added before serving.

162. Creole rice
RISO ALLA CREOLA

Ingredients:
- 1 cup rice
- 5 oz butter
- 30 pearl onions
- 4 oz tomato sauce
- 4 grated carrots

Rinse the rice and place in a saucepan together with the whole onions, butter, tomato sauce, carrots, salt, pepper and water (which should be 1 inch over the rice). Cover and cook over a high to medium flame for 15 minutes without stirring. Then uncover and continue to cook over a slow flame for an additional 30 minutes without stirring.

163. Italian style tortellini
TORTELLINI ALL'ITALIANA

Make the **tortellini** as in recipe 57, adding:
- 1 tbsp dried **mushrooms** (soaked in warm water and chopped)
- 8 crushed **walnuts**

Cut the tortellini dough with a pizza cutter. Cook them briefly in boiling water, drain and season with:
- **butter**
- **Parmesan cheese**
- **velouté sauce** (recipe 655)

164. Polenta
POLENTA

Slowly pour into 1 quart plus 1 cup cold salted water:
- 1 lb **polenta** or **cornmeal**

Put the saucepan on the fire and stir continually for 20 minutes (timing from when it comes to a boil). Spread this paste on a marble counter in inch-thick layers and when it has cooled, cut into rectangles slightly smaller than 2 × 3 inches. Place these on a baking sheet greased with butter and spread them with **Parmesan cheese** and a few dots of **butter** before putting in a medium oven. These may also be seasoned with tomato sauce, "subisso" sauce (recipe 686) or others according to taste. It is also excellent fried in a skillet.

165. Polenta from Lodi
POLENTA LODIGIANA

Ingredients:

- **1 cup cornmeal**
- **1 qt milk**

Prepare the polenta as in recipe 164, adding salt, and turn off the burner. While still hot, spread it on a marble surface. After it has cooled, cut it in disks with a small mold. Join the disks two by two, placing a slice of **Gruyère cheese** in the middle. Dip in **beaten eggs**, then in **bread crumbs** and fry in hot olive oil.

166. Neapolitan pizza
PIZZA ALLA NAPOLETANA

In **½ cup milk** dissolve **1 to 2 oz yeast** and keep warm for 30 minutes. Then add:

- **1 lb flour**
- **2 beaten eggs**
- **salt**
- **enough warm water** to achieve the right consistency (similar to bread dough)

Flatten into the bottom of a large baking sheet to a thickness of ½ inch.

Cover with slices of **mozzarella** (which should first be drained to remove excess liquid) and chunks of drained, peeled **ripe tomatoes**. Sprinkle with:

- **bread crumbs**
- **oregano**
- **salt**
- **pepper**
- **a few drops of olive oil**

Let it rise in a warm place, then bake in a very hot oven (up to 500°F) until the crust is crisp.

167. Potatoes 'pizzaiola' style
PATATE ALLA PIZZAIUOLA

Ingredients:

- **4 lb potatoes**
- **1 lb onions**
- **10 oz fresh cheese**
- **10 oz fresh ripe tomatoes** (first peel and remove seeds)
- **olive oil**

Peel the potatoes and slice in ¼-inch slices, then place in salted water for 30 minutes (to remove excess starch). Cover the bottom of a baking dish with olive oil and line with a layer of potatoes. Cover this with thick slices of fresh cheese (mozzarella or Sicilian primosale or scamorza) followed by a layer of sliced onions with a few chunks of tomatoes. Sprinkle with salt, pepper, oregano and repeat the layers until finished; the top layer should be potatoes, cheese and tomatoes but no onions. Sprinkle with bread crumbs and oregano and add a few drops of oil on top before placing in a medium oven. Crisp up the top under the broiler before serving.

168. Potatoes and spinach
PATATE AGLI SPINACI

Follow recipe 137, substituting the cabbage with **spinach**.

169. 'Ciupe' (a Spanish dish)
CIUPE (PIATTO SPAGNOLO)

Alternate layers of:

- **sliced onion**
- **sliced peeled potatoes dotted with butter**

sliced tomatoes

grated cheese

Finish with a layer of potatoes covered with butter and a generous sprinkling of cheese. It must be baked at 350°F for 45 minutes until the onions are well cooked and the tomato juice has been absorbed. In Spain it is also seasoned with cayenne.

170. Stuffed potatoes
PATATE RIPIENE

Choose **potatoes** of the same size, peel and cut in half. Meanwhile prepare a filling composed of:

dried bread (from which the crusts have been removed)

finely chopped onion and parsley

butter

pepper

a raw egg to bind

Mix thoroughly, then dig out the center of the potatoes, being careful not to break through the outside shell. Fill with the stuffing, then tie with a string across the top. Place in a deep saucepan and brown in butter over a medium flame until they are cooked. Serve while piping hot.

171. Tapioca potatoes
PATATE CON TAPIOCA

Peel **3 lb potatoes** and slice ½ inch thick, spreading them in an ovenproof dish alternately with layers of **sliced onions**. Add water to cover and pour over the top:

6 tbsp tapioca

½ tsp salt

Place **3 or 4 tbsp butter** in the center and bake in a medium oven for an hour and a half.

172. Potatoes with Marsala wine
PATATE AL MARSALA

Choose **small potatoes** of the same size, peel and place in a wide saucepan to form only one layer. Fry gently in butter and oil and when half-cooked, add:

salt

a glass of dry Marsala wine

When uniformly golden brown, serve immediately. This dish can also be made with sliced potatoes and slivers of onion, using potatoes of various sizes.

173. Potatoes 'puviredda' style (pauper's potatoes)
PATATE ALLA PUVIREDDA

Place **potatoes** under the glowing coals of a barbecue and when soft, take off the jackets and season with a **salmoriglio sauce** (recipe 972).

174. Eclectic potatoes
PATATE IN TUTTI I MODI

Peel the **potatoes** and cut in ½-inch slices; cook in a double boiler and season with any of the sauces in this book (see chapter on "Sauces and Stuffings") which all combine well with potatoes. These may also be placed in a saucepan and cooked directly in the sauce of your choice.

175. Potatoes 'sfincione' style (like Sicilian deep pan pizza)
PATATE A SFINCIONE

Peel the **potatoes** and slice in ¼-inch slices, then spread in a baking dish in layers alternately with:

- slices of onion
- grated **caciocavallo** (or any sharp dry cheese)
- a pinch of oregano
- a spray of olive oil

176. Parsley potatoes
PATATE AL PREZZEMOLO

Peel and cook **whole potatoes** in a double boiler and serve hot with the following sauce: Dissolve **1 tbsp flour** in **1 tbsp butter** and add **2 tbsp finely chopped parsley**. Lightly fry these ingredients, stirring continually, and then add enough water to bring to the desired consistency and simmer until thickened. Add salt and pepper before serving.

177. Potatoes in 'salmoriglio'
PATATE AL SALAMORIGLIO

Peel and steam the **potatoes** in a double boiler (see recipe 894). Place on a platter, pressing them lightly with a fork and season with **salmoriglio** (recipe 972).

178. Potatoes 'subisso' style
PATATE AL SUBISSO

Boil or steam peeled **potatoes**, then cut in cubes and serve with **subisso sauce** (recipe 686).

179. Potatoes with cabbage
PATATE AL CAVOLO CAPPUCCIO

Shred the **cabbage** and sauté in a small quantity of olive oil; put a lid on the saucepan and allow to simmer over a slow flame. Meanwhile, slice freshly boiled **potatoes** into very thin slices and place in an ovenproof dish, alternating layers of potatoes dotted with butter and layers of cooked cabbage. The top layer of potatoes should be covered with a thin **béchamel** (recipes 652 and 653). Place under the broiler to brown the top and serve in the baking dish.

180. Potatoes and brown butter
PATATE AL BURRO NERO

In an ovenproof dish spread alternating layers of:

- **3 lb potatoes**, peeled and sliced in ½-inch slices
- onion
- a pinch of salt and pepper

Add water to cover and cook over a slow flame. In another pan put:

- **5 oz butter**
- chopped parsley

Melt the butter and cook until the butter has darkened. When the potatoes have absorbed all of the cooking water, put them in a serving dish and pour the browned butter over them. (If the potatoes are soft before having absorbed all the water, drain off the excess water and serve immediately with the above butter sauce.)

181. Potato 'pasticcio' French style (potato pie)
PASTICCIO DI PATATE ALLA FRANCESE

Cook the **potatoes** as in the foregoing recipe and put them through a food mill with a grating of **lemon grind**; place in a saucepan over a low flame and mix continually, adding a chunk of **butter**. Continue stirring and add:

> **milk in small doses**
>
> **a spoonful of sugar**

Let cool and beat in:

> **4 raw egg yolks**

Then fold in:

> **4 stiffly beaten egg whites**

Mix thoroughly and butter a mold or an oven-proof dish, sprinkle with **bread crumbs** and fill with the potato mixture. Bake in the oven for 45 minutes and brown under the broiler before serving.

182. Gruyère potatoes
PATATE AL GRUVIERA

Cook **6 large potatoes** in a double boiler using yellow potatoes if available. Put them through a food mill and spread a 1-inch layer in an oven-proof dish. Cover with alternating layers of:

> **grated Gruyère cheese**
>
> **butter**
>
> **a pinch of pepper**

Finish with a layer of potatoes, which should then be covered with grated Gruyère and Parmesan.

Cover with an earthenware lid for 15 minutes then bake until the top is browned.

183. Wafer-thin fried potatoes
PATATE FRITTE AD OSTIA

Peel raw **potatoes** and slice in paper-thin slices (with a truffle slicer if possible, so they are of uniform thickness). Put in very hot olive oil (without adding salt) until they are crisp and brown, then drain on paper towel and sprinkle with salt.

184. Potato puffs
PATATE SOFFIATE

Peel and slice **potatoes** lengthwise in ¼-inch thicknesses. Fry in olive oil over a medium flame until almost done, then remove from the pan and drain on paper towel until they are almost cool. Replace in very hot olive oil a few at a time, moving continually, until they puff up and become golden brown. Remove and serve hot.

185. Parisian style fried potatoes
PATATE SALTATE ALLA PARIGINA

Peel **potatoes** and place whole in hot butter in a saucepan and stir until they are golden brown. Drain and add salt before serving.

186. Italian style fried potatoes
PATATE SALTATE ALL'ITALIANA

Follow the above recipe, but use **already-boiled potatoes** and serve without draining off the excess butter.

187. Sicilian style fried potatoes
PATATE SALTATE ALLA SICILIANA

Boil the **potatoes** and cut into thin slices. Sauté in a butter and olive oil mixture in a covered frying pan. When a crust has formed, turn out on a plate in a solid mass and slide back into the pan to brown the other side. Serve with **lemon** on the side.

188. French potato salad
PATATE ALL'INSALATA ALLA FRANCESE

Slice boiled peeled **potatoes** while still hot and season with:

> **extra virgin olive oil**
> **vinegar**
> **salt**
> **pepper**
> **chopped herbs**

(Some cooks prefer to substitute the olive oil with fresh cream.)

189. 'Picchio-pacchio' potatoes
PATATE AL PIK-PACCHIO

Select small **potatoes** of more or less the same size, steam in a double boiler and peel. Place the steamed potatoes in a saucepan with picchio-pacchio **sauce** (recipe 647), stew for a few minutes and serve immediately.

190. Oven-roasted potatoes
PATATE AL FORNO

Peel **potatoes** of the same size, then place them in a baking dish with butter and olive oil and a pinch of salt. Place in the oven until they are golden brown. These are then served on a **bed of lettuce** with a **sauce** of your choice.

191. Potato 'pasticcio' Italian style (potato pie)
PASTICCIO DI PATATE ALL'ITALIANA

Peel the **potatoes**, boil and put through a food mill, then mix with:

> **grated Parmesan**
> **beaten eggs** (one egg for each pound of potatoes)
> **salt**
> **pepper**

Pour half the potato mixture into a baking dish that has been greased with butter and sprinkled with **bread crumbs**. Cover the layer of potatoes with slices of **mozzarella** or other fresh cheese and then add the remaining potatoes. Bake in a medium oven until golden brown.

192. Lyonnaise potatoes
PATATE ALLA LIONESE

After boiling peeled **potatoes** in salted water or steaming in a double boiler, slice them and place in a saucepan. Cover them with an **onion sauce** (recipe 681), heat up without bringing to a boil and serve immediately.

193. Potatoes countrified style
PATATE ALLA PROVINCIALE

In a saucepan, place:
- 1 tbsp butter
- 6 tbsp olive oil
- a grating of lemon rind
- chopped parsley
- onions
- a clove of crushed garlic
- a pinch of nutmeg
- salt
- pepper

Peel and boil the **potatoes**, then slice into the above sauce until they have absorbed the oil. Squeeze some fresh **lemon juice** on top and add a sprinkling of **grated cheese** before serving.

194. Fricasseed potatoes
PATATE IN FRICASSEA

Peel and slice raw **potatoes** in ½-inch slices and spread in a saucepan with **dots of butter** and the **juice of 1 lemon**. Barely cover with salted water and stew until done. Turn out onto a platter and cover with **fricassee sauce** (recipe 662).

195. Potatoes with peas
PATATE CON PISELLI

Prepare as in recipe 37 and place in a saucepan with **butter**, adding a few ladles of **vegetable broth** (recipes 43 to 51). Serve in individual

dishes covered with **velouté sauce** (recipe 655) or another sauce of your choice.

196. Potatoes with Corvo wine
PATATE AL VINO CORVO

Combine and sauté in a saucepan:
- butter
- pepper
- salt
- parsley
- chopped onion

Add:
- a few ladles of broth
- a glass of white Corvo wine

When simmering, add sliced **boiled potatoes** and cook until the sauce has evaporated.

197. Stewed potatoes
PATATE A SPEZZATINO

Lightly fry **chopped onion** in olive oil or butter and then add:
- diced peeled potatoes
- peppers
- chopped parsley
- a pinch of saffron
- a glass of white wine

Simmer until the potatoes are cooked and serve with **cumin**.

198. Potatoes with walnuts
PATATE ALLE NOCI

Follow the above recipe and add **12 crushed walnuts** to round out the dish with proteins. These are also delicious served with pine nuts.

199. Potatoes 'alla castellana' (Chatelaine's potatoes)
PATATE ALLA CASTELLANA

After steaming the **potatoes** in a double boiler, roll in **flour** and fry in hot olive oil. Place on a serving dish and cover with **tomato sauce**.

200. English style potatoes
PATATE ALL'INGLESE

Cook the **potatoes** in a double-boiler (recipe 904), slice and place in a saucepan with:

> **butter**
> **salt**
> **pepper**
> **nutmeg**

Toss well, then serve with **Worcestershire sauce** or **ketchup**.

201. Soft-boiled new potatoes
PATATINE NUOVE IN CAMICIA

Choose **tiny new potatoes** the size of a walnut and place in a food mill (without peeling); sprinkle with water and a generous handful of cooking salt, then put through the food mill. Toss into water to remove the salt, dry on absorbent paper and fry in butter with salt. These should be eaten with the peel that gives a unique flavor to the dish.

202. Potatoes with cream
PATATE AL FIOR DI LATTE

In a saucepan, cook over a slow flame:

> **1 tbsp butter**
> **flour**
> **salt**
> **pepper**
> **ground nutmeg**
> **parsley**
> **chopped onion**

Pour in a **cup of cream**. Fry the **potatoes** in butter or steam in a double-boiler (recipe 904), then serve with the above sauce.

203. Jacket potatoes
PATATE IN GIACCHETTA

Boil **potatoes** without peeling and serve in the cooking water in a soup dish. These should be peeled on the plates and eaten steaming hot with **fresh butter** and **salt**.

204. Parisian style potatoes
PATATE ALLA PARIGINA

Put a pat of butter in a saucepan with a **chopped onion**. When the onion becomes transparent, add:

> **1 cup water**
> **peeled whole potatoes**
> **salt**
> **pepper**
> **a handful of chopped herbs**

Cook uncovered over a slow flame, pressing from time to time.

205. Steamed potatoes
PATATE A VAPORE

Peel **potatoes** and sprinkle with salt, then place in a double boiler. The potatoes are cooked when a fork goes in easily. Serve with **butter** or a **sauce** of your choice.

206. 'Locandiera' (innkeeper's) potatoes
PATATE ALLA LOCANDIERA

Steam peeled **potatoes** and then cut in slices, and place in a saucepan with:

  butter
  parsley
  chopped herbs
  salt
  pepper
  a few drops of vinegar

Heat and serve.

207. 'Montanara' (mountain-dweller's) potatoes
PATATE ALLA MONTANARA

After cooking **potatoes** as in recipe 205, mash with a potato masher; for every pound of potatoes, add:

  4 oz melted butter
  2/3 cup cream
  1 slice of bread (first remove the crusts)
    soaked in milk

Combine then add to the potatoes:

  3 tbsp grated cheese
  salt

  pepper

Stir well then add:

  4 egg yolks
  4 egg whites, beaten until stiff

Mix again and place in an ovenproof dish, then put in a medium oven until ready.

208. Potatoes with sage
PATATE SALVIATE

Peel medium-sized **potatoes** and make a slit with a knife, inserting **a leaf of sage**. Then fry in an equal quantity of butter and olive oil, turning until they are evenly browned. Douse with a small quantity of **white wine** and serve with a **sauce of your choice**.

209. Red beans 'alla cantiniera' (wine-keeper's beans)
FAGIUOLI ROSSI ALLA CANTINIERA

Cook **dried beans** in water with a pinch of salt and one of baking soda. When almost done, drain and rinse. Combine in a saucepan:

  a pinch of flour
  a dot of butter
  some chopped herbs
  the cooked beans
  a glass of red wine

Allow to finish cooking.

210. Lentils 'alla cantiniera'
LENTI ALLA CANTINIERA

Prepare **lentils** as in the above recipe.

211. Birdie style beans
FAGIUOLI ALL'UCCELLETTO

In water with salt and a pinch of baking soda, boil:

> dried white (cannellini) beans

Drain and place in a pan with:

> oil
>
> a cupful of fresh peeled tomatoes
>
> chopped celery hearts
>
> onions

When well amalgamated, add **salt** and **cayenne** and serve.

212. New beans
FAGIUOLI NUOVI

Take **shelled beans** and toss into boiling water. When half cooked, add salt. When ready, drain and add **cream**, **butter** or **olive oil** before serving.

213. White beans 'alla locandiera'
FAGIUOLI BIANCHI ALLA LOCANDIERA

Soak the **beans** in water overnight then cook with a pinch of baking soda, adding salt halfway through the cooking time. Drain when done and place in a frying pan with:

> sautéed butter
>
> chopped parsley
>
> onions
>
> carrots
>
> sweet peppers

Allow to thicken and serve.

214. Baked agnellotti
AGNELLOTTI AL FORNO

Cook **agnellotti** as in recipe 217 and after boiling, place in an ovenproof dish and cover with slices of **fried eggplant**; sprinkle with **Parmesan cheese**, dampen with **velouté sauce** and bake in a slow oven.

215. Agnellotti in béchamel
AGNELLOTTI ALLA BESCIAMELLA

Cook **agnellotti** as in recipe 216 then spread in a baking dish and cover with **béchamel** (see recipes 652–653), sprinkle with **cheese** and a few chunks of **butter**, then put in the oven until golden brown.

216. Agnellotti Sardinian style
AGNELLOTTI ALLA SARDA

Peel **four eggplants**, dice and sprinkle with salt, let drain in a colander, then rinse and dry. Fry the eggplant cubes in hot olive oil and after draining, mix with:

> 3 oz grated Parmesan cheese
>
> 1 chopped onion sautéed in oil
>
> finely chopped parsley
>
> 10 crushed walnuts
>
> pepper
>
> a few leaves of basil or sage

Combine all these ingredients with an egg. On the side, prepare a dough with:

> 1 lb of semolina
>
> a pinch of saffron dissolved in warm water
>
> salt to taste

Knead and then roll on a floured board to the

thickness of a nickel. Place the above filling in small mounds on one half of the rolled dough and then cover with the other half and cut around each mound in squares with a wheeled pizza cutter. Allow to dry and then cook briefly in abundant water. Drain, place in baking dish in layers and cover with:

> velouté sauce or tomato sauce
> grated Parmesan cheese

Put in oven until it forms a golden crust.

217. Green ravioli
RAVIOLI AL VERDE

Make a **pasta dough** (see recipe 533) with **1 ½ lb flour** and roll out to ⅛ inch thickness. For filling, mix:

> 1 cup boiled, drained and
>   chopped spinach
> 1 cup ricotta
> salt
> pepper

Place this filling in small mounds on half of the rolled pasta dough and then fold over the other half and cut with a pizza cutter. Boil in abundant water and drain, then place on a serving dish covered with a **velouté sauce** (recipe 655) and **grated Parmesan cheese**, or with **spinach** and **béchamel**.

218. Gnocchi pie with pizzaiola sauce
GNOCCATA ALLA PIZZAIUOLA

In order to make good gnocchi in an hour and a half follow this recipe: boil **1 quart water** with salt and spices. When it is boiling rapidly, pour in **6 oz semolina**, stirring continually. Allow to thicken, then remove from the flame and let cool. Stir in:

> 4 beaten eggs
> 2 oz grated Parmesan cheese
> 2 oz Gouda or Edam cheese

Mix until well amalgamated. Pour into a greased baking dish and cover with:

> chunks of peeled tomatoes
> a few slices of fresh cheese
> a sprinkling of bread crumbs
> oregano
> minced garlic
> pepper

Add a few drops of olive oil and bake in a medium oven until crusty on top.

219. Heavenly gnocchi
GNOCCHI DEL PARADISO

Prepare the paste for **fried milk fritters** as in recipe 615, but cut them in rounds with a glass rim. Spread all the leftover strips on the bottom of a buttered baking dish and place the rounds on top. Sprinkle with **cheese**, a few dots of **butter**, and cook under a broiler until golden brown.

220. Potato gnocchi Florentine style
GNOCCHI DI PATATE ALLA FIORENTINA

Boil **2 lb peeled potatoes** and put through a ricer. Add:

> 2 oz crushed walnuts
> 5 oz grated Parmesan cheese

3 whole eggs

spices

salt

Knead, adding a spray of **semolina** until the right consistency for forming ½-inch thick finger-shaped gnocchi. Cut these in 1-inch lengths and drop in boiling **broth** (see recipes 44 and 51) for a few minutes and serve as a minestra topped with **grated cheese**. If you prefer, you can boil them in salted water, removing with a strainer, and then season with cheese and velouté sauce (recipe 650).

221. Sicilian style gnocchi
GNOCCHI ALLA SICILIANA

Make a pasta with:

2 lb hard grain semolina

Knead thoroughly until it is white and dry enough to cut, then form finger-shaped sticks and cut in ½-inch pieces. Press the pieces lightly with your thumb on a grater from the top down until they roll up into a shell and leave to dry on a kitchen towel for one or two hours. Cook (see recipe 232) and after draining, put back in the dry saucepan and mix with the following sauce: Fry **eggplant slices** (see recipe 269), then dice and combine with:

thick tomato sauce

olive oil

12 crushed walnuts

Pour half this sauce onto the gnocchi and mix, sprinkling with **Parmesan cheese**. Place the gnocchi and sauce in a baking dish, cover with the remaining sauce, sprinkle with Parmesan and put in a hot oven until a crust has formed.

222. Potato gnocchi with bread crumbs
GNOCCHI DI PATATE AL PANGRATTATO

Ingredients:

1 lb potatoes

5 oz bread crumbs

1 egg

3 oz caciocavallo (or other dry, medium sharp cheese)

2 oz butter

tomato or velouté sauce

Peel and boil the potatoes, then drain and put through a food mill while still hot. Add the bread crumbs, eggs and half the cheese. When well mixed, form into little balls and press flat, then boil in salted water until they come to the surface. Drain and season before serving with the remaining cheese, butter and tomato sauce.

223. Green gnocchi
GNOCCHI VERDI

Follow recipe 224 but substitute **greens** (either spinach, or other leafy greens) which have been boiled in salted water, drained and put through a food mill. Season with **béchamel** (recipe 652) to which some of the spinach has been added.

224. Red gnocchi
GNOCCHI ROSA

Ingredients:

10 oz semolina

5 eggs

3 oz grated Parmesan cheese

tomato sauce

4 oz butter

Make a batter with the semolina, a little tomato sauce, a pinch of salt, 2 oz butter and water. Place over a low flame stirring continually and when it has thickened and is of a uniform consistency, remove from the flame. When it has cooled beat in the eggs with salt and stir well. Drop small nuggets of the batter into boiling water with the tip of a tablespoon and cook for 4 to 6 minutes. Remove with a strainer and season in the serving dish with tomato sauce and butter.

225. Gnocchi 'alla golosa' (glutton's gnocchi)
GNOCCHI ALLA GOLOSA

Cook:

9 oz semolina

1 quart of milk

3 oz butter

a pinch of salt

nutmeg

When the semolina is well cooked, cool by spreading on a marble surface and knead, adding:

4 whole eggs

5 yolks

more uncooked semolina if necessary to reach the right consistency

Mix well and add:

3 oz Parmesan cheese

3 tbsp butter

8 oz ricotta

When well mixed, form 1-inch finger-shaped sticks and cook in boiling water and remove with a draining ladle. When they are all cooked, douse with a **Spanish sauce**, **velouté sauce** or **white sauce** (see recipes 649 and 650), sprinkle with Parmesan and serve.

226. Stale bread gnocchi
GNOCCHI DI PAN DURO

Ingredients:

1 lb stale bread

9 oz semolina

1 egg

4 oz grated Parmesan cheese

3 tbsp butter

Soak the bread in water until thoroughly wet; remove the crusts, squeeze well and mix with the semolina, the egg and a pinch of salt. Roll this paste into walnut-sized balls, cover with flour and flatten slightly. Drop into salted boiling water and when the gnocchi rise to the surface, drain and season with butter and Parmesan, adding **tomato sauce** if you wish.

227. Homemade gnocchi Roman style
GNOCCHI ALLA ROMANA CASALINGHI

Boil in 1 quart salted water:

10 oz semolina

As soon as it thickens, take off the flame and stir in:

4 eggs

Spread on a marble counter greased with butter. When cool, cut into rounds; place the bits and pieces of cuttings on the bottom of a buttered baking dish and cover with a layer of the rounds and sprinkle with **grated Parmesan cheese**. The top layer should be dotted with butter. Put in a hot oven or under a broiler until crusty brown.

228. Roman gnocchi with tomato sauce
GNOCCHI ROMANI AL POMODORO

In **1 quart boiling milk**, pour:

10 oz of semolina

Add a pinch of salt. When the paste is thick, bind with **4 beaten eggs** and spread on a marble surface greased with butter. The paste should be spread to a ½-inch thickness. When cool, cut in disks with the rim of a glass and place the gnocchi in an oven dish in layers, covering each layer with **grated cheese**, except the last. Top with dots of butter and place in a hot oven until a golden crust has formed. Serve with **tomato sauce** on the side.

229. Extra rich gnocchi Roman style
GNOCCHI ALLA ROMANA ARRICCHITI

Ingredients:

10 oz semolina

1 qt milk

3 oz caciocavallo (or other medium-sharp cheese)

2 oz butter

a pinch of saffron dissolved in water

6 eggs

Boil the milk in a saucepan and pour in the semolina, then add the saffron and salt and mix continually. When the pasta has thickened, add half the cheese and the egg yolks and take off the flame.

Spread one inch thick on a marble board greased with butter and when it has cooled, cut

in disks; place these in a baking dish in layers, sprinkling the cheese over each. Finally, add the remaining butter and put in the oven.

230. Pisan style gnocchi
GNOCCHI ALLA PISANA

In **1 pint of milk**, pour:

10 oz semolina

Stir constantly. When it comes to the boil add:

4 oz cream

a pinch of salt

some nutmeg

When this is dense, add:

4 whole eggs

4 egg yolks

Pour out on a marble surface. Knead the pasta, adding:

4 oz grated Parmesan cheese

2 additional oz semolina

4 oz ricotta

1 oz skinned, crushed almonds

When well mixed, roll into balls the size of a hazelnut and press slightly to flatten, or else in finger-shaped, inch-long sticks. Roll them in flour and drop in boiling water. When cooked, remove and place in a hot serving dish while the others are cooking. Sprinkle with Parmesan and season with **velouté sauce** (recipe 650).

231. Twice-cooked gnocchi
GNOCCHI DI RICUPERO

Take the leftovers from the **timballo** in recipe 258 (it is worth making a double portion to have leftovers), slice and cut in squares or rounds. Then place on a baking sheet, sprinkle with **butter** and **cheese** and put in a hot oven until crisp.

232. Pasta with butter and directions for cooking
PASTA AL BURRO E MODO DI CUOCERLA

Pasta should always be cooked in abundant water. The following proportions may serve as a guide: **1 lb pasta** in no less than **8 quarts water**, (but even the smallest quantity of pasta requires at least 1 quart water). Drop the pasta (macaroni, spaghetti, penne, etc.) in rapidly boiling water, add a tsp salt when the water is boiling, and stir well. When it is cooked to the desired consistency, take off the flame, pour in ½ quart cold water and drain immediately. Excellent served with a pat of **butter** and **grated Parmesan cheese**.

233. Pasta with tomato sauce
PASTA AL SUGO DI POMODORO

Cook as in the above recipe, serve with the **tomato sauce** in recipe 646 and **Parmesan cheese**.

234. Vermicelli with mock clams
VERMICELLI ALLE VONGOLE (PSEUDO)

In olive oil, sauté:

    minced onion

When transparent, add:

    a clove of crushed garlic
    some chopped zucchini blossoms
    a pinch of saffron dissolved in warm
      water
    chopped parsley
    salt
    pepper

During cooking add a cup or two **tomato sauce** (see recipe 646). When the pasta is cooked and drained (see recipe 232 above), place in a dry saucepan and pour in half of the above sauce. Stir, serve in individual dishes, and add the remaining sauce.

235. Pasta with sardines still in the sea (a vegetarian version of the Sicilian 'pasta with sardines')
PASTA CON LE SARDE A MARE

Boil some **wild fennel leaves** if available; if not, substitute leaves from domestic fennel, add salt and drain when cooked, but save the water. Chop the fennel leaves and put in a saucepan where you have sautéed in some **chopped onion** in abundant **olive oil**. Add:

    a handful of pine nuts
    small black raisins (uva passita)
    a pinch of saffron dissolved in hot water
    salt
    pepper

Cook the **pasta**, which for this dish should be large macaroni, long like spaghetti but with a large hole in the center (see recipe 232 for instructions on cooking), in the water you have saved from the fennel leaves. When cooked, drain and put back in a large dry saucepan and mix with half the above sauce, then place in an oven-proof dish and cover with the remaining sauce, sprinkle with toasted, crushed **almonds**, and place in a hot oven for 10 to 15 minutes. Some like to add **picchio-pacchio sauce** (see recipe 647).

236. Sicilian style pasta
PASTA ALLA SICILIANA

Prepare a sauce with:

> **concentrated tomato paste:**
> **chopped fried eggplant**
> **10 shelled and crushed walnuts** in place
> > of meat

Cook the pasta (as in recipe 232), which should be **large ring-shaped anelli**, then drain and put in a saucepan with two thirds of the sauce and a generous sprinkling of **Parmesan cheese**. Mix, put in an ovenproof dish, add the remaining sauce with slices of **fresh caciocavallo cheese**, then sprinkle with Parmesan and put in the oven after dotting the top with butter.

237. Capuchin pasta (with cauliflower)
PASTA ALLA CAPPUCCINA

In olive oil, sauté:

> **chopped onion**

Add:

> **finely chopped boiled cauliflower**
> **a pinch of saffron dissolved in**
> > **warm water**

pepper
salt
small black raisins (uva passa)
pine nuts

Cook the pasta, preferably **small macaroni**, as in recipe 232, and when it has been drained, put in a dry saucepan and add half the sauce. Mix well and place in individual dishes then add the remaining sauce with a pinch of **cumin** or **grated cheese**.

238. Vermicelli 'alla finanziera'
VERMICELLI ALLA FINANZIERA

Prepare a good **Spanish sauce** (recipe 649), sauté some **truffles** and **mushrooms** sliced to look like liver, and add to the sauce. Cook the **vermicelli** (see recipe 232), season with half the sauce and **Parmesan**, place in individual dishes, then add more Parmesan and the remaining sauce. Spread on top some of the **mock eggs** in recipe 466 and dot with **butter** before serving.

239. Pasta with a glaze sauce
PASTA GLASSATA

Cook the **pasta** (see recipe 232) and pour into a dry saucepan after draining. Add **velouté sauce** (as in recipe 650) and **grated Parmesan cheese**, then mix rapidly and place in individual dishes. Before serving, sprinkle with Parmesan and add more of the velouté sauce.

240. Pasta served Gangi style
PASTA ALLA GANGITANA

Put 4 quarts water in a large pan. When it begins to boil, add:

1 small head of cauliflower, diced
a pinch of salt

When cooked, take out with a slotted ladle and place the cooked cauliflower in **a pint of good tomato sauce** (recipe 646). Add:

small black passolina raisins
pine nuts

Cook **2 lb pasta** (preferably a large form) in the water where the cabbage was boiled (adding fresh water to reach the necessary quantity) and when ready, drain and put in a saucepan with half of the sauce and mix well. Place in dishes and add the rest of the sauce with a sprinkling of **Parmesan cheese**.

241. Vermicelli 'alla carrettiera' (carter style)
VERMICELLI ALLA CARRETTIERA

Sauté in olive oil:

long slivers of onion
2 cloves of garlic
pepper
parsley
oregano

On the side prepare some **bread crumbs** by toasting in a frying pan with oil and salt. Cook the **vermicelli** (recipe 232), then drain and place in the pan with the onion mixture and stir until the sauce has been absorbed. Place in individual dishes and sprinkle with the bread crumbs before serving.

242. Pasta with 'caponata'
PASTA A CAPONATA

Ingredients:

6 oz green olives
2 lb tomatoes
2 stalks celery
½ cup olive oil
3 oz capers
2 onions
1 ½ lb pasta (preferably pasta with a hole in the center, such as rigatoni, shells, etc.)

Fry the chopped onion in olive oil and when transparent, add the tomatoes (that have previously been put through a food mill and drained), the pitted chopped olives, chopped celery and capers. Add salt and pepper and cook until the celery is tender, adding water if necessary. When the sauce is thoroughly amalgamated and has thickened adequately pour in **3 tbsp wine vinegar**.

When this has evaporated, remove from the flame. Cook the pasta, drain, and mix in a saucepan with half the sauce. Allow the pasta to cool, then place in individual dishes and add the remaining sauce. This dish should be served at room temperature, garnished with:

pickles
capers
fresh mint leaves

243. Macaroni in béchamel
MACCHERONI ALLA BESCIAMELLA

Cook the **macaroni** as usual (recipe 232), mix with **half of the sauce** in recipe 652, place in an oven-proof dish and spread the remaining sauce on top, sprinkling with a generous quantity of **Parmesan cheese**. Dot the top with butter and put in a hot oven until golden brown.

244. French style macaroni
MACCHERONI ALLA FRANCESE

Ingredients:

> 1 ¾ lb Neapolitan macaroni
> 5 oz butter
> 8 oz Gruyère cheese
> 3 oz grated Parmesan cheese
> 1 pint milk

Boil the macaroni and drain when al dente (that is, chewy, or resistant to the bite), placing in a saucepan with butter, Gruyère and milk, and stirring well. When it is thoroughly amalgamated, place in dishes and serve with Parmesan.

245. Spaghetti with walnuts
SPAGHETTI ALLA NOCI

Ingredients:

> 1 ¼ lb spaghetti
> ⅓ cup crushed walnuts
> 3 oz bread crumbs
> a pinch of spices

Cook the spaghetti (see recipe 232), season with **sautéed onion** and add the bread crumbs (which have been toasted in a frying pan with olive oil) and then sprinkle the walnuts over the top before serving.

246. Lasagne with ricotta
LASAGNE CON RICOTTA

Prepare the **sauce** in recipe 221, cook some **wide lasagne** following the instructions in recipe 232, drain, and place in a dry saucepan. Combine:

> half the sauce
> some Parmesan cheese
> ricotta that has been broken up with
>   a fork

Spread in a baking dish, adding slices of ricotta on top along with the remaining sauce. Sprinkle with Parmesan before placing in the oven to brown.

247. Homemade taglierini (thin noodles) Sicilian style
TAGLIERINI DI CASA ALLA SICILIANA

Ingredients:

> 1 ¾ lb fine semolina
> 3 eggs
> 2 oz butter
> 4 oz Parmesan cheese
> sauce

Put the semolina in a mound on a marble surface or floured board, and make a well in the center, then break the eggs directly into the well with a pinch of salt. Knead (see recipe 633), adding the quantity of water necessary to give the right consistency for rolling. When the dough has been kneaded for at least 15 minutes, roll it out to a ⅛-inch thickness and cut in very thin ribbons. Cook briefly as in recipe 232 and season with **butter**, **cheese** and **sauce** or with the sauce in recipe 221.

248. Macaroni 'pasticcio' as in Romagna
PASTICCIO DI MACCHERONI
ALLA ROMAGNOLA

Ingredients:

- 1 lb macaroni
- 5 oz Parmesan
- 3 oz truffles
- 2 oz butter
- 1 tbsp dried mushrooms that have been soaked in warm water and squeezed dry
- 2 finely chopped fried eggplant slices
- 1 cup béchamel (see recipe 652)
- 10 walnuts
- 10 oz pastry crust (see recipe 643)

Boil the macaroni in salted water, draining while still al dente. Make a filling with truffles, the chopped eggplant and mushrooms, seasoning with pepper, salt and nutmeg. Put the macaroni in a saucepan on the fire and add:

- ½ cup velouté or Spanish sauce (recipes 649-650)

Stir until absorbed. Then put the pasta in a baking dish in layers, sprinkling each with Parmesan and the crushed, shelled walnuts, then pour a béchamel and more of the filling over the pasta and dot with butter. Cover with a sheet of pastry dough, making certain it adheres to the sides of the dish. You may make some decorative pattern on the dough with the leftover cuttings, brush with egg white and put in the oven for 20 to 30 minutes.

Timballo is not to be confused with timbale, often used in American cooking to refer to a dish somewhere between a custard and a soufflé, made in individual portions. Timballo, instead, indicates a dish with a carbohydrate base (such as semolina, pasta or potatoes) and a variety of other ingredients, baked in a large round or rectangular baking dish, generally 5 or 6 inches in height, or else steamed in a mold. The baking dish or mold is first oiled and spread with bread crumbs or cheese. The cooked timballo may be served directly from the baking dish or turned out onto a platter and covered with sauce (in either case, it is of a rather solid consistency, unlike other casserole dishes).

249. The Queen's timballo
TIMBALLO REGINA

Ingredients:

- 8 oz rice
- 4 lb potatoes
- 1 pint milk
- 6 eggs
- 3 oz grated Parmesan cheese
- 3 tbsp truffles or mushrooms

Prepare a **Milanese risotto** (recipe 155), and a potato purée, then combine these with 2 raw eggs and half the Parmesan, salt and pepper. Now make a béchamel (as in recipes 652–653) and scramble the remaining 4 eggs in butter. Mix the scrambled eggs with the béchamel, the chopped truffles and the remaining Parmesan. Butter a baking dish and line with bread crumbs, then put in half the rice and potato mixture, cover with the egg and béchamel filling, and close with the remaining rice and potato. Bake in a hot oven 20–30 minutes.

250. 'Aprileno' timballo
TIMBALLO APRILENO

Follow the preceding recipe, but substitute the truffles with:

- 6 oz peas
- 4 oz carrots
- 3 tender artichokes

These should all be steamed in a double boiler.

251. Green timballo with mozzarella
TIMBALLO VERDE ALLA MOZZARELLA

Ingredients:

- 2 lb potatoes
- 10 oz shelled peas
- 9 oz spinach
- 3 oz Parmesan cheese
- 6 oz mozzarella
- 4 eggs

Cook the peas and make a dense purée with the potatoes (boil and put through a food mill or ricer). Cook the spinach and put through the food mill. Combine all three, stirring in the 4 beaten eggs, Parmesan, salt and pepper. Butter and line a baking dish with **bread crumbs**, pour half the mixture into the dish, cover with sliced mozzarella and add the remaining potato/vegetable mixture and bake in a hot oven for 20–30 minutes.

252. Macaroni timballo with béchamel, 'finanziata' style
TIMBALLO DI MACCHERONI ALLA BESCIAMELLA FINANZIATA

Ingredients:

- 4 eggs
- 12 shelled and crushed walnuts
- 2 oz butter
- 5 oz Parmesan cheese
- 2 truffles
- 1 lb macaroni

Boil the macaroni al dente, drain and put aside. Sauté the truffles and walnuts in butter and bind with 1 tbsp flour. Whip the egg whites until stiff, stir in the macaroni, truffles, egg yolks and Parmesan and place in a mold or a baking dish lined with **pastry crust** (see recipe 643). Put in a hot oven for 15–20 minutes, then turn out on a serving dish and serve with **béchamel** (see recipe 653) on the side.

253. Green timballo with Gruyère
TIMBALLO VERDE AL GRUVIERA

Ingredients:

- 2 lb spinach
- 18 oz fidellini pasta (thin noodle-like strips)
- 4 eggs
- 3 oz butter
- 5 oz Gruyère cheese
- 1 pint milk

Boil the spinach and put through a food mill, then mix with **béchamel** (recipes 652–653). Cook the pasta, drain and stir in the 4 beaten eggs, half the spinach and béchamel mixture and the grated Gruyère (keep 1 tbsp Gruyère to spread on the bottom of the baking dish). Pour the mixture into a buttered mold, place in a pan of water and cook over a low flame for 2 hours. Separate from the sides of the mold with a knife and turn out on a serving platter, covering with the remaining spinach sauce.

254. Semolino timballo
TIMBALLO DI SEMOLINO FARCITO

Ingredients:

- 3 ½ cups milk
- 9 oz semolina
- 4 oz butter
- 4 oz Parmesan cheese
- 4 eggs

Cook the semolina in milk, stirring continually and when it is dense, take off the flame and allow to cool. While still lukewarm, add the eggs and Parmesan, stirring briskly. Pour half of the semolina mixture in a baking dish or mold (which has been buttered and spread with **bread crumbs**). Make a hole in the center and fill with a **stuffing** of your choice (see stuffings and fillings), cover with the rest of the semolina and bake in a hot oven.

255. Glutton's timballo
TIMBALLETTE GOLOSETTE

Make:

- a pea purée (recipe 63)
- a potato purée (recipe 74)

Make the purées thicker than those called for in the recipes, then combine the two with **beaten raw eggs** (calculate 3 eggs for every pound of purée). Add ½-inch cubes of **mozzarella** and pour the mixture into individual molds which have been **buttered** and sprinkled with **grated cheese**. Place in the oven for about 15 minutes and turn out onto a serving plate.

256. Egg timballo 'alla molinara' (miller's wife style)
TIMBALLO D'UOVA ALLA MOLINARA

Into a saucepan, pour:

- a pint of milk
- a pinch of salt

Place over a low flame; then add:

- 5 oz semolina

Stir continually. When it has thickened, remove from the flame and let cool. Whip **8 egg whites** until stiff, and fold these into the semolina paste. Add:

- 8 egg yolks
- 3 oz Parmesan cheese

Pour into a baking dish which has been buttered and sprinkled with grated **Gruyère cheese**. Place this in a larger dish with two or three inches water, and cook over a low flame. Turn out on a plate to serve.

257. Timballo lined with macaroni shells
TIMBALLO A CHIOCCIOLA

Cook **wide pasta strips** as in recipe 232, then butter a baking dish. After draining the pasta, take one noodle and roll it across the bottom of the dish, until it is wound around itself like a shell. Continue with other pieces of pasta until the sides of the dish are lined with the rolled pasta. Cut the remaining noodles in pieces and put in a saucepan, adding the sauce prepared as follows. In a saucepan mix:

- 1 tbsp of melted butter
- 1 tbsp of flour
- a cup of good broth (recipes 43 to 51) or, if not available, a cup of salted water
- a spoon of caramel sauce (see recipe 889)

Add **chopped mushrooms** and allow to thicken over a low flame. When the sauce has thickened, add **a few mock eggs** (recipe 466). Pour this over the pasta in the saucepan, sprinkle with **Parmesan cheese** and **crushed shelled walnuts**. When the mixture has condensed, pour into the center of the baking dish and cover with a few unseasoned noodle strips you will have set aside; press them down on the top and allow to cool before putting the timballo into a hot oven for 10 to 15 minutes. Turn out on a platter to serve.

~~~~~~~~~~~~~~~~

258. Timballo Valguarnera style
TIMBALLO ALLA VALGUARNERA

Prepare the following sauce: **chopped onion** sautéed in butter with:

- 10 oz peas
- 4 artichokes
- a small cauliflower cut in quarters

Dampen with a sprinkling of water and when cooked add:

- 1 tbsp flour
- some chopped herbs
- salt
- pepper

On the side, cut some **Gouda** (or **Edam**) **cheese** and **Gruyère** into small cubes and prepare a baking dish with butter and a lining of **bread crumbs**. Cook **1 ¼ lb whatever pasta** you wish (see instructions in recipe 232), drain and mix in a dry saucepan with some **tomato sauce** and **grated cheese**, then pour into the baking dish. Make a well in the center and fill with the above vegetable filling and cubes of cheese.

Cover with the remaining pasta and place in a medium oven for 45 minutes. Then turn out on a platter and serve.

259. 'Aurora' timballo
TIMBALLO AURORA

Prepare a **cream sauce** (see recipes 652 to 654) with a pint of milk. Cook briefly, drain then butter **1 lb fidellini** (very thin noodles) or **capelli d'angelo** (hair-like noodles), following the instructions in recipe 232. Place half of the pasta in a buttered baking dish which has been lined with **pastry dough** (recipe 543). Make an opening in the center and add the previously prepared cream and cubes of **fresh cheese**, possibly mozzarella. Cover with the remaining pasta and put in a hot oven.

260. Macaroni timballo 'falso grasso' (seemingly rich)
TIMBALLO DI MACCHERONI (FALSO GRASSO)

Cook **1 1/2 lb small macaroni**, drain and mix in a saucepan with the **sauce** in recipe 221, then butter and line the bottom of a baking dish with bread crumbs. Pour in half of the pasta, make a hole in the center and pour in the sauce with:

peas

small chunks of fresh cheese

diced fried eggplant slices

12 crushed walnuts

Cover with the remaining pasta and put in a hot oven for 15–20 minutes.

261. Dried bread pie
TONDO DI PAN DURO ALLA CASALINGA

Another way of using stale bread is the following:

1 1/2 lb bread

5 eggs

3 oz Parmesan cheese

3 tbsp tomato sauce

Put the bread in water until it is thoroughly soaked, take off the crusts and squeeze out the excess liquid, then put through a food mill. Sauté **chopped onion** in butter, then add the sauce and **chopped parsley**. Beat the eggs and mix everything together with the Parmesan cheese. Place in a buttered baking dish lined with bread crumbs and cook over boiling water until it solidifies. Turn out on a platter to serve.

262. Scottish bread and milk pudding
BODINO SCOZZESE DI PANE E LATTE

Ingredients:

1 3/4 lb bread

2 qt milk

4 oz butter

2 oz Parmesan or Cheshire cheese

Sauté **chopped onion** briefly in 1/3 of the butter and add the milk. Slice the bread, spreading each slice with butter and a sprinkling of salt, then place in layers in a baking dish, covering each layer with cheese. Pour over the milk and bake in a medium oven for 45 minutes.

263. Italian rice pudding
BODINO DI RISO ALL'ITALIANA

Make a **risotto with Corvo wine** (1 lb of rice) and put half of this in a buttered baking dish. Cover with the following sauce:

chopped sautéed onion

6 oz chopped cauliflower

1/2 cup wine

Bind with **flour**; add:

salt

pepper

pine nuts

a fistful of small black raisins (uva passa)

Place the remaining risotto on top and put in a hot oven for 30 minutes. Turn out on a plate and serve with a sauce of your choice (see Sauces).

264. White pudding
BODINO CANDIDO

In **2 quarts milk**, cook:

1 lb rice

3 oz peeled and chopped almonds

Stir continually, adding water if necessary to keep it fluid. Remove from the flame and add:

salt

white pepper

3 oz grated Gruyère cheese

4 beaten eggs

Pour half of this in a mold which has been buttered and sprinkled with Gruyère, and cover with slices of **mozzarella** or other fresh cheese. Finally, put the remaining rice on top and steam over a pan of boiling water for 3 hours, then serve with **béchamel**.

265. Red pudding
BODINO ROSSO

Make a **red risotto** (recipe 161); when cool, beat in **4 eggs** and pour half of the rice into a buttered baking dish and sprinkle with **Gruyère cheese**. Cover this with the following sauce:

chopped sautéed onion

6 oz chopped peeled tomatoes or **2 oz tomato concentrate**

Cook in a saucepan until thickened, then combine with:

4 oz Gruyère

4 oz Gouda (or **Edam**) cut in cubes

parsley

salt

pepper

Finally, add the remaining rice on top and steam over a pan of water. Put out on a platter and cover with **tomato sauce** to serve.

266. Green pudding
BODINO VERDE

Boil **1 lb spinach** and put through a food mill, saving the water in which it was boiled. In **2 oz butter**, sauté:

1 chopped onion

Add the **rice** and stir until it turns transparent, then add half of the spinach purée along with the cooking water, and stir until the rice is cooked. Remove from the fire and add **4 beaten eggs**, then pour half this mixture in a mold which has been buttered and lined with **Gruyère cheese**. Place on top **4 artichokes** which have been chopped and cut in segments along with:

6 oz peas

salt

pepper

finely chopped parsley

Cover with the rest of the rice and place the mold in a pan of boiling water. Put the remaining spinach in a saucepan over a low flame, add **1 tbsp flour** and slowly pour in **1 pint of warm milk**. Allow to thicken, adding salt and pepper to taste. When the cooked pudding has been turned out on a plate, cover with the spinach sauce.

267. Polenta pudding
BODINO DI POLENTA

Make the **polenta** as in recipe 164, putting half in a buttered mold and covering with slices of **mozzarella** or other **fresh cheese**. Pour over the remaining polenta before it cools and cook by placing the mold in a pan of boiling water for one hour. Turn out on a plate and cover with a **fricassee sauce** (see recipe 762) to serve.

Luncheon dishes, vegetables, legumes and side dishes

TRAMESSI, VERDURE, ORTAGGI, LEGUMI E CONTORNI

268. Sicilian 'caponata'
CAPONATA ALLA SICILIANA

Dice **5 whole eggplants** into ½-inch cubes, sprinkle with salt and let stand in a colander until they have shed their bitter liquid, about 30 minutes. Rinse the eggplant well and let dry.

In a large sauté pan, fry the eggplants in **½ cup of olive oil** for 5 to 10 minutes. The pan should be hot, but not smoking.

Place the cooked eggplant on kitchen paper to soak up excess oil.

Set the eggplants aside and prepare a sauce with:

2 lb diced tomatoes

1 thinly sliced head of celery

2 oz capers

4 oz pitted, chopped olives (soak before cooking to eliminate excess salt)

Cook the above sauce over low heat until the celery becomes translucent and the sauce begins to thicken. Add:

a dash of vinegar

a pinch of sugar

Allow to simmer for 10 minutes. Serve cold over the fried eggplant, garnished with:

capers

gherkins

269. Eggplants 'a beccafico'
MELANZANE A BECCAFICO

Preheat oven to 350°F.

To prepare the eggplant: Cut **5 eggplants** length wise into 1-inch strips. Sprinkle with salt and let stand in a colander until they have shed their bitter liquid, about 30 minutes. In a large sauté pan, fry in olive oil, turning once, and cooking until both sides are golden brown. Place the cooked eggplant on kitchen paper to soak up excess oil.

To prepare the topping: Lightly brown **bread crumbs** in olive oil, salt, and pepper. Add a handful of **pine nuts** and **raisins**.

To serve: Spoon the bread crumb mixture on to the eggplant slices and fold over lengthwise, then place each folded eggplant slice in an ovenproof dish. Separate the strips with **bay leaves**, sprinkle with **olive oil**, and bake for 20 to 30 minutes. Serve hot or cold, adding a few drops of **lemon juice** before serving.

270. Eggplants 'a funghetto' or 'trifolate' (stewed in oil)
MELANZANE A FUNGHETTO O TRIFOLATE

Dice **5 eggplants** into ½-inch cubes, and, in a large sauté pan, fry gently in olive oil with:

> crushed garlic
>
> salt
>
> pepper

Stir frequently, cooking for about 15 minutes or until the egglant is soft, and adding **chopped parsley** just before the eggplant is finished cooking. Sprinkle with a few drops of **lemon juice** before serving.

271. Eggplant Parmesan
MELANZANE ALLA PARMIGIANA

Preheat oven to 350°F.

Slice **5 eggplants** into ½-inch round slices. Salt them and let stand in a colander for at least 30 minutes. Rinse, dry, and, in a large sauté pan, fry gently in olive oil, turning once and cooking until both sides are golden brown. Place the strips in layers in a large ovenproof dish, alternating with:

> thick tomato sauce
>
> grated Parmesan cheese

The top layer should be cheese. Place in the oven and cook for 25–30 minutes.

272. Grilled breaded eggplants
ARROSTO DI MELANZANE PANATE

Slice **5 eggplants** into half inch slices, sprinkle with salt and let stand for 30 minutes in a colander. Rinse and dry. Coat with **olive oil** and **bread crumbs** and then grill (or place under the broiler), sprinkling occasionally with olive oil.

273. Grilled eggplants
MELANZANE ALLA GRIGLIA

Slice **5 eggplants** in half lengthwise. Add salt and pepper and sprinkle with olive oil. Allow the eggplants to absorb the oil for about 30 minutes. Grill and season with a dressing of:

> olive oil
>
> lemon
>
> parsley

274. Eggplants 'a skapici'
MELANZANE A SKAPICI

Skapici indicates a Sicilian way of cooking remnants of tuna fish. Adapted here for eggplant.

Make a "**picchio-pacchio**" **sauce** (see recipe 647) and add to **5 sliced fried eggplants**, prepared as in recipe 269. Add a little **vinegar** and cook for 10 minutes. Serve cold with a sprinkling of **chopped mint**.

275. Fricasseed eggplants
MELANZANE IN FRICASSEA

Gently fry **5 sliced eggplants**, prepared as in recipe 269, place in a serving dish and cover with a **fricassee sauce** (see recipe 662).

276. Eggplants, Chilean style
MELANZANE ALLA CILENA

Preheat oven to 350°F.

Halve **5 eggplants** and boil in salted water. Allow to cool and spoon out the flesh of the eggplant. Set the skin aside. Chop the flesh finely and mix with:

- peeled tomatoes
- grated Parmesan cheese
- chopped parsley
- bread crumbs
- salt
- cayenne pepper

Fill the skin with this mixture. Top with small knobs of **butter** and bake in an oven-proof dish for 20–30 minutes.

277. Stuffed eggplants
MELANZANE IMBOTTITE ALLA CASALINGA

Take **4 small eggplants**. Make four small splits lengthwise in each eggplant. Stuff each with:

- a slice of cheese
- a sliver of garlic
- a leaf of mint
- salt
- pepper

In a large sauté pan, lightly brown all sides of the eggplant in olive oil, add **tomato sauce,** and then simmer on medium heat until fully cooked, or, if you prefer, bake at 350°F for 25 minutes or until the eggplant is tender.

278. Turnips with velouté sauce
NAVONI ALLA VELLUTINA

Cook the **turnips** in a double boiler, place in a serving dish, garnish with **croutons**, and pour over a **light velouté sauce** (see recipe 655).

279. Turnips in a sauce of your choice
NAVONI IN VARIE SALSE

Cook the **turnips** as specified in a double boiler and serve with a **sauce of your choice** (see Sauces on pages 181–191).

280. Turnips with potatoes
NAVONI CON PATATE

Steam **turnips** and **peeled potatoes** until tender. Set aside. In a sauté pan over medium heat, melt a knob of **butter** and add:

- a spoonful of flour
- a little water
- salt and mustard

Cook until combined, and pour over the turnips. Garnish with **fried croutons** and serve.

281. Cauliflower served as you wish
CAVOLFIORI IN TUTTI I MODI

Boil or steam **cauliflower** and pour over any **sauce** of your choice (see Sauces on pages 181–191).

282. Cauliflower stalks as you wish
TORSI IN TUTTI I MODI

As above, with **cauliflower stalks**.

283. Artichokes as you wish
CAVCIOFI IN TUTTI I MODI

Clean **4 artichokes**, taking off the outside leaves and cutting off two-thirds of the top. Trim around the outside, leaving only the heart and a few of the inside leaves. Boil or steam and halve. Place in a serving dish and add a **sauce** of your choice.

284. Cauliflower with eggs
CAVOLFIORI ALL'UOVO

A simple cauliflower omelet. Ingredients:
- one head cauliflower, about ¾ lb
- 1 tbsp of olive oil
- 2 oz Parmesan cheese
- 6 eggs
- 2 oz butter

Mince the cauliflower and, in a medium sauté pan, cook it in olive oil. Set aside. Beat the eggs and add the grated Parmesan cheese, along with a pinch of salt. In a seperate sauté pan, on medium heat, melt 2 oz butter and pour the eggs into in the pan. Add the cauliflower, turning when the eggs set and become golden brown (use a plate to flip).

285. Cauliflower with cheese sauce
CAVOLFIORI AL FORMAGGIO

Preheat oven to 350°F.

Steam the **cauliflower**. Toss the florets in a **white sauce** (see recipe 661), sprinkle with **grated Parmesan cheese**. Place in an ovenproof dish. Pour over the remaining white sauce, add more cheese and a little melted **butter**, sprinkle with finely grated **bread crumbs**, and bake in the oven.

286. Cauliflower with butter
CAVOLFIORI AL BURRO

Steam the head of one **cauliflower**. Then, in a medium sauté pan, melt **butter** and add the cauliflower with:
- salt
- pepper
- your favorite herbs

Serve with **fried croutons**.

287. Cauliflower with Bolognese sauce
CAVOLFIORI AL RAGÙ

Steam the **cauliflower** with a sprinkling of salt. Place half the cauliflower in a buttered pan, top with:

> knobs of butter
>
> salt
>
> pepper

Add the remaining florets and cover with **tomato sauce**. Cook over a low flame until combined.

288. 'Drowned' cauliflower
CAVOLFIORI AFFOGATI

Pour some olive oil in a medium sauté pan over medium heat, amd add:

> some chopped garlic
>
> salt
>
> pepper
>
> a glass of wine

Throw in the **florets of one cauliflower**, cover, and cook over a slow fire.

289. Brussels sprouts with velouté sauce
CAVOLINI DI BRUXELLES IN SALSA VELLUTINA

Preheat oven to 350°F.

Clean **Brussels sprouts** and cook as you wish. You can steam or roast the sprouts in the oven. When cooked, place the brussels sprouts in a baking dish on **velouté sauce** (see recipe 650).

Sprinkle with **cheese** or **béchamel sauce** and cook in the oven until the cheese has melted.

290. German cabbage
CAVOLI ALLA TEDESCA

To pickle the cabbage: Shred **white cabbage** into fine strips, having removed the outside leaves. Spread a layer of salt in the bottom of a small wooden cask, cover with a 3-inch layer of cabbage, sprinkle with:

> juniper seed
>
> peppercorns
>
> bay leaves

Press lightly with a wooden spoon. Add another layer of cabbage, and again sprinkle generously with salt, juniper seed, peppercorns and bay leaves. When the cask is three-quarters full, cover with cloth and a lid that fits tightly into the cask. Put a heavy weight on top (rocks, or whatever). As fermentation begins the lid sinks down and the water eliminated must be drained off. However, the cabbage must be kept constantly immersed. After a month the cabbage is ready. Remove the weight, wash the cloth and after taking out the amount of cabbage to be used, the cask must be covered again, together with the weight, after removing the excess water. The cabbage can be cooked as indicated below, or any way you prefer.

To cook: After rinsing repeatedly, place the cabbage in a pan with:

> **oil** and **butter** (half and half)
>
> chopped mushrooms
>
> juniper berries

a glass of white wine

salt

pepper

consommé (see recipe 47)

Cook over a gentle flame for 30 minutes to 1 hour, depending on how you prefer your cabbage. It can stew for up to 6 hours. When the cabbage is cooked, serve garnished with **fried croutons**.

291. Cauliflower with béchamel
CAVOLFIORI ALLA BESCIAMELLA

Preheat oven to 350°F.

Steam cook the **cauliflower** and place in an ovenproof dish, cover with **béchamel** (see recipes 652–653). Sprinkle with **Parmesan cheese**, top with knobs of **butter**, and bake in the oven.

292. Chards with béchamel
CARDI ALLA BESCIAMELLA

Follow the above recipe, substituting **chard**.

293. Artichokes with béchamel
CARCIOFI ALLA BESCIAMELLA

Same recipe as for cauliflower (see recipe 291), substituting **artichokes**.

294. Brussels sprouts with béchamel
CAVOLINI DI BRUXELLES ALLA BESCIAMELLA

Follow the cauliflower recipe (recipe 291), substituting **Brussels sprouts**.

295. Cabbage Sicilian style
CAVOLO CAPPUCCIO ALLA SICILIANA

Cut **white cabbage leaves** into ½-inch strips, wash well, and place in a pan with:

a glass of white wine

2 or 3 cloves of chopped garlic

a spoonful of tomato concentrate

a generous quantity of olive oil

Cover and cook for about an hour, stirring frequently.

296. Sweet-sour cabbage
CAVOLO CAPPUCCIO AD AGRO-DOLCE

Cut a **cabbage** into ½-inch strips and place in the pan with:

oil

garlic

salt

pepper

a small glass of vinegar

2 teaspoons of sugar

Cook over a gentle heat for 30 minutes or longer, depending on your taste. Can also be served cold.

297. Artichokes Gangi style
CARCIOFI ALLA GANGITANA

Clean the **artichokes**, cutting off the tops and paring the bottoms into cone shapes. Steam and fill with **caponata** (see recipe 268). Set them in a serving dish with the cones up and pour **mayonnaise** over them (see recipes 671–672).

298. Stuffed artichokes 'alla villana' (rustic style)
CARCIOFI RIPIENI ALLA VILLANA

Choose your **artichokes** carefully, clean by taking off the outside leaves and cutting off the points. Toast **bread crumbs** in a pan over medium heat with a little oil. Stir in:

chopped parsley

some sliced garlic or onion as preferred

Use the above mixture to stuff the artichokes. Set them in a saucepan with the stem ends down. Season with oil and a little water, cover tightly, and cook over a low heat for about an hour.

299. Artichokes with mayonnaise
CARCIOFI ALLA MAJONESE

Steam **artichokes** and then allow them to cool. Arrange artfully on a serving dish. Cover with **mayonnaise** (see recipes 671–672) and garnish with:

peppers

chopped gherkins

parsley

whatever else takes your fancy

300. Provincial artichokes
CARCIOFI ALLA PROVINCIALE

Preheat oven to 375°F.

Remove the tough, thorny parts of the artichokes, cut in quarters, and cook as follows: place **artichokes** in a roasting pan with:

oil

garlic

salt

pepper

Cook until tender, about 1 hour, and finish by squeezing a **lemon** and some **parsley** over the artichokes. Serve.

301. Stuffed artichokes à la barigoule
CARCIOFI FARCITI ALLA BARIGOULE

Remove the tough, thorny parts of **artichokes** and fill with a stuffing of:

bread crumbs

chopped herbs

small pieces of mushroom

Put in a pan with a knob of **butter**, cover, and cook. Take out the artichokes when they are soft, add a **spoonful of flour** to the butter and when the mixture is nicely browned, thin by adding some **broth** or water, a little at a time (see recipes 43 to 51). Pour over the artichokes in the serving dish.

302. Fricasseed artichokes
CARCIOFI IN FRICASSEA

Remove the tough, thorny parts of **artichokes** and steam. Take out of the steamer and place in a serving dish, pour over the **fricassee sauce** (see recipe 662) and garnish with **fried croutons**.

303. Artichokes with different sauces
CARCIOFI SALSITI IN TUTTI I MODI

Remove the tough, thorny parts of **artichokes**, place in a serving dish and dress with whatever **sauce** you wish (see Sauces, pages 187–198).

304. Grilled artichokes
CARCIOFI ALLA GRIGLIA

Halve the **artichokes**, remove the outside leaves, and cut out the thorny parts. Sprinkle the inside part with:

    chopped parsley
    a little garlic
    salt
    pepper
    olive oil

Grill and serve with a dressing of:

    olive oil
    lemon juice
    oregano

305. Artichokes 'alla giudea' (Jewish artichokes)
CARCIOFI ALLA GIUDEA

Choose wide, flat Roman **artichokes**. Clean well and cut off the tops, gently opening out the leaves as much as possible. Dust with salt and pepper and plunge into a pan of hot olive oil with the leaves down and the stalks uppermost. Press downwards gently so that the leaves spread out and turn regularly so that both sides cook evenly. When they are golden brown (about 10 minutes) remove from the pan and serve upside-down, without adding any further oil.

306. 'Let me be' artichokes
CARCIOFI A LASCIAMI STARE

After carefully cleaning and removing the tops of the **artichokes**, thinly slice. Pour a little oil in a sauté pan over medium and place a layer of the artichoke slices in it, dust with **bread crumbs** mixed with:

    Parmesan cheese
    salt
    pepper
    parsley
    grated onion

Make 4 or 5 layers, sprinkling each layer with a little oil. Cook for 45 minutes, without even looking at them.

307. Zucchini with béchamel
ZUCCHINI ALLA BESCIAMELLA

Follow the recipe 291, substituting cauliflower.

308. Stuffed zucchini
ZUCCHINE RIPIENE

Scoop out the **zucchini** pulp and fill the shell with **rice** (see recipe 155), or whatever other filling you wish (see recipes on filling 702–709). Place in a pan with butter and a little water and cook, turning a few times.

309. Stuffed zucchini in tomato sauce
ZUCCHINI IMBOTTITI AL POMODORO

Follow the above recipe but cook the zucchini in **tomato sauce** (see recipe 646).

310. Zucchini with butter and eggs
ZUCCHINI AL BURRO ED UOVO

Cut **zucchini** into square shapes and cook as follows: In a sauté pan over medium heat, slightly sauté the zucchini in butter, adding salt and pepper. As soon as they are cooked, bind them together with:

> **4 beaten egg yolks** to which **a cup of broth** has been added (recipes 44 and 51)

Garnish with **fried croutons** and serve hot.

311. Asparagus in white sauce
ASPARAGI IN SALSA BIANCA

Boil or steam **asparagus** tied together in a bunch. Don't allow them to overcook. Place on a napkin in a dish and serve hot. Serve **white sauce** on the side (see recipe 661).

312. Asparagus with oil
ASPARAGI ALL'OLIO

Cook as above, cool, and serve with the **sauce** in recipe 650.

313. Asparagus with peas
ASPARAGI CON PISELLINI

Chop up the tender parts of **asparagus** and steam together with **peas**. Stir in a pan with:

> **melted butter**
> **salt**
> **pepper**
> **herbs**

Serve with **fried croutons**.

314. Fricasseed asparagus
ASPARAGI ALLA FRICASSEA

Steam **asparagus** and place on a napkin in a serving dish. Serve the **fricassee sauce** separately in a sauce boat (see recipe 662).

315. Asparagus with cheese
ASPARAGI AL FORMAGGIO

Steam the **asparagus** and place in an ove-nproof dish, sprinkle the points with **Parmesan cheese**, top with small knobs of **butter**, and cook in a 350°F oven until golden brown, about 10 to 15 minutes.

316. Asparagus with a variety of sauces
ASPARAGI IN VARIE GUISE

After steaming **asparagus**, serve with whatever **sauce** you please (see Sauces, pages 187–198).

317. Fricasseed green beans
FAGIOLINI VERDI IN FRICASSEA

Cook the **green beans** in a steamer and pre-pare some **chopped onion**, sautéed with a little **garlic** and **butter**. Toss in the beans, and cook for a few minutes. Beat together **4 egg yolks** for every 2 lb of beans, and mix in:

> the juice of a lemon
> salt
> pepper
> chopped parsley

Pour over the beans and as soon as the mixture is firm serve hot, garnished with **fried croutons**.

318. Green beans with black butter
FAGIOLINI AL BURRO NERO

Steam cook and place in a serving dish, pour the **sauce** in recipe 668 over the beans, and serve.

319. Green beans
FAGIOLINI VERDI

Snip off the heads and tails and steam, dusting with a little salt. Toss in a sauté pan over medium heat with melted **butter** and serve with **croutons**.

320. Green beans in milk
FAGIOLINI LEGATI AL LATTE

Steam the **green beans** and put in a pan with:

> fresh butter
> a little flour
> salt
> pepper
> nutmeg
> a glass of milk

Lightly simmer for a few minutes, add a little **mozzarella cheese**, and serve with **fried croutons**.

321. Celery
SEDANO

Choose the heart of the **celery** and the whiter leaves, and follow the recipe for cooking chards (see recipe 358). Serve the celery with **croutons** and a sauce of your choice.

322. Celery with cheese
SEDANI AL FORMAGGIO

Cook as for recipe 358, place in an oven-proof dish, sprinkle with **Parmesan cheese**, top with small knobs of **butter**, and cook in the oven until golden brown.

323. Celery with mustard
SEDANI ALLA MOSTARDA

Remove the green leaves from **celery**, clean without chopping, arrange the **stalks** so they fan out in the serving dish, and serve a **mustard sauce** separately (see recipe 685).

324. Country-style chicory
CICORIA ALLA CAMPAGNUOLA

Steam the **chicory** and toss in a pan with:
- olive oil
- chopped garlic
- salt
- pepper
- a glass of dry white wine

325. Cooked chicory salad
CICORIA COTTA ALL'INSALATA

Steam the **chicory**, cool, and serve with a **salad dressing**.

326. Wild chicory
CICORIA SELVAGGIA

The most tender leaves and the heart of the **chicory** can be eaten raw in a salad.

327. White chicory
CICORIA BIANCA

Steam **chicory**, allow to cool, and serve with **melted mozzarella**.

328. Onions with cream
CIPOLLE ALLA CREMA

Steam some **white onions**. Melt a little butter in a pan and add the onions, which have been lightly dusted with:
- flour
- salt
- pepper

Pour a little **milk** in and continue stirring until the mixture is nicely blended. Serve with **fresh cream**.

329. Stewed onions
CIPOLLE STUFATE

Brown some **flour** and **butter** very lightly in a pan over medium heat, and add:
- red wine
- broth (see recipes 43 to 51)
- onions cut in quarters

Stir together with:
- 2 cloves
- bay
- thyme leaves

Cook until the sauce is quite thick and serve with **croutons**.

330. Stuffed onions
CIPOLLE FARCITE

Preheat oven to 400°F.

Lightly steam **onions** and remove from cooking when still fairly firm. Spoon out the inside of the onions. Knead together a stuffing of:
- grated Parmesan cheese
- egg yolks
- bread crumbs that have been soaked in milk

Fill onions with stuffing. Place in an oven-proof dish with knobs of **butter** and bake in the oven, about 20 to 30 minutes.

Cover with a **velouté sauce** (see recipe 650) and serve with **fried croutons** and crescents of **flaky pastry**.

331. Stuffed onions (or potatoes or eggplants)
CIPOLLE RIPIENE (PATATE O MELANZANE)

Preheat oven to 400°F.

Choose **12 nice big onions** of about the same size and make a hole in the center, extracting it from the root side. Chop the onion you have removed together with:

4 oz bread crumbs

1 egg

2 oz ground walnuts

salt

parsley

cayenne pepper

If the mixture is slightly dry add a little **milk**, and if too runny, extra bread crumbs. Stuff the onions with the above mixture and bake in a greased oven-proof dish, about 40 minutes. Pour a **béchamel** (see recipes 652–653) on and serve.

332. Baby onions in béchamel
CIPOLLETTE ALLA BESCIAMELLA

Peel the **onions** and caramelize (see recipe 334) or steam. Pour a **béchamel** over the dish and serve (see recipes 652–653).

333. Peas, English style
PISELLI ALL'INGLESE

In salted boiling water, blanch:

½ lb peas

Drain in a colander. Melt **1 tbsp butter** in a pan and add the peas. Pour **a glass of cream** over the dish and serve garnished with **croutons**.

334. Candied peas
PISELLI ALLA CARAMELLA

Take **2 lb very tender peas**, and place in a pan with a knob of **butter** and a little **water**. As soon as they are cooked push to one side of the pan, leaving a corner dry. Melt **a spoonful of sugar** until it is slightly caramelized, tilt the pan so that the peas slip into the caramel, adding a little water if necessary, and as soon as the two have blended together, serve garnished with **croutons**.

335. Peas in vol-au-vent
PISELLI IN VOLA AL VENTO

Follow recipe 291 and then put the **peas** in pastry cases (see recipe 538), without adding Parmesan, and warm in the oven.

336. Peas with butter
PISELLI AL BURRO

Blanch tender peas in salted boiling water. When done cooking, strain and toss in the pan with a wedge of **butter**. Serve garnished with **fried croutons**.

337. Mushrooms 'trifolati' (cooked in oil)
FUNGHI TRIFOLATI

Chop the **mushrooms** and cook in **butter** and **olive oil** together with:

- finely chopped garlic
- parsley
- salt
- pepper

Serve with a sprinkling of **lemon juice**.

338. Sautéed mushrooms
FUNGHI SALTATI

Finely chop and sauté in **butter** with little salt. Serve with **croutons**.

339. Roast mushrooms
FUNGHI ARROSTITI

Use **large mushroom caps**, brush with **oil**, dust with **salt**, and put under the broiler. Sprinkle with chopped **herbs** and squeeze a few drops of **lemon juice** over the mushrooms before serving.

340. Mushrooms with Marsala
FUNGHI AL MARSALA

In a medium sauté pan over low heat, cook **mushrooms** in butter and after 5 minutes add:

- a small glass of Marsala

After simmering for 15 minutes add:

- a little flour dissolved in a cup of water
- a pinch of salt
- pepper
- chopped herbs

Stir for a few minutes until the mixture thickens. Serve with **croutons**.

341. Mushrooms served on crostoni
CROSTONI AI FUNGHI

Crisply fry some large rounds of **bread** (crostoni) in butter or oil and place on a serving dish.

Spoon over the **fricasseed mushrooms** (see next recipe) and dust with **chopped truffles**.

342. Fricasseed mushrooms (version one)
FUNGHI IN FRICASSEA N. 1

In a medium sauté pan, melt a chunk of **butter** and stir in ½ tbsp **flour**. Toss in the **mushrooms**. Add a little **broth**, or simply water, and cook. Bind with **egg yolks**, squeeze a few drops of **lemon juice** over the mixture, and sprinkle with chopped **parsley** before serving.

343. Fricasseed mushrooms (version two)
FRICASSEA DI FUNGHI N. 2

In a medium sauté pan, sauté **mushrooms** in **butter** with:

salt

pepper

chopped parsley

As soon as they are cooked add:

2 or 3 egg yolks dissolved in a cup
of water

the juice of half a lemon

Serve with cream.

344. Mushrooms with béchamel
FUNGHI ALLA BESCIAMELLA

As in recipe 291, substituting mushrooms.

345. Mushrooms with bread crumbs
FUNGHI AL PANGRATTATO

Preheat oven to 350°F.

Grease a baking tin with oil, place the mushrooms in it, dusting with bread crumbs. Add:

chopped parsley

salt

oregano

garlic

Sprinkle with oil. Bake in the oven and squeeze a little lemon juice over the dish before serving.

346. Tomatoes 'al naturale'
POMIDORI AL NATURALE

Halve the tomatoes sideways and top with:

chopped herbs

olives

some finely-grated onion if you choose

Dust with salt and pepper, sprinkle with oil and a few drops of lemon juice, and serve.

347. Filled tomatoes
POMIDORI RIPIENI

Preheat oven to 375°F.

Remove the core and seeds without breaking the skin. Prepare a mixture of toasted bread crumbs in a pan with a little oil. Mix in:

some grated cheese

chopped parsley

Fill the tomatoes. Bake in a greased oven-proof dish for 15 to 20 minutes.

348. Tomatoes 'alla pizzaiola'
POMIDORI ALLA PIZZAIUOLA

Preheat oven to 375°F.

Lay out slices of fried bread in an oven-proof dish. Place cored tomatoes (as described in recipe 347 above) in the dish and fill with mozzarella. Add:

a few tiny pieces of garlic

salt

oregano

pepper

Bake for 15 to 20 minutes.

349. Stuffed tomatoes
POMIDORI FARCITI

Remove the seeds and core, stuffing as indicated in recipe 706. Bake in a 375°F oven for 15 to 20 minutes.

350. Tomatoes with bread crumbs
POMIDORI AL PANGRATTATO

Preheat oven to 375°F.

Remove the core and seeds, leaving the tomatoes intact. Toast some **bread crumbs** in a pan with a little oil. Add:

- capers
- chopped olives
- salt
- pepper

Stuff the tomatoes. Bake for 15 to 20 minutes.

351. Tomatoes Genoese style
POMIDORI ALLA GENOVESE

Preheat oven to 375°F.

Halve the **tomatoes** sideways and place each one over a slice of raw **potato**. Dust with:

- bread crumbs
- parsley
- onion
- salt
- pepper

Put a small knob of **butter** on each one and bake in the oven for 15 to 20 minutes.

352. Truffles cooked in oil
TARTUFI TRIFOLATI

Pound a little **garlic** and **parsley** together, and put in a sauté pan with:

- butter
- sliced truffles
- salt
- a pinch of herbs

- some pepper

Cook and squeeze a few drops of **lemon juice** over the dish before serving. Garnish with **fried croutons**.

353. Stuffed truffles
TARTUFI FARCITI

Clean and peel the **truffles**, empty out one side and fill with a **stuffing** (see recipes 702 to 709). Place in a pan with:

- butter
- wine
- the finely chopped insides of the truffles

When cooked bind with a little **flour**, stirring for a minute or two until combined. Garnish with **croutons** and serve.

354. Truffles 'alla marinara' (Sailor style)
TARTUFI ALLA MARINARA

Slice the **truffles** and sauté in **butter** with:

- onion
- chopped parsley
- salt
- pepper

Pour in a small glass of **red wine** and allow to evaporate, thickening the mixture by adding a little **flour**. Garnish with **croutons** or **crescents** and serve.

355. Truffles, oyster style
TARTUFI AD OSTRICA

Clean some white **truffles**, chop, and place in **oyster shells**. Dust with **salt** and **pepper**, and sprinkle with **lemon juice**.

356. Cucumbers 'alla locandiera' (innkeeper style)
COCOMERI ALLA LOCANDIERA

Toss **cucumbers** with:
> **parsley**
>
> **minced onion**
>
> **salt**
>
> **pepper**

Garnish with **croutons** and serve.

357. Cucumbers with béchamel
COCOMERI ALLA BESCIAMELLA

Prepare as in recipe 356 and cover with a **béchamel sauce** (recipes 652–653).

358. Chard (preparation)
CARDONI (COTTURA)

Cut the **tender white parts** and the **root of chard** into 2-inch strips, removing the stringy bits. Soak in cold water, into which a **lemon** has been cut in quarters, for about an hour, or until they whiten. Drain and cook by steaming or cooking in a large sauté pan with **butter**. Prepare according to the following recipes.

359. Chard with béchamel
CARDONI ALLA BESCIAMELLA

Preheat oven to 350°F.

Prepare the **chards** as in recipe 358, and then place them in an oven-proof dish, and pour a **béchamel sauce** over them (see recipes 652–653). Dust with **Parmesan cheese** if you wish, top with little pieces of **butter**, and brown in the oven, about 15 minutes.

360. Steam cooked chards
CARDONI IN UMIDO

Prepare as in recipe 358, then place the **chards** in a sauté pan with:
> **oil**
>
> **garlic**
>
> **parsley**

Add:
> **a cup of water** to which **a spoonful of flour** and **lemon juice** have been added
>
> **salt**
>
> **pepper**

Serve as soon as the liquid thickens. **Croutons** go well with this dish.

361. Stuffed lettuce
LATTUGA FARCITA

Blanch a handful of nice big **lettuce leaves** (Bibb or other leafy lettuce) for 5 minutes in boiling water. Spread out on a dish towel. Put a spoonful of whatever **stuffing** you choose into each one (see recipes 701 to 709). Roll the leaves up lengthwise like kebabs. Arrange them one beside the other in a pan with salt and pepper and a little butter. Cook over a low flame. Serve the dish covered in a **velouté sauce** (recipe 650).

362. Spinach
SPINACI

Chop **spinach** and put into a sauté pan with **2 tbsp of butter,** and cook over a gentle heat for 10 minutes. Add:

> a little salt
>
> nutmeg
>
> a pinch of flour
>
> **enough milk to make it slightly more liquid**

Blend the ingredients together and serve with **fried croutons.** Fresh cream can be served over the dish.

363. Carrots, Flemish style
CAROTE ALLA FIAMMINGA

Cut the **carrots** and blanch in boiling water for 5 minutes. Put in a pan with:

> **butter**
>
> **broth** (see recipes 43 & 51)
>
> **a little sugar**

Cook until the broth is almost absorbed, add more butter, **chopped herbs** and a little broth. Serve garnished with **fried croutons** if you wish.

364. Fried carrots
CAROTE FRITTE

Peel the **carrots** and cut into fingers, dust with **salt,** and leave to drain for an hour. Roll in **flour**

and toss the individual fingers in **beaten egg,** before frying lightly.

365. Fricasseed beets
BARBABIETOLE ALLA FRICASSEA

After boiling and peeling **beets,** cut into slices and place in a heated dish. Pour a **fricassee sauce** (see recipe 662) over them and serve garnished with **fried croutons.**

366. Turnips in milk
RAPE AL LATTE

Peel and dice the **turnips** before steam cooking. Then put the turnips in a sauté pan and barely cover with **milk.** Add:

> salt
>
> white pepper
>
> **a good-sized wedge of butter**

As soon as they come to the boil, blend in **4 beaten egg yolks.** Serve with **croutons.**

367. Mixed root vegetables cacciatore
RADICI VARIE ALLA CACCIATORA

Peel and dice:

> **6 carrots**
>
> **6 turnips**
>
> **6 rutabagas**

Melt a good-sized piece of **butter** and put the roots in a large sauté pan with:

> **a glass of water**
>
> **a small glass of dry white wine**

20 chopped olives

salt

pepper

parsley

When they are parboiled add **peeled pearl onions**. When these are fully cooked, blend in **2 egg yolks**, garnish with **fried croutons**, and serve.

368. Tortiglione peas
TORTIGLIONE DI PISELLI

In salted boiling water, blanch:

2 lb peas

Drain and put in a dish with a generous sprinkling of **Parmesan cheese**, and bind with **5 egg yolks** and **the juice of one lemon**. Arrange the mixture in a spiral shape like tortiglione pasta and make a hole in the middle. Fill this with **mushroom stuffing** (see recipe 702). Heat and serve with a garnish of **fried croutons**.

369. American-style peppers
PEPERONI ALL'AMERICANA

Preheat oven to 375°F.

Remove the seeds from **6 large peppers**. To prepare the stuffing, in a large sauté pan combine:

a cup of finely chopped, peeled, seedless
    tomatoes

half a cup of chopped onion

a spoonful of butter

salt

pepper

Cook until the ingredients begin to thicken, and add:

5 oz bread crumbs

4 oz grated Parmesan cheese

If the mixture is too runny, more bread crumbs can be added. Finally, add:

chopped parsley

grated nutmeg

Fill the peppers and arrange in an oven-proof dish, pour a little **melted butter** over each one, and cook in the oven until golden brown, about 15 to 20 minutes.

370. Stuffed peppers
PEPERONI IMBOTTITI

Preheat oven to 375°F.

Halve the **peppers** lengthwise, remove the seeds, and fill with:

béchamel

Mozzarella cheese

Bake in the oven about 15 to 20 minutes or until golden brown. **Stuffing** can also be used (see under "Fillings," pages 198 to 200).

371. Savoy cabbage rolls
ROLLATINI DI VERZE

Preheat oven to 350°F.

Blanch the **white leaves of one cabbage** and fill with:

cooked rice

butter

slivers of fresh cheese or mozzarella

Roll up as for skewers, place in an oven-proof

dish or baking tray, dust with **Parmesan cheese** and drizzle with **broth** (see from recipes 43 to 51), top with little knobs of **butter**, and bake in the oven, about 15 minutes.

372. Savoy cabbage rolls with béchamel
ROLLATINI DI VERZE ALLA BESCIAMELLA

Prepare as above but use a **filling** (see recipes 702–709) and cover with **béchamel** (see recipes 652–653). Dust with **cheese**, pour a little melted **butter** over the dish, and bake in the oven until golden brown.

373. Vegetable harlequinade
ARLECCHINATA DI LEGUMI

Take **red and yellow peppers**, cut them into small square shapes, mix together with:

- 1 lb cup peas
- 1 lb cup chopped mushrooms
- 8 oz blanched green beans (cut into square shapes)

Drain the vegetables well and put in a pan with:

- butter
- salt
- pepper

Heat for 10 minutes and serve with a garnish of fried **croutons**.

374. Fennel with béchamel
FINOCCHI ALLA BESCIAMELLA

The same recipe as for cauliflower (see recipe 291), substituting fennel.

375. Cucumber with mayonnaise
CETRIOLO ALLA MAJONESE

Peel and slice the **cucumber** and sprinkle with salt. Leave to drain in a colander for at least 30 minutes. Arrange over slices of **boiled potato** in a dish, cover with **mayonnaise** (see recipes 672–673), and decorate with capers, gherkins, and olives.

376. Mock tuna 'a skapici'
BURLA DI TONNO A SKAPICI

A dish known as "tonno a skapici' is extremely popular dish in Sicily. It is made with slices of fried tuna fish covered in cipollata (onions cooked to a purée-like consistency in oil and a little water). The following is a clever imitation.

Cut a **yellow squash** into 4-inch slices. Dust with salt and leave for around 30 minutes.

In a medium sauté pan, fry in **oil** and then arrange in a serving dish.

To garnish, brown a generous amount of the **sliced onions** in the oil left in the pan. Throw away the extra oil, pour in a **small glass of vinegar**, and allow to evaporate. Put the cipollata over the squash. Sprinkle with **chopped mint** and serve cold.

377. Mushrooms in special onion sauce
FUNGHI AL SUBISSO

Chop the **mushrooms** any way you wish and cook in butter. Pour **special onion sauce** (see recipe 686) over the dish and serve garnished with **croutons** or flaky **pastry crescents**.

378. Grilled eggplant with lemon
MELANZANE GRIGLIATE AL LIMONE

Halve the **eggplants** and make slits in the flesh into which salt is to be generously sprinkled together with:

>   lemon juice
>   oregano
>   salt
>   pepper

Place on the grill and while they are cooking squeeze a little more **lemon juice** in the slits and brush with oil.

379. Eggplants Sardinian style
MELANZANE ALLA SARDEGNUOLA

Preheat oven to to 350°F.

Choose **6 nice big eggplants**, halve lengthwise, and scrape out the pulp, leaving the shells whole. Dust with salt and leave to drain in a colander for 30 minutes. Rinse, dry, and deep fry. Finely chop the pulp, and fry lightly with:

>   a little garlic
>   onion

>   parsley
>   salt
>   pepper

Allow the mixture to cool and make into a stuffing by adding:

>   **8 oz crustless bread soaked in milk**
>   **4 oz grated Parmesan cheese**
>   **2 eggs**

Mix together, fill the eggplant shells, and then bake in the oven, about 20 to 30 minutes.

380. American style tomatoes
POMIDORI ALL'AMERICANA

Peel the **tomatoes** and remove the seeds, cut into quarters, toss in **flour**, **salt**, and **pepper**, roll in **beaten egg** and **bread crumbs**, and fry. Pour a **béchamel** over the dish (see recipe 652) before serving.

381. Spinach with egg
SPINACI ALL'UOVO

Boil and chop the **spinach** and put in a pan with:

>   butter
>   salt
>   pepper

As soon as it is well seasoned add:

>   **slivers of 3 hard-boiled egg whites**
>   **3½ oz milk**
>   **a little flour** (or other thickening agent)

Heat up. Arrange on a plate, pour **fresh cream**

over the dish, and garnish with the **grated hard-boiled egg yolks**.

382. Stuffed peppers
PEPERONI FARCITI

Blanch the **peppers**, remove the stems, seeds, and skin. Fill with **stuffing** (see recipes 702 to 709), sprinkle with small knobs of **butter**, and bake in the oven until golden brown.

383. Stuffed zucchini, Italian style
ZUCCHINE FARCITE ALL'ITALIANA

Cut **zucchini** into 2-inch pieces, peel, and take out the pulp from one side only. Fill with **stuffing** (see recipes 702 to 709), fry gently in **butter**, and arrange in a serving dish as soon as the pieces are well cooked and golden brown. Cover with a **velouté sauce** (recipe 650).

384. Stuffed potatoes, Italian style
PATATE FARCITE ALL'ITALIANA

Choose large **potatoes** all the same size. Peel, halve, and hollow out each half. Fill with the same **stuffing** as used in the previous recipe. Put the two halves together, tie up with raffia or cotton string, and lightly fry (giving the mixture a slightly more liquid consistency with a little **wine**) until golden in color. Serve a **salmi sauce** (recipe 699) separately. Tie the strings with bows and leave these on when serving.

385. Stuffed eggplants, Italian style
MELANZANE FARCITE ALL'ITALIANA

Follow the same recipe as above and bake in the oven, without putting the two halves back together.

386. Sicilian 'frittella' (fresh vegetable medley)
FRITTELLA SICILIANA

Ingredients:
- 2 lb green peas
- 6 artichokes
- 2 lb green fava beans
- 9 oz onions
- olive oil

Cut the onions into strips and lightly fry. Throw in the beans and peas, which need to be fresh and tender. Cover and cook over a low heat. After 10 minutes, add the artichokes that have been carefully cleaned and cut into 8 pieces. Add salt and pepper and a little water if necessary. Cover and cook slowly until the vegetables are done but not overcooked. Dissolve **2 teaspoons of sugar** and **two of vinegar** in the sauté.

387. Tomatoes, Chilean style
POMIDORI ALLA CILENA

Peel **2 lb nice round tomatoes** and remove the core and seeds, leaving the shells whole.

To make the filling, lightly fry a grated **onion** in **2 oz butter** and toast **5 oz bread crumbs** in a pan with **2 oz butter**. Cool and stir in:

4 oz grated Parmesan cheese

salt

pepper

parsley

other chopped herbs

Stuff the tomatoes and place in a greased dish. Bake the tomatoes in the oven until golden in color. This dish can be served with any of the **hot sauces** in the Sauces, pages 187–198.

388. Cauliflower au gratin
CAVOLFIORE GRATINATO

Steam cook a nice big **cauliflower**, place in an oven-proof dish, sprinkle with equal amounts of:

grated Parmesan cheese

bread crumbs

Dust with **chopped parsley**, and pour a little melted **butter** over the dish. Bake until golden brown.

389. Cauliflower with creamed tomato
CAVOLFIORI AL POMODORO CREMATO

Steam cook the **cauliflower** and serve with a **tomato sauce** made with **butter**. Pour **fresh cream** over the dish before serving.

390. Mushrooms on toast
FUNGHI AL PANE TOSTATO

Ingredients:

20 oz mushrooms

10 oz tomatoes

4 oz butter

sliced bread

Lightly fry the sliced bread. Peel the mushrooms and fry in butter, salt, and pepper. Slice the tomatoes and arrange on the buttered toast, spoon over the mushrooms, sprinkle with chopped **parsley**, and bake for 10–15 minutes.

391. Harvest pie
PASTICCIO DI HARVERT

Parboil **1 ¼ lb potatoes** and slice together with:

2 carrots

8 oz turnip cabbage

3 boiled onions

Boil **1 lb chestnuts**, remove both the outside and inside skins, and cut into quarters. Bind all the ingredients together with **2 tbsp tapioca** that has been soaked in water for several hours. Add:

4 hard-boiled eggs

Put in an oven-proof or pie dish, and season with salt and pepper. Cover with a layer of **flaky pastry** and bake in the oven.

392. Sautéed beets
BARBABIETOLE SALTATE

Cook as for the above recipe. Slice and sauté in butter, salt, and pepper. Place in a serving dish and cover with **fresh cream**.

393. Brussels sprouts with chestnuts
CAVOLINI DI BRUXELLES CON CASTAGNE

Melt **1 oz butter**, and add:

> **Brussels sprouts**
> **the same amount of peeled green**
>   **chestnuts**

Cook in a steamer. Cover and leave to thicken slightly over a gentle heat. Serve with any **sauce** you wish or with **fresh cream**.

394. Zucchini risotto
ZUCCHINI AL RISOTTO

Make **8 oz Corvo risotto** (see recipe 156), empty out the **zucchini** after scraping the skin, fill with the risotto and gently fry in butter, sprinkling with a little **white wine** from time to time.

395 Carrots and turnip with cabbage
CAROTE E CAVOLRAPE

Chop the same amount of each of the **vegetables** and after steam cooking, sauté in:

> **butter**
> **salt**
> **pepper**

Garnish with **fried croutons** and serve with a **sauce** of your choice.

396. Green beans in sauce
FAGIOLINI VERDI SALSITI

Top and tail and cut the **green beans** in three. Toss in **butter** and '**picchio-pacchio**' sauce (see recipe 652). Serve garnished with fried croutons or flaky pastry crescents.

397. Beets in sauce
BARBABIETOLE SALSITE

Wash, remove the roots, and boil in salted water. Once cooked, remove the skins, slice thinly, and serve hot with a **sauce** of your choice, garnished with **fried croutons**.

398. Beets with onions
BARBABIETOLE CON CIPOLLE

Cook and slice **beets** as above; strew strips of **baked onion** on the beets, dust with:

> **ground walnuts**
> **chopped parsley**

Season with a dressing made of:

> **oil**
> **lemon juice**
> **salt**
> **pepper**

Serve cold.

399. Beets with béchamel
BARBABIETOLE ALLA BESCIAMELLA

Boil the **beets**, slice them, and peel and cover with **béchamel** (see recipe 652). Bake until golden brown.

400. Onions Spanish style
CIPOLLE ALLA SPAGNUOLA

Choose **6 large Spanish onions**. Cut out the core, fill with a **stuffing** (see recipes 702 and 709), and bake until done. Serve with a **Spanish sauce** (see recipe 649).

401. Ciaulini tomatoes
POMIDORI CIAULINI

Choose some **large but fully ripe tomatoes** and remove the core and seeds. Dust with a little salt and place upside down in a colander to drain. Make some **mayonnaise** (see recipes 672–674) and mix in:

3 hard-boiled eggs

20 chopped olives

Fill the tomatoes with the mixture.

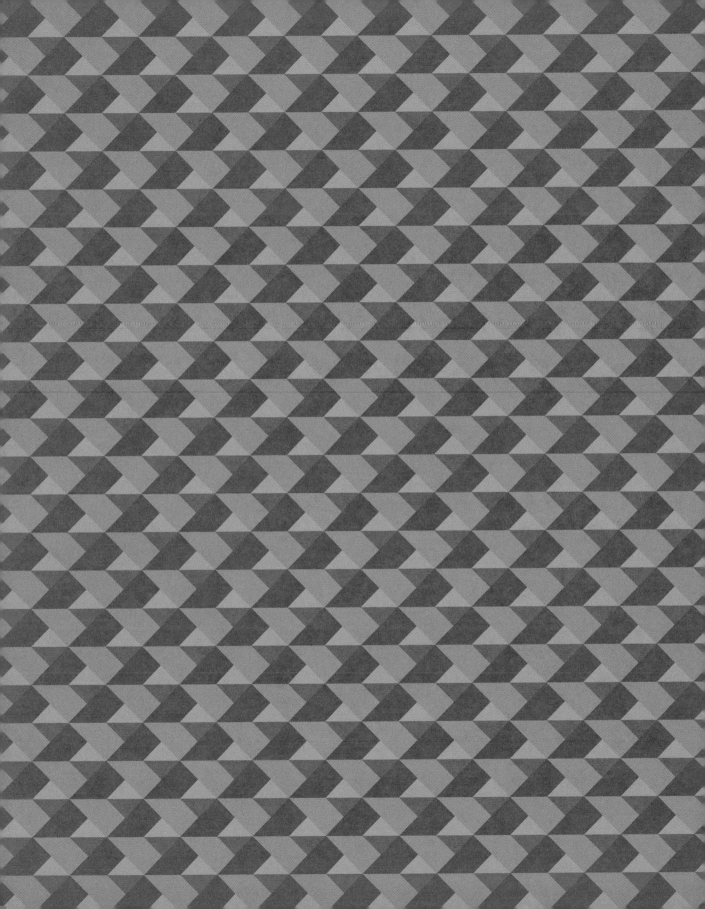

Main dishes, casseroles and soufflés

PIATTI FORTI, UMIDI E FLAN

402. Sicilian pancakes
PANTALONI ALLA SICILIANA (PANCAKES)

Follow the recipe for **sweet pancakes** (recipe 768), and fill with a stuffing of:

- fried, diced eggplant
- Parmesan cheese
- a few ground walnuts
- parsley
- a few chopped dried mushrooms
- salt
- pepper

Roll the pancakes around the stuffing and arrange in an oven-proof dish, cover with **tomato sauce**, dust with Parmesan and either bake in a 400°F oven or put under the broiler until a nice golden crust is formed.

403. Pancakes sautéed in béchamel
FRITTELLE SALTATE ALLA BESCIAMELLA

Cook as above, but instead of tomato sauce cover with **béchamel** (see recipes 652–653), dusting with:

- Parmesan cheese
- butter

Bake until the sauce has a nice golden crust.

404. Vegetarian meatballs
GRANATINE DI PSEUDO-CARNE

Make the **eggplant stuffing** described in recipe 708, but give it a slightly firmer consistency by adding **bread crumbs** and **an egg white**. Make the dough into small, slightly flattened balls, and, in a large sauté pan, fry in **olive oil**. Serve with a homemade **tomato sauce** (see recipe 646), or any other sauce you choose. Serve with French fries.

405. Vegetarian kidneys with Marsala wine
PSEUDO-ROGNONI AL MARSALA

There is of course no such thing as a vegetable kidney—but mushrooms in a good Marsala sauce get close to the classic dish. Use some good **mushrooms**, either fresh or canned (never the dried variety). Chop into kidney shapes and sauté in butter with:

- onion
- chopped parsley
- salt
- pepper

Add a little **wine** occasionally during cooking. When the mushrooms are almost fully cooked, pour in **a small glass of Marsala**, and allow this to evaporate. Thicken with **flour** and garnish with **fried croutons**.

406. 'Cacimperio'
CACIMPERIO

This is a simple, savory egg dish. Ingredients:

14 oz Fontina cheese
2 oz butter
4 egg yolks
as much milk as is needed

Dice the fontina or other fresh cheese and soak in milk for two hours. After two hours, drain the cheese. In a medium sauté pan, melt some butter, and stir in the cheese and a cup of milk. Keep stirring, without allowing the mixture to boil. When the fontina is completely liquefied remove from the stove, add the egg yolks and put back over the flame for a few minutes, stirring continuously. Serve hot, if possible with a sprinkling of chopped **truffles** or other fine **mushrooms**.

407. Vegetarian tripe 'alla pizzaiola'
PSEUDO-TRIPPA ALLA PIZZAIUOLA

Preheat oven to 350°F.

There is a long tradition of vegetable pâtés and tripes. This recipe gets close to a tripe "alla pizzaiola" by mixing mushrooms with tomato, garlic, and oregano. Ingredients:

8 oz mushrooms
8 oz Parmesan cheese

8 oz tomato concentrate
4 oz butter
½ cup olive oil

Lightly fry a finely chopped onion in oil and blend in the tomato concentrate, garnish with parsley, a clove of garlic, a few leaves of basil and very finely chopped sage. Cut the mushrooms into strips (in the manner of tripe) and, in a separate pan, sauté in the butter. When the mushrooms are cooked, mix with the tomato sauce, and transfer the mixture to an an ovenproof dish and dust with Parmesan. Finish the dish with:

a few pieces of peeled garlic
some bread crumbs
a little oregano

Bake in the oven for about 10 minutes.

408. Vegetarian tripe, Sicilian style
PSEUDO-TRIPPA ALLA SICILIANA

Preheat oven to 350°F.

This recipe uses pancakes baked in a tomato sauce, cheese, and herbs to aproximate the texture of a tripe. Make **pancakes** (see recipe 768) but omit the sugar.

Next, roll the pancakes, and cut into strips that resemble tripe. Dress these with a thick **tomato sauce** and **grated caciocavallo cheese**. Sprinkle with:

bread crumbs
oregano
oil

Bake in the oven for about 10 minutes.

409. Sautéed pancakes with cheese
FRITTELLE SALTATE DI FORMAGGIO (PANCAKES)

Follow the recipe for **sweet pancakes** (number 768), but omit the sugar, fill with a thick **béchamel** (see recipes 652–653) and small pieces of fresh **caciocavallo cheese**. Grease a baking tin with **butter**, arrange the rolled pancakes in the tin, dust with Parmesan, sprinkle with a **velouté sauce**, and cover. They can be cooked under the broiler or in a 400°F oven until they form a golden crust.

410. Ricotta balls
POLPETTE DI RICOTTA

Ingredients:

    12 oz ricotta cheese
    3 oz grated caciocavallo cheese
    8 ground walnuts
    3 eggs
    salt
    spices
    chopped parsley

Mix all the ingredients together, toss nuggets of the mixture into flour and use your hands to form small balls. In a large sauté pan, fry the balls in **olive oil**. To serve, cover with **tomato sauce** (see recipe 646) or any other sauce of your choice.

411. Spicy 'berlingozzo'
BERLINGOZZO PICCANTE

Preheat the oven to 350°F.

Make a **béchamel** (see recipes 652–653). Next, beat **8 egg whites** with a pinch of salt until they are stiff, and fold in:

    the béchamel
    8 egg yolks
    2 oz Parmesan cheese

Pour into a greased, oven-safe ring mold and dust with **breadcrumbs**. Cook in the oven for 40 minutes to 1 hour, until the the top of the ring is golden brown. When cool, turn out on to a serving plate.

412. Spinach 'berlingozzo'
BERLINGOZZO DI SPINACI

Follow recipe 421, adding two handfuls of **spinach** that has been cooked in butter or olive oil.

413. Curried 'berlingozzo'
BERLINGOZZO AL CURRIE

Follow recipe 421, adding a teaspoonful of **curry** (see recipe 893).

414. 'Berlingozzo' with truffles
BERLINGOZZO TARTUFATO

Follow recipe 411, adding **2 or 3 chopped truffles** and laying a few slices in the greased mold.

415. 'Berlingozzo' with herbs
BERLINGOZZO ALL'ERBETTE

Follow recipe 411, adding a little bunch of finely chopped **herbs** that have been lightly fried in **butter**.

416. Tomato mousse
SPUMA DI POMODORO

Preheat oven to 350°F.

In a sauté pan, lightly brown:

onion

garlic

basil

parsley

salt

pepper

Add:

2 lb of tomatoes, chopped

Cook, and when the mixture begins to thicken, remove tomatoes from it, put it through a food mill and return to the pan. Blend the **whites of 8 eggs** and the sauce together with the **yolks**. Stir continuously and add **2 oz of grated Parmesan**.

Pour into a greased mold and bake for 40 minutes to 1 hour, until the top of the ring is golden brown. When cool, turn out on to a serving plate.

417. Potato mousse
SPUMA DI PATATE

Preheat oven to 350°F.

Boil **1 lb potatoes** and put through a food mill, then mix with **10 oz bread crumbs** that have been soaked in **milk**, squeezing off any excess moisture. Beat **5 egg whites** until stiff, and add:

the egg yolks

6 ½ oz grated Parmesan cheese

salt

pepper

Blend in with the potatoes and bread crumbs.

Put the mixture in a greased soufflé dish or oven-proof dish, leaving it space to rise. Bake in the oven for 40 minutes to 1 hour.

418. Cauliflower mousse
SPUMA DI CAVOLFIORI

Steam a nice big **cauliflower**, break up with a fork and mix in **half a pound of bread crumbs** that have been soaked in milk. Put through a food mill, and add:

8 egg whites that have been beaten stiff with a pinch of salt

the egg yolks

4 oz of grated Parmesan cheese

Pour into a greased soufflé dish or oven-proof bowl and bake in the oven, about 30 to 40 minutes.

419. Pea mousse
SPUMA DI PISELLI

Follow the above recipe with **1 lb of boiled peas** put through a food mill.

420. Fava bean mousse (fresh or dried)
SPUMA DI FAVE VERDI O SECCHE

Follow the above recipe, using the same quantity of **fava beans**.

421. Foie gras mousse (made with ricotta cheese and black truffles)
SPUMA DI FEGATO GRASSO

Make the mixture described in recipe 546 and fold in:

8 stiffly beaten egg whites
1 egg yolk

Pour into a soufflé dish or oven-proof bowl and bake.

422. Milk and egg soufflé
FLAN DI LATTE ED UOVA

Preheat oven to 400°F.

Make **2 pints of béchamel** (see recipes 652–653), and fold in:

8 stiffly beaten egg whites
the egg yolks

Pour into a greased mold and steam cook.

423. Green and white soufflé
FLAN BIANCO-VERDE

Ingredients:

2 pints of béchamel (see recipes 652-653)
a generous amount of spinach
6 eggs
2 oz butter

Boil the spinach and put through a food mill, mix with half the béchamel and 3 eggs. Mix the rest of the sauce with the 3 remaining eggs. Choose a smooth ring or savarin mold and pour in the mixture. Steam cook until it is firm. Turn upside down onto a serving plate, filling the center with **peas** or any other vegetable sautéed in **butter**.

424. Green bean soufflé
FLAN DI FAGIOLINI

Ingredients:

1 ½ lb tender green beans
half an onion
parsley leaves
4 oz of butter
2 tbsp flour
2 cups milk
4 oz grated Parmesan cheese
8 eggs

Top and tail the beans and cook in boiling, salted water. Toss into a pan with the lightly fried onion, parsley and half the butter. Add a little extra liquid until they are well cooked, put through a sieve or blend otherwise. Make a béchamel with the milk, flour and the remainder of the butter. Mix with the bean purée while still hot, and add the beaten eggs and grated Parmesan. Grease a ring mold with butter and pour in the mixture. Steam cook until firm and turn onto a plate when cool.

425. Cauliflower soufflé
FLAN DI CAVOLFIORI

Boil, chop and lightly fry the **cauliflower** in **2 oz of butter**, and put through a food mill. Mix with:

1 pint of béchamel (see recipes 652-653)
8 beaten eggs
4 oz of grated Parmesan cheese

Pour into a greased mold and steam cook.

426. Carrot and beet flan
FLAN DI CAROTE O DI BARBABIETOLE

Follow the above recipe, using **1 lb of boiled carrots** or **beets** instead of the cauliflower.

427. Vegetarian huntsman's pie
FLAN DI CACCIA (PSEUDO)

Lightly fry an **onion** in **2 oz butter**, gradually add **a glass of dry red wine**. Mash in:

> **10 oz of ricotta cheese**
>
> **salt**
>
> **pepper**
>
> **herbs**

Put through a food mill and add:

> **8 beaten eggs**
>
> **grated truffles**

Put a few slices of the truffles around the bottom and sides of a ring mold. Steam cook and when it is nice and firm turn over a plate before serving.

428. Spinach soufflé
FLAN DI SPINACI

Boil **1 lb spinach** in a tiny amount of water, chop, and put through a food mill. Then follow the recipe for cauliflower.

429. Artichoke soufflé
FLAN DI CARCIOFI

Clean and wash **6 artichokes**, cut into 8 segments, and cook in a minimum of salted water. When they are nice and soft, put through a sieve

and follow the recipe for green beans (see recipe 424), adding an extra **egg** if you like.

～～～～～～～～～

430. Chard or pepper soufflé
FLAN DI CARDONI O DI PEPERONI

Follow recipe 424, choosing nice big white **chards**, which are to be cut into little pieces before boiling. A pound of Neapolitan **peppers** may be used as an alternative.

431. Tomato soufflé
FLAN DI POMODORO

Put **4 ½ lb tomatoes** through a food mill to make about 2 pints of liquid (add more tomatoes if necessary), and melt **4 oz corn flour** in this (without heating). Add:

> **2 oz butter**
>
> **a pinch of salt**

Stir continuously over a low heat until it begins to thicken. Remove from the heat and as soon as it cools a little add:

> **8 beaten eggs**
>
> **6 oz grated Parmesan cheese**

Pour into a greased ring mold and steam cook.

432. Celery soufflé
FLAN DI SEDANI

Chop and cook the **celery** in a little boiling water. As soon as it is done put through a food mill and follow the recipe for the green bean soufflé (see recipe 424)

433. Fennel soufflé
FLAN DI FINOCCHI

Follow the recipe for the green bean soufflé (see recipe 424).

434. Green pea soufflé
FLAN DI PISELLINI VERDI

Ingredients:

- 28 oz shelled peas
- 4 oz butter
- 1 ¼ oz flour
- 8 eggs
- 2 oz Parmesan cheese
- 1 pint milk

Lightly fry half a **chopped onion** with half the butter, toss in the peas with salt and pepper. As soon as they are cooked put a third through a food mill. Blend the rest of the butter, flour, and milk together. Mix in the whole peas and the purée, the beaten eggs and the grated Parmesan, without heating the mixture. Put in a greased ring mold and steam cook. The peas can all be put through the sieve and puréed if preferred. Dried peas can also be used for this recipe (12 oz).

435. Zucchini soufflé
FLAN DI ZUCCHINE

Ingredients:

- 1 ¼ lb zucchini
- 1 ½ oz Parmesan cheese
- 8 eggs
- 2 oz butter
- 1 pint béchamel

In the butter, lightly fry:

- **half an onion**
- **chopped celery**
- **carrots**
- **a generous amount of parsley**

Add a little water if needed. Toss in the zucchini strips with salt and pepper. When they are well cooked put through a food mill, adding the Parmesan, the beaten eggs and the béchamel (see recipes 652–653). Put in a smooth greased mold and steam cook.

436. Pumpkin soufflé
FLAN DI ZUCCA GIALLA

Follow the above recipe but use **pumpkin** (or other orange squash).

437. Mushroom flan
FLAN DI FUNGHI

Ingredients:

- 1 ¼ lb fresh mushrooms
- 8 eggs
- 2 oz butter
- 4 oz grated Parmesan cheese
- 1 pint béchamel

Cut into ¼ inch strips. Lightly fry in butter with salt and pepper, adding extra liquid if needed. As soon as they are well cooked mix in the béchamel (recipes 652–653), the beaten eggs and grated Parmesan, and steam cook in a mold that has been greased with butter.

438. 'Salpicone' in shells (a savoury bake in custard shells)
SALPICONE IN TERRINE O CONCHIGLIE

In a pan with **2 oz of butter**, lightly fry a **chopped onion** and sauté **½ lb good quality chopped mushrooms**; season with:

> salt
>
> herbs
>
> nutmeg
>
> a little parsley
>
> pepper

When well cooked, add a little **wine**, remove from the heat and add:

> some mock new-laid eggs (see recipe 466)
>
> 4 raw yolks
>
> a pinch of cayenne pepper
>
> a few chopped black truffles

Fill custard shells, top with extra truffles and a small knob of **butter**, and bake in the oven.

439. Mushroom and egg bake
TERRINE DI FUNGHI ALL'UOVO

Sauté some good quality chopped **mushrooms** in **butter**, and season with:

> salt
>
> pepper
>
> nutmeg

Cool and mix together with:

> ½ pint cream
>
> 8 egg yolks

Put in an oven mold and bake for 15 minutes.

440. Milk 'spools' with mock new-laid eggs
SPOLETTE DI LATTE CON OVETTI PSEUDO-NEONATI

Into **1 pint of milk**, blend:

> 8 oz corn flour
>
> a pinch of salt

Cook over a low heat, stirring until the sauce thickens. Pour it out onto a marble surface that has been rubbed with butter. As soon as it cools, cut into spool shapes. Arrange these in the middle of an oven-proof dish and garnish with **mock eggs** (see recipe 466). Dust with **Gruyère cheese** and bake until golden brown. Pour a **velouté** or **Spanish sauce** around the sides (see recipes 649–650) and serve hot garnished with **fried croutons** or flaky **pastry crescents**.

441. Nut-flavored milk disks
DISCHI DI LATTE NOCCIOLATI

Prepare the milk as in the previous recipe, adding **4 oz ground hazelnuts**. Cut into disks, arrange in a greased baking tin or oven-proof dish, dust with **caciocavallo cheese**, pour a little melted **butter** on, and bake in the oven. Serve with whatever **sauce** you please.

442. Pasha chops (a savory rolled in cabbage or lettuce leaves)
BRACIOLINE DEL PASCIÀ

Blanch leaves of **lettuce** or **Savoy cabbage** and fill with a mixture of:

ricotta cheese

ground walnuts

chopped parsley and onion

salt

pepper

Roll the leaves over like kebabs. Place in a baking dish and cover with a **velouté** or **tomato sauce** and heat in a low oven. These are also excellent when rolled in flour, tossed in beaten egg and bread crumbs, and fried.

443. The Maharaja's platter
TERRINE DEL MARAHJA

Ingredients:

12 oz ricotta

3 oz Parmesan

2 lb spinach

2 oz butter

½ cup wine

onion

truffles

curry

parsley

nutmeg

4 eggs

Lightly brown the chopped onion in the butter and add the ricotta, boiled spinach, **a teaspoonful of curry** (see recipe 893), parsley, salt, and nutmeg. Cook for 10 minutes, adding the wine and stirring continuously. Put through a sieve, mix in the egg yolks, and then the stiffly beaten whites and the Parmesan. Fill a terrine or oven-proof dish, garnish with **black truffles**, and bake in the oven.

444. Vegetarian meat loaf
ARROSTO IN CASSERUOLA

Mix together **1 lb of the following legumes**: lentils, beans, and dried peas. Cook slowly with a **carrot** and a pinch of **baking soda**, without adding salt and pouring in a little boiling water occasionally until they are well cooked, but not too liquid. Put through a food mill and mix with:

chopped parsley

onion flavoring

nutmeg

6 ground walnuts

salt and pepper

3 oz grated Parmesan

2 eggs

enough bread crumbs to give the mixture consistency

Roll it into a large sausage shape and place in an oven-proof dish with **butter** and **a sprig of rosemary**. Brown in the oven then remove the rosemary, pour **in half a glass of good dry white wine**, add a little **flour** and allow to thicken over a low flame. Place on a serving platter and garnish as you please.

445. German style vegetarian scallops
SGALOPPINA ALLA TEDESCA

Make the same legume mixture as for the '**meat loaf**' above (see recipe 444) but instead of forming a sausage shape, make walnut-sized pellets. Flatten these a little between the palms of your hands, and sauté in **butter** over a gentle flame.

446. Vegetarian steaks
BISTECCHE IN TEGLIA

Make the 'meat loaf' mixture in recipe 444 and shape it like a meat roast. Slice as you meat into generous ½-inch slices. Sauté in **butter** and garnish with **French fries** or **salad**.

447. Medallions in salmi
MEDAGLIONI AL SALMI

Arrange **6 slices of fried bread rounds** in a buttered baking dish. Lay a slice of 'meat loaf' (see recipe 444) over each of these. Heat in the oven and pour a generous amount of **salmi sauce** (recipe 699) over the dish, sprinkling with minced **black truffles**.

~~~~~~~~~~~~~~~~~~~

448. Vegetarian cutlets English style
COTOLETTE DI PROTOSE ALL'INGLESE

Ingredients:

> **10 oz minced peanuts**
> **5 oz boiled mashed potatoes**
> **6 oz crustless bread**
> **chopped parsley**
> **a grated onion**
> **salt**
> **pepper**

Mix the ingredients together, shape into a cutlet, roll in **flour**, then soak in **beaten egg**, coat with **bread crumbs** and fry.

449. British rice
RISO BRITANNICO

Wash **16 oz rice**, boil in water until cooked, and then drain. Add:

> **a quart of milk**
> **a knob of butter**
> **salt**
> **pepper**

Cook until the rice has soaked up all the milk. Butter an oven-proof dish and cover with layers of the rice, alternating with layers of **grated cheese**. Top the last layer with little pieces of butter. Bake until golden brown.

450. Palermitan vegetarian meatballs
POLPETTINE PALERMITANE

Ingredients:

> **12 oz bread crumbs**
> **4 oz walnuts**
> **4 oz caciocavallo cheese**
> **2 eggs**
> **parsley**
> **onion**
> **tomato sauce**

Gently fry the onion in butter and dissolve into a purée with **half a glass of wine**. Make a mound of bread crumbs on a pastry board and fill the center with the sautéed onion, grated cheese, ground walnuts, chopped parsley, salt, pepper, and 2 eggs. Knead and add extra bread crumbs or egg if needed. Make into meatball shapes and fry. Serve with a good **tomato sauce**.

451. Mock Scotch haggis
HAGGIS SCOZZESE

Ingredients:

  10 oz flour
  10 oz bread crumbs
  5 oz butter
  1 tbsp rolled oats
  6 eggs

Mix all the ingredients together with half the melted butter, put in a greased mold with the remaining butter and boil for around 4 hours.

452. Herb scallops
SGALOPPINE ALLE FIN'ERBE

Follow the recipe for the mock woodcock balls (recipe 453), without the truffles. Brown in **butter** and lightly fried **onion**. Sprinkle with:

  parsley
  chopped herbs

Garnish as you choose.

453. Vegetarian woodcock
TORNATI DI PSEUDO-BECCACCIA

Ingredients:

  1 oz dried mushrooms
  30 walnuts
  6 oz flour
  ½ cup Marsala wine
  6 oz butter

  as many truffles as you wish

Clean the mushrooms well and chop finely. Grind the nuts, chop the **parsley** and any other herbs you please. Melt the butter and stir in the flour until they are nicely blended. Remove from the heat and add the other ingredients, mixing continuously. Before it cools make spoonfuls of the mixture into small balls. When cool, lightly fry these in butter and moisten with Marsala. Arrange in a serving dish with chopped truffles and garnish with **fried croutons** or **vegetables** cooked in butter.

454. English style vegetarian meat-balls
POLPETTE ALL'INGLESE

Ingredients:

  1 lb lentils
  6 oz onions
  2 oz beets
  12 walnuts
  chopped parsley
  thyme
  1 tbsp tomato concentrate
  spices

Cook the lentils with a pinch of **baking soda**. Boil the beets, peel, and chop. Brown the onion, moistening with **wine**. Mix all the ingredients together and put through a food mill. Work in the ground walnuts and chopped parsley and make the mixture into "meat balls," giving it a firmer consistency by adding **bread crumbs** if necessary. Fry and serve.

455. Italian style chops in gravy
BRACIOLINE ALL'ITALIANA

Ingredients:

- 6 medium-sized potatoes
- 4 oz chopped onions
- 12 ground shelled walnuts
- salt
- pepper
- parsley
- 4 oz butter
- whatever bread crumbs are needed

Boil the potatoes and put through a ricer, mix with the onions (that have been lightly fried in half the butter) and the well-ground walnuts, parsley, salt, pepper, **eggs**, and as many bread crumbs as are needed to give the mixture a fairly thick consistency. Make into cutlets, brush with butter, and bake briefly in the oven. Remove from the oven and thicken the butter with:

- a little flour
- a small glass of wine

Simmer for a minute or two. Pour this gravy over the cutlets and serve hot with a garnish of your choice.

456. Irish style chops
BRACIOLINE IRLANDESI

Ingredients:

- 6 tbsp wholemeal bread crumbs
- 4 oz Cheddar or grated Gruyère cheese
- parsley
- onion
- a little less than 1 oz finely chopped dried mushrooms that have been left to soak in water

- 4 eggs

Mix all the ingredients together, add salt and pepper and, if needed, wholemeal bread crumbs. Make into small cutlets. Fry in boiling **oil** for a few minutes and serve with French fries.

457. York Pudding
BODIANO DI YORK

Combine:

- 4 oz bread crumbs
- 6 eggs
- 4 oz boiled chopped onion
- generous amount of chopped parsley
- 10 ground walnuts
- enough **cream** to give the mixture a fairly firm consistency

Season with salt and pepper, grease small molds, fill half full, and bake in the oven for around 20 minutes. Remove from the oven and serve with a good **fricassee** or **salmi sauce** (see under Sauces).

458. Scottish loaf
FORMATA SCOZZESE

Ingredients:

- 12 oz bread crumbs
- 4 oz ground peanuts
- 6 eggs
- 4 boiled chopped white celery hearts
- 1 pint milk

Beat the eggs with a little salt and pepper and mix together with the other ingredients. Put in a greased mold and cook in a double boiler.

459. Vegetable sausages
SALSICCIOTTI VEGETALI

Boil and chop:

6 carrots

4 medium-sized onions

2 turnip cabbages

Cook **12 oz dried shelled peas** separately. Mix all the ingredients together with:

12 ground walnuts

finely chopped parsley

salt, pepper

4 eggs

bread crumbs as needed to make the
    mixture easier to mold

Make into small sausages, toss in beaten egg then in bread crumbs, and fry.

Eggs

UOVA

460. Almond eggs
UOVA MANDORLATE

In a cup of **boiling milk**, soak:

    a cupful of bread crumbs

Add:

    6 beaten eggs

    salt

    pepper

    4 oz ground almonds

Place the egg mixture in serving molds and cook in a double boiler. Serve when the eggs are firm.

461. Eggs empress style
UOVA ALL'IMPERATRICE

Hard-boil **eggs**, shell, and cut in half, removing the yolks.

    Make a pesto sauce by grinding together:

    an onion

    a clove of garlic

    a bunch of parsley

    a bunch of mint

    salt

    pepper

Add a little **vinegar**. Mix in the egg yolks and put through a food mill. Fill the whites with the pesto mixture and cover with good **mayonnaise**. Sprinkle with **capers** and **chopped gherkins**. Garnish with **lettuce** or **boiled potatoes**.

462. Fricasseed eggs
UOVA IN FRICASSEA

Poach the **eggs** in water (recipe 479) then arrange on a slice of **fried bread** and pour **fricassee sauce** over the eggs (see recipe 662).

463. Eggs with sage
UOVA SALVIATE

Hard boil **8 eggs**.

    Make a pesto sauce by grinding together:

    2 oz capers

    3 sage leaves

    8 cloves of garlic that have been boiled for 10 minutes

    2 oz crustless bread that has been soaked in **vinegar** and **lemon juice** and seasoned with salt and pepper

Put through a food mill. Pour the pesto sauce over the bottom of the serving dish and arrange the hard boiled eggs whatever way you choose, dusting with chopped **sage** and other **herbs**.

464. Egg terrine with truffles
TERRINE D'UOVA TARTUFATE

Finely chop **6 hard-boiled eggs** and arrange in individual custard cups. Dice **8 oz mozzarella** or any other fresh, non-fermented cheese, and place over the eggs. Cover with a **béchamel** (see recipes 652–653), sprinkle with **chopped truffles**, top each cup with a small knob of **butter**, and bake in a 325°F oven until the cheese is melted.

465. Eggs stuffed with vegetarian chicken
UOVA FARCITE AL POLLO (PSEUDO)

Hard-boil **6 eggs**, halve them and remove the yolks, which are to be mixed into the **vegetarian chicken stuffing** (see recipe 707). Fill the egg white halves with the filling, rounding them off so that they appear to be whole. Roll in **flour**, toss first in **beaten egg** and then in **bread crumbs**, and fry in oil.

466. Mock new-laid eggs
OVETTI O UOVA PSEUDO-NEONATI

Put **hard-boiled yolks** through a food mill. Mix the egg yolk purée with enough **raw egg white** to be able to mold them into small balls of irregular sizes, like new-laid eggs. Throw into slowly boiling water and remove as soon as they are firm. The remaining hard-boiled whites can be used as in the following recipe.

467. Stuffed yolkless eggs
UOVA FARCITE SENZA TUORLI

To use up **hard-boiled egg whites**, once the yolks have been used for other dishes, fill with a **stuffing** of your choice, preferably one done with vegetarian chicken. Toss in **flour**, then in **beaten egg** and **bread crumbs**. Fry in hot oil, and garnish before serving.

468. Eggs 'alla marinara' (sailor-style) or in green sauce
UOVA ALLA MARINARA O IN SALSA VERDE

Grind together:
   fresh mint
   parsley
   a little crustless bread that has been soaked in **vinegar** or **lemon**
Put through a food mill, and season with:
   oil
   salt
   pepper
Hard-boil **eggs**, then shell, halve and remove the yolks without breaking the whites. Mash the yolks and mix with the green sauce, adding salt and pepper as well as a small quantity of finely-chopped **garlic**. Fill the egg halves, arrange in a serving dish, and cover with the remaining sauce.

469. Monk's eggs
UOVA ALLA MONACALE

Hard-boil **6 eggs**, then shell and halve. Remove the yolks and mix with:

> **the same amount of ricotta**
> **6 oz grated Parmesan cheese**
> **8 ground walnuts**
> **salt**
> **pepper**
> **chopped parsley**

Stuff the egg halves, roll in **flour**, toss in **beaten egg** and **bread crumbs**, and fry.

470. Eggs with herbs
UOVA ALL'ERBETTE

Place in a pan:

> **some parsley**
> **chopped onion**
> **salt**
> **pepper**
> **a glass of white wine**
> **½ tbsp butter** dusted with **flour**
> **chopped herbs**

Boil for 15 minutes. In the meantime, poach eggs as in recipe 479. As soon as the sauce has thickened, cover the eggs with the sauce, dust with **bread crumbs** that have been toasted in a pan with butter, and serve.

471. Scrambled eggs
UOVA STRAPAZZATE

Put raw beaten **eggs** in a pan with a wedge of **butter** and cook slowly, stirring continuously. Optionally, add:

> **a few tablespoons of heavy cream**
> **chopped herbs**
> **grated Parmesan cheese**

Remove the eggs from the heat as soon as they are firm and serve.

472. Scrambled eggs with 'picchio-pacchio' sauce
UOVA STRAPAZZATE AL PIK-PACCHIO

Make a "**picchio-pacchio**" sauce (see recipe 647) and mix in with:

> **raw eggs**
> **a knob of butter**
> **salt**
> **pepper**

Stir continuously in a pan over moderate heat until the eggs are firm. Serve with **fried croutons**.

473. Eggs with peas, French style
UOVA COI PISELLINI ALLA FRANCESE

Blanch **peas** in boiling, salted water and drain. Arrange **fried croutons** in an oven-proof dish and sprinkle with **beaten eggs** mixed with the peas. Cook under the broiler or bake over a charcoal fire until firm.

474. 'Aurora' eggs
UOVA ALL'AURORA

Halve some **hard-boiled eggs**, remove the yolks, and put these in a bowl with:

a knob of butter

chopped herbs

salt

a little grated nutmeg

a little crustless bread soaked in milk (after squeezing out the excess moisture)

Mix all the ingredients together. Fill the egg white halves, arrange in a greased oven-proof dish and cover with a layer of **béchamel** (see recipes 652–653). Bake in 325°F oven after topping with small pats of butter, about 10 minutes.

475. Eggs in individual custard cups
UOVA IN TERRINE

Put a small drop of melted **butter** together with some **chopped herbs** in individual custard cups, break an **egg** into each mold, cover with **grated Parmesan cheese**, bake in a 350°F oven until the egg whites are firm, and serve in the terrines.

476. Mirror-image eggs with asparagus
UOVA ALLO SPECCHIO CON ASPARAGI

Chop the tips and tender parts of some **asparagus** into small pieces, blanch in boiling water, and put in a pan with:

a little butter

parsley

chopped onion

Cook, with a pinch of **flour** and moisten with a little **water**. Simmer, adding a little salt, then

place in a oven-proof dish, break **eggs** on top, and season with a little salt, pepper, and nutmeg. Cover and place the dish over a charcoal fire or in a 350°F oven, until the egg whites are firm.

477. Eggs with sauce
UOVA SALSITE

Place as many **whole eggs** as you want in boiling water and boil for 5 minutes. Then plunge them into cold water. Shell, without damaging the whites. The eggs should be parboiled and fairly soft to the touch. Serve whole with a **white** or **green sauce**, or **hot spicy sauce**, or any other you choose.

478. Eggs in Indian style béchamel
UOVA ALLA BESCIAMELLA INDIANA

Cut some **hard-boiled eggs** into round wheel shapes and mix with a **béchamel** (recipes 652–653), to which a **teaspoonful of curry** has been added (see recipe 893). Sprinkle with little knobs of **butter** and **cumin** and bake in a 325°F oven.

479. Poached eggs
UOVA INSACCATE

Boil a pan of salted water (¾ full) to which **2 tablespoons of vinegar** have been added (the acetic acid evaporates once the water boils). As soon as the water boils, break the **eggs** into the pan one by one. When cooked, remove with a skimming spoon and serve on a platter with a **sauce** of your choice (see Sauces, pages 187–198).

480. Florentine style eggs
UOVA ALLA FIORENTINA

Halve **9 hard-boiled eggs**. Remove the yolks and grind these together with:

4 oz butter

6 oz fresh ricotta

4 oz grated Parmesan cheese

a little salt and pepper

Place this mixture in a pan and add:

the yolks of 4 raw eggs

4 stiffly beaten whites

Mix well and stir continuously over a low heat until the mixture thickens. Fill the hard-boiled egg white shells with the above and spoon the remaining mixture into an oven-proof dish, arranging the stuffed eggs on top. Cover with a **béchamel** with **spinach** (see recipes 652–653), sprinkle with **Parmesan**, and pour over a little melted **butter**. Heat in a 350°F oven before serving.

481. Eggs with black butter
UOVA AL BURRO NERO

Break **eggs** into an oven-proof dish. Cook in a 350°F oven until the egg whites are firm. Pour a **black butter sauce** over the eggs and serve (see recipe 668).

482. Eggs 'in carrozza' (in coach)
UOVA IN CARROZZA

Fry the **eggs** one by one and place on a slice of **fried bread**. Fry slices of **fresh cheese** and arrange one of these over each egg, cover with a generous helping of homemade **tomato sauce**, and serve.

483. Eggs 'a spezzatino' (stew)
UOVA A SPEZZATINO

Halve **hard-boiled eggs**. Lightly fry chopped **onion** in oil and sprinkle with warm water in which **saffron** has been dissolved. Add the egg halves, and sprinkle with:

chopped parsley

salt

pepper

Cover the pan and cook until the eggs take on the yellow saffron color. Serve with **fried croutons** on the side.

484. Egg soufflé
TIMBALLO D'UOVA

Stiffly beat **8 egg whites** and mix with:

1 pint béchamel (see recipes 652–653)

8 oz grated Parmesan cheese

10 ground walnuts

a generous amount of chopped parsley

the egg yolks

Pour into a greased mold sprinkled with bread crumbs. Bake in the oven and turn onto a serving platter.

485. Eggs in shells (with cream and mushrooms)
SALPICONE D'UOVA IN CONCHIGLIA

Chop **4 hard-boiled eggs** into tiny pieces and mix with:

> the same quantity of mushroom stuffing (see recipe 705)
>
> **4 tablespoons of cream**
>
> cayenne pepper

Arrange in shells, pour over a little melted **butter** and bake in 325°F oven, about 10 minutes.

486. Pancake and fried egg rolls on skewers
BRACIOLINE DI UOVA FRITTE

Make some fairly small **pancakes** (see recipe 768). Fill with a stuffing of:

> bread soaked in milk
>
> grated Parmesan cheese
>
> a little lightly fried onion
>
> chopped parsley
>
> salt
>
> pepper

Roll these up and place on skewers, alternating with pieces of **bread**. Sprinkle with **béchamel**, roll in **flour**, toss in **egg** and then **bread crumbs**, and fry.

487. Eggs 'alla pizzaiola'
UOVA ALLA PIZZAIUOLA

Put oil in a baking tin or oven-proof dish and add **6 beaten eggs**. Cover with:

> thin slices of fresh cheese
>
> peeled tomato halves

Dust with:

> salt
>
> pepper
>
> oregano
>
> chopped garlic

Bake in a 350°F oven, about 20 minutes.

488. Egg and lettuce salad
UOVA CON LATTUGHE ALL'INSALATA

Cut **hard-boiled eggs** into quarters and place on a bed of **shredded lettuce**. Crush a few of the yolks and mix with:

> mustard
>
> vinegar
>
> olive oil
>
> salt
>
> pepper

Pour over the eggs.

489. Boiled eggs in cheese jackets
UOVA IN CAMICIA

Poach some **eggs** (see recipe 479) and allow to cool on a napkin. Thinly slice some **fresh cheese** and blanch in boiling water for a second or two, then wrap the slices around the eggs. Roll in **flour**, toss in **beaten egg** and then in **bread crumbs**, and deep fry.

490. Eggs 'all'ortolana' (eggs in tomato shells)
UOVA ALL'ORTOLANA

Choose **tomatoes** that are big enough to hold an egg each, empty out the seeds, sprinkle with salt, arrange in an oven-proof dish, and break an **egg** into each tomato. Add:

a slice of fresh cheese
a little butter

Bake in a 350°F oven.

491. Eggs on clouds
UOVA NUVOLATE

Beat **egg whites** until stiff and add:

a little chopped onion
parsley
salt
pepper

Pour into a greased oven-proof dish, fill the center with **a cup of cream** and arrange the **raw yolks** symmetrically over the whites. Cook in a 350°F oven until egg whites are firm and serve.

492. Herb omelet
FRITTATA ALL'ERBETTE

Break **eggs** into a bowl with:

salt
pepper
finely chopped herbs

Beat well, melt a little **butter** in a pan and add the eggs. When they begin to solidify, flip, and cook until golden brown. Serve at once.

493. Eggs with mushrooms
UOVA AI FUNGHI

Remove the **yolks** from **12 hard-boiled eggs** (without breaking them).

In a pan, cook:

chopped mushrooms
butter
salt
pepper

Add the chopped **egg whites**. Scoop the mixture into a serving dish, arranging the hard-boiled yolks on top and garnishing with **fried croutons**.

494. Eggs Chilean style
UOVA ALLA CILENA

Make **Chilean style eggplant** (see recipe 276) and place a **fried egg** over each one. Cover with **tomato sauce** and serve.

495. Anemone eggs
ANEMOLE D'UOVA

Beat **6 eggs** and make 6 small open-face omelets, turning over with the help of a plate. Make a paste with:

ricotta
grated Parmesan cheese
salt
pepper

Spoon this over the egg 'frittate' and roll them up. Arrange in an oven-proof dish, dust with Parmesan, cover with a **velouté sauce**, and place in a 350°F oven until it forms a golden crust.

496. Sultan's eggs
UOVA ALLA SULTANA

Cook some **stale bread** in **milk**. When it begins to thicken, add **5 oz grated Parmesan cheese**. Stiffly beat **5 egg whites** and mix the bread together with the **egg yolks**. Choose a pan big enough for three-quarters of the mixture, pour in **two glasses of broth**, and bring to the boil. Put in the bread and egg mixture without stirring or touching in any way (it must stay intact). Move by holding the pan handle and shaking. When it is nice and firm, cool and strain off the broth. Turn into a plate, thicken the broth slightly and pour over the savory pudding.

497. Woodman's eggs
UOVA ALLA BOSCAIUOLA

Mix together:

    ½ pint of red wine
    ½ pint of broth (see under Broths),
        although water will do

Add:

    a few sprigs of herbs
    1 onion
    1 clove garlic
    salt
    pepper
    spices

Boil for 10 minutes and remove to the edge of the burner so that it continues to simmer. Break the **6 fresh eggs**, one by one, into the liquid. Take them out with a skimming spoon as soon as they are cooked. Arrange on **fried croutons** on a heated plate. Reduce the broth and bind with:

    2 oz butter
    1 tbsp flour

Pour this sauce over the eggs and serve.

498. Eggs 'al subisso' (in a deluge)
UOVA AL SUBISSO

Make an **omelet** and cut it into noodle-like strips. Arrange on a heated plate and pour over the **'subisso' sauce** (see recipe 686). Heat slightly before serving.

499. Squash soufflé
UOVA ZUCCATE

Ingredients:

    6 eggs
    4 oz Parmesan cheese
    1 lb squash
    3 oz butter
    4 oz almonds

Choose a tender squash that easily dissolves when it cooks and cut it into little pieces. Cook in salted water and put through a food mill. As it cools, add 2 oz butter, the skinned, chopped almonds, and the cheese together with the beaten eggs. Add a little salt. Pour the liquid into an oven-proof dish and sprinkle with the remaining Parmesan and some bread crumbs. Top with small pats of butter and bake in the oven.

500. Spinach eggs
UOVA SPINACIATE

Ingredients:

- 8 eggs
- 1 pint milk
- 3 oz butter
- 1 lb spinach

Boil the spinach in salted water, drain, and put through a food mill. Melt 2 oz of the butter with **a heaping tbsp of flour** and slowly stir in the milk, simmer for a minute or two, and add the spinach. Pour over the poached eggs (recipe 479) and serve.

501. Truffled eggs
UOVA TARTUFATE

Make a **béchamel** (recipes 652–653) and add the **finely chopped truffles**. Cool and mix in:

- beaten eggs
- Parmesan cheese

Pour into a baking tin or oven-proof dish, sprinkle with **bread crumbs**, pour over a little melted **butter**, and bake in the oven.

502. Rosé eggs
UOVA ROSATE

Follow the previous recipe, substituting **tomato sauce** in the place of truffles.

503. Egg medallions in fricassee
MEDAGLIONI D'UOVA IN FRICASSEA

Ingredients:

- 8 oz crustless bread
- 10 eggs
- 4 oz butter
- 4 oz Parmesan cheese
- 2 lemons
- 1 cup milk

Soak the bread in the milk. Beat the egg whites with a pinch of salt until stiff. Mix in the bread, 7 of the egg yolks, and the grated Parmesan. Melt the butter in a pan and add half the mixture. As soon as the bread becomes firm, turn and cook the other side. Do the same with the remaining bread mixture. Stir last 3 egg yolks with:

- the lemon juice
- ½ cup water
- a generous amount of chopped parsley

Add:

- ½ tbsp flour
- salt
- pepper

Stir for a minute or two over a low heat until the sauce thickens and pour over the medallions previously prepared.

504. 'Casate' eggs (baked with cheese sauce)
UOVA CASATE

Break the **eggs** into an oven-proof dish, and

cover with:

> slices of fresh cheese
> a béchamel (see 652–653)
> small pats of butter

Bake in a 350°F oven.

505. Eggs any style
UOVA IN TUTTI I MODI

Poach **eggs** (see recipe 479), or hard-boil. Place in a serving dish. Cover with any **Duke of Salaparuta sauce** or let the sauce decide the name of the recipe.

506. Eggs with green sauce
UOVA CON SALSA VERDE

Hard-boil the **eggs**, halve, and place in a serving dish. Mix the yolks with a little **Florentine green sauce** (recipe 660) and fill the egg whites with this mixture before covering with the remaining sauce.

507. Hidden eggs
UOVA CELATE

Make a **ravioli pasta** and roll out to the thickness of a coin. Make a **béchamel** (see 652–653) with twice the amount of flour. Mix in:

> grated Parmesan cheese
> curry powder
> cayenne pepper

Put half a spoonful of the mixture on a rectangular strip of the pasta, place half a hard-boiled **egg** over this, cover with a little more of the mixture, fold the strip of pasta in two, and cut with a pastry cutting wheel. Press the edges together and fry in oil, or boil in water or broth for 5 minutes.

508. Cauliflower omelet
FRITTATA AL CAVOLFIORI

Follow recipe 492, but add cauliflower prepared as in recipe 291.

509. Simple omelet
FRITTATA SEMPLICE

Follow recipe 492, but without adding any herbs.

510. Cheese omelet
FRITTATA AL FORMAGGIO

Follow recipe 492, adding some good-quality **grated Parmesan cheese** before cooking.

511. Mushroom omelet
FRITTATA AI FUNGHI

Follow recipe 492, adding **chopped mushrooms** that have been cooked in **butter**.

512. Truffle omelet
FRITTATA AI TARTUFI

Follow recipe 492, adding **chopped truffles**.

513. Asparagus omelet
FRITTATA AGLI ASPARAGI

Follow recipe 492, but before turning the omelet over, throw in a handful of **tender boiled asparagus**.

514. Sicilian style omelet
FRITTATA ALLA SICILIANA

Stiffly beat **10 egg whites**, then grate:
>   4 oz bread
>   4 oz Parmesan cheese

Finely chop:
>   a fistful of parsley
>   an onion

Mix all the ingredients together, including the **egg yolks**. Pour into a pan with oil, and as it takes on nice golden color gradually fold it over into a roll. Serve the roll with **French fries** on the side.

515. Tomato omelet
FRITTATA AL POMODORO

Follow the above recipe, and then slice the **omelet** into small wheel shapes, arrange on a heated plate, and cover with a homemade **tomato sauce** (recipe 646).

516. Spinach omelet
FRITTATA AGLI SPINACI

Make a **simple omelet** (recipe 492), and before turning add boiled chopped **spinach** that has been sautéed in **butter**.

517. Onion omelet
FRITTATA ALLA CIPOLLA

Slice a **large onion** into strips and lightly fry in a little **butter** over a moderate flame. Before the onion browns, pour in:
>   6 beaten eggs
>   salt
>   pepper
>   chopped parsley

Cook the omelet, flipping half way through cooking.

518. Walnut omelet
FRITTATA ALLE NOCI

Follow recipe 492, adding a **ground walnut** for each egg.

519. Macaroni omelet
FRITTATA AI MACCHERONI

Stir cooked, chopped **macaroni** into the beaten **eggs**, add a generous helping of **grated Parmesan cheese**, and fry, without folding over.

520. Bread or ricotta omelet
FRITTATA AL PANE OD ALLA RICOTTA

Fry slices of **bread** and arrange these over **eggs**, which have just been poured into the pan (see recipe 492). Flip the omelet so that the bread is covered by the egg. Ricotta is also excellent prepared this way.

521. Fondue 'alla castellana' (Chatelaine's choice fondue)
FONDUTA ALLA CASTELLANA

In a pan, melt:

> 4 oz butter

Add:

> 1 ½ oz flour
> 4 egg yolks
> ½ cup milk

Boil all the ingredients together for 2 minutes, stirring continuously. Remove from the heat and stir in:

> 4 oz grated Parmesan cheese
> 4 oz Gruyère cheese
> salt
> pepper
> nutmeg
> two stiffly beaten egg whites

Fill custard cups or small terrines to a third from the top and bake in a 350°F oven.

522. Fondue 'alla cittadina' (Citizen's choice fondue)
FONDUTA ALLA CITTADINA

Put in a pan:

> 6 egg yolks
> 1 oz flour

Mix the ingredients well, and pour in:

> a glass of heavy cream
> 2 oz fresh butter cut into small pats

Stir continuously over a low heat for 3 minutes. Take off the heat and mix in:

> 8 oz grated Parmesan cheese
> 6 oz Gruyère cheese
> some finely diced truffles or other mushrooms

Add:

> salt
> pepper
> a small pinch of grated nutmeg
> 2 stiffly beaten egg whites

Fill small terrines with the mixture to a third from the top and cook in a 350°F oven.

523. Puffed-up omelet
FRITTATA SOFFIATA

This particular omelet has to be cooked and served in individual portions. Stiffly beat **egg whites** with a pinch of salt and put a single portion in a dish, quickly mixing in an **egg yolk**. Toss into a frying pan with a little melted **butter**. Push the mixture toward the middle of the pan with a spatula turning until you have made a nice puffy ball. Serve at once, otherwise it will deflate.

524. Tricolor omelet
FRITTATA BANDIERA

Make **three simple omelets** (see recipe 492). In the first, add cooked **spinach**, in the second **tomato**, and in the third use only the whites (the yolks can go into the tomato omelet). Arrange these on a plate with the "white" omelet in the middle.

525. Vegetarian tripe omelet 'all'olivetana'

FRITTATA PSEUDO-TRIPPA ALL'OLIVETANA

'All'olivetana' likely refers to a 14th-century Benedictine monk who belonged to a monastic community on Mount Oliveto, near Siena.

Make **small, round omelets** (see recipe 492) and turn these over without folding with the help of a plate. Cut into strips. Grease a baking dish and toss in a first layer of these strips. Sprinkle with:

> **Parmesan cheese**
> **chopped parsley**
> **pepper**
> **thick tomato sauce**

Continue until you have four or five layers and top with **slices of fresh cheese** (provola, mozzarella or Gruyère, etc.). Sprinkle some more grated Gruyère, and small flecks of **butter** on top. Bake in 350°F oven until golden brown.

526. Puff pastry bake 'alla borghigiana'

SFOGLIATELLA ALLA BORGHIGIANA

Make the **small round omelets** as above. Grease a baking dish and sprinkle with **bread crumbs**. Lay a first omelet on the bottom and then a layer of **cheese stuffing** (see recipe 706).

Alternate with more omelets and further layers of cheese stuffing (4–5 of each), cover with bread crumbs, top with pats of **butter**, and bake in a 350°F oven until the cheese melts and the casserole is combined.

527. Farm fresh eggs

UOVA A BERE

Boil enough water to just cover your eggs. Break the **eggs** into the boiling water, take the pan off the heat and count 6 minutes before taking the eggs out of the water.

528. Eggs with curry

UOVA AL CURRIE

Into a pan with **1 oz butter**, stir:

> **1 tbsp flour**
> **1 tsp curry powder** (see recipe 893)

Slowly dilute by stirring in **broth** (see recipes 43 to 51). As soon as the mixture thickens, put in the sliced **hard-boiled eggs**. Serve lukewarm or at room temperature.

529. Eggs sunny side up

UOVA AD OCCHIO

Grease some small baking tins or oven-proof molds with butter and break **two eggs** into each. Bake in a 350°F oven until the white is firm and peel the film of white off the yolk with a fork, without breaking it. Add salt and pepper, cook until the eggs are slightly firmer, and serve.

530. Eggs with a mince sauce

UOVA ALLA SALSA TRITATA

Cut **hard-boiled eggs** into quarters, place in a dish, cover with a **"mince" sauce** (recipe 695), and serve.

531. Puffed eggs
SOFFIATO DI UOVA

Heat oven to 350°F. Ingredients:

6 eggs

½ pint milk

3 tbsp flour

2 oz butter

salt

Mix the flour with some of the milk, add the egg yolks, and beat well, pouring in the milk a little at a time. Stiffly beat the egg whites with a pinch of salt and fold in with the yolks.

Pour into a greased dish and bake for 20 minutes or until the egg whites have set. Serve hot in the same dish.

532. Eggs in a savory bread soup
UOVA IN PANATA

Ingredients:

1 lb stale bread

6 eggs

½ cup cream

2 oz butter

Soak the bread in water and when well soaked remove the crust and squeeze out the excess liquid. Melt the butter in a pan and add the bread, stirring continuously. Once the bread and butter have amalgamated, remove from the heat and stir in the cream a little at a time. Transfer the bred to a large bowl. Next, mix in the eggs one at a time, making sure each one is blended in before adding the next. Mix diced **cheese cubes** in last. Fry tablespoonfuls of the mixture and serve.

Batters, pastry dough and savory pies

PASTE, PASTETTE, PASTICCI E PASTICCERIA PICCANTE

533. How to make pasta
MANIERA D'IMPASTARE

Take whatever flour you decide to use and heap it up with a "well" in the center, where the liquid (water, eggs, butter) is to be poured. Stir the liquid slightly with the fingers of your right hand so that the flour falls slowly into the well. Once all the liquid has been absorbed, lightly work the dry flour into the moist flour by rubbing the dough between the palms of your hands. Then begin kneading the dough, pressing down from the wrists, and folding the dough over on itself. Sprinkle with a little extra water if too dry. The dough can be divided into two separate parts, so that they can be kneaded contemporaneously, one with each hand, as described above. Part of the technique consists of occasionally beating the strip of pasta against the working surface. It can be considered adequately kneaded when it is smooth and white, a process that takes at least 30 minutes.

534. Pastry for cold pies
PASTA PER PASTICCI FREDDI

For a pie 4 inches in diameter use **12 oz flour**, piling into a mound with a hole in the center. Add:

- **about ⅓ oz butter**
- **1 egg**
- **a pinch of salt**
- **½ glass of tepid water**

Knead the pastry as in recipe 533. Grease a springform baking mold (4 to 6 inches in diameter), place the dough in it and press down with your fingers to ¼ inch thickness. Bake in an oven for 30 minutes. Allow to cool and remove from the pan. This pastry shell can then be filled with one of the following.

535. Pastry for muffins or bignés
PASTA DA MUFFOLETTE O BEGNETTE

See recipe 750 for bignés. These can also be filled with a stuffing or spicy seasoning.

536. Ravioli pasta
PASTA PER RAVIOLI

Ingredients:

- 12 oz flour
- 3 oz butter
- 1 egg
- a pinch of salt
- water as needed

Mix all the ingredients together and knead until the dough is smooth and white. Roll out the pastry (approx. ⅛ inch thick) and make the ravioli (see recipe 53).

537. Pastry for sweet pies
PASTA PER TORTE

Mix:

- 2 lb flour
- 2 eggs
- 4 oz butter
- half a glass of milk
- 1 tbsp of confectioner's sugar

Work into a soft smooth dough. This pastry does not require kneading.

538. Flaky pastry crust
PASTA SFOGLIA

It is strongly recommended that whoever intends making this dough should see it done at least once by an expert. We shall nevertheless attempt to describe it. In hot weather the butter should come from the icebox. The working surface should be marble, and iced water should be used. In winter, however, the water should be tepid.

On a marble working surface, put:

- 12 oz of flour

Make a well in the center, and add:

- a pinch of salt
- 2 egg yolks
- a walnut-sized knob of butter
- a glass of water

Make into a dough starting with the inside 'well', crumbling the mixture between your fingers and then kneading for approx. 20 minutes. Mold the dough into a fairly moist ball, which should be wrapped and left in a dish cloth for 20 minutes. Sprinkle flour over the marble surface and roll out the pasta into a rectangle, twice as long as it is wide. Soften **8 oz of butter** in a floured table napkin and flatten to half the size of the rolled pastry dough. Place the butter on the pastry and fold the other half of the pastry over it, sealing the edges together so that the butter doesn't ooze out. Both the pastry and the butter should be the same consistency, so that they can be rolled out together. Roll the pastry into a rectangle once more, and fold in three this time. Lightly sprinkle the marble with flour and continue this procedure every 45 minutes, seven times in the winter and six in the summer. The pastry can be used five minutes after the final rolling.

539. Yeast batter for deep frying
PASTETTA LIEVITATA PER FRIGGERE

Dissolve **1 lb flour** in enough **milk** so the batter isn't either too liquid or too thick. Add **1 oz brewer's yeast** and leave to rise in a warm place. Any kind of vegetable can be cut into strips, dipped in this batter, and deep fried. If the vegetables are tough they should be blanched in boiling water for a few minutes before being battered and fried.

540. Egg batter for deep frying
PASTETTA ALL'UOVO PER FRIGGERE

Beat together:

3 eggs

2 egg yolks

a pinch of salt

Gradually add enough **flour** to make a fairly liquid batter. This must be used straight away to coat vegetables or whatever else is to be deep fried.

541. Shortcrust pastry (recipe 1)
PASTA FROLLA N. 1

In a bowl, place:

2 cups flour

4 oz butter

a pinch of salt

Cut in the butter until the mixture resembles fine crumbs. Add:

1 beaten egg

sufficient water to make a soft but manageable dough

Roll out and leave for 15 minutes. Fold over four or five times and then roll out to the thickness you need.

542. Sweet shortcrust pastry (recipe 2)
PASTA FROLLA DOLCE N. 2

Ingredients:

10 oz flour

4 oz powdered sugar

4 oz butter

3 egg yolks

Mix the flour and powdered sugar together. Soften the butter in a double boiler. Mix with the flour and sugar to make a soft dough, adding a little water if needed. This pastry does not require kneading, however if kept for a day or more in the icebox it becomes lighter.

543. Savory shortcrust pastry
PASTA FROLLA PICCANTE

Follow the recipe above, adding a pinch of **salt** instead of the sugar.

544. Cannolo pastry (traditional Sicilian pastry filled with ricotta cheese)
PASTA PER CANNOLI

Ingredients:

10 oz flour

1 oz cocoa

2 oz butter

1 oz sugar

1 egg

Mix the flour, cocoa, and sugar together, make into a heap with a small well in the center, and break in the egg and a little water. Make into a soft dough. Form small pellets and roll these out very thinly into rounds 6 inches in diameter. Roll around 1 inch thick bamboo or tin tubes and seal the two extremities by dampening a little and pressing together. Deep fry in oil and butter and remove from the tubes as soon as they cool. Fill with:

fresh ricotta (see recipe 874)
diced candied fruit

Sprinkle with powdered sugar. Cannoli are also excellent with Moca cream.

~~~~~~~~~~~

545. Vegetarian hare pie
PSEUDO-PASTICCIO DI LEPRE

Ingredients:

4 oz black beans
12 oz ricotta
4 oz butter
1 cup dry red wine
spices and herbs
onion

If using dried beans, add a pinch of baking soda, and cook until they are almost mushy. (You can also use canned black beans.) Put through a food mill. In a seperate sauté pan, lightly fry the onion in the butter until transparent, adding the wine as the onion cooks. Add:

the ricotta
herbs
a clove of garlic
2 cloves
salt
spices

Cook, scraping and stirring the mixture until it acquires a thick consistency. Color with **carmelized sugar** and put through a food mill. Mix in with bean purée, add **diced truffles or other mushrooms**, and put in a terrine or pastry shells (recipe 534). Serve cold.

546. Vegetarian Strasbourg foie gras
PSEUDO-PASTICCIO DI FEGATO GRASSO DI STRASBURGO

Ingredients:

14 oz ricotta
4 oz butter
2 oz coconut oil
½ cup dry red wine
black truffles
½ cup cream
1 large onion

Cook onion in butter until transparent, adding the wine as it cooks, and then add:

the ricotta
herbs
spices
salt
nutmeg
a clove

Cook, scraping and stirring the mixture until it acquires a thick consistency. Color with **caramelized sugar** and put through a sieve, pouring in the cream. Add a generous amount of diced black truffles, place in a terrine, and cover with a layer of melted butter. The foie gras can also be served in a pastry shell (see previous recipe.)

547. Vegetarian foie gras
PSEUDO-PASTICCIO DI FEGATO GRASSO

Ingredients:

- 6 oz lentils
- 10 oz ricotta
- 4 oz butter
- ½ cup red wine
- truffles
- 1 large onion
- herbs
- spices

Boil the lentils with a pinch of baking soda and when they are well cooked put through a sieve. Gently fry the onion, adding the wine as it cooks, and stir in the ricotta, chopped herbs, nutmeg, 2 cloves, salt, and pepper. Remove the cloves and mix the onions, ricotta, and herbs with the lentils. Simmer for a minute or two, stirring continuously. Add small cubes of black truffles and put in a terrine or pastry shell (see recipes above).

548. 'Panovato' pie (a tasty bread pudding)
PASTICCIO PANOVATO

Make a pastry for a cold pie (see recipe 534) and fill as follows:

- 16 oz diced, fresh, crustless bread (½ inch cubes)
- 4 eggs beaten into ½ cup cream
- 12 ground walnuts
- 6 oz grated Parmesan cheese
- chopped parsley
- salt, pepper
- 2 oz peeled pistachios

Mix the above ingredients together and put in a pastry shell. Bake in a moderate oven for about 15 minutes. Serve cool.

549. Harvest pie
PASTICCIO DELLA RACCOLTA

Ingredients:

- 12 oz potatoes
- 1 carrot
- 3 onions
- the tough part of a cauliflower

Boil the above ingredients for 15 minutes, and then strain and stew until well cooked. Mix the following ingredients together:

- 6 oz boiled chestnuts cut into quarters
- 1 tbsp tapioca soaked in water for 4 hours
- 2 chopped hard-boiled eggs
- salt
- pepper
- enough milk to soften the mixture

Add the stewed vegetables and put into a large, shallow mold. Cover with a layer of **shortcrust pastry** (recipe 541), brush with **beaten egg yolk**, and cook in the oven.

550. Lentil pie
PASTICCIO DI LENTICCHIE

In salted water, cook:

- 1 lb lentils

Put through a food mill. Mix in:

- 4 eggs
- 6 oz grated Parmesan cheese
- a small glass of Marsala wine

Pour into a pastry shell and bake. Serve cold.

551. Mushroom pie
PASTICCIO DI FUNGHI

Follow recipe 545. Instead of the beans add:

    10 oz mushrooms that have been sautéed
        in butter

Serve hot.

552. Artichoke and spinach pie
PASTICCIO DI CARCIOFI E SPINACI

Ingredients:

    10 artichokes
    2 ½ oz butter
    3 oz grated Parmesan cheese
    8 bunches of spinach
    12 oz shortcrust pastry (recipe 534)

Clean the artichokes, making sure all the hard, thorny bits have been removed. Cut in four. Cook in salted water with half a lemon. When half cooked removed from the heat. Cook the spinach separately, chop, put in a pan together with the artichokes, and finish cooking with salt, pepper and 2 oz butter. Mix the remainder of the butter with a tablespoon of flour and bind together with a little water. Arrange the artichokes in an oven-proof dish and add the cheese with the blended flour and butter. Cover with pastry crust and bake in the oven.

553. Vegetarian pheasant pie
PASTICCIO DI FAGIANO (PSEUDO)

Ingredients:

    1 oz oatmeal flour
    14 oz ricotta
    ½ cup dry white wine

    4 oz butter
    truffles or mushrooms
    onion
    carrots
    spices

Cook the onion, carrots, and chopped parsley in butter, adding the wine as they cook. Mash in the ricotta, adding salt, oatmeal flour, and spices. Simmer for a minute or two, remove from the heat, put through a food mill, mix in the cubes of black truffle, and pour into a pastry shell (see recipe 534). This dish can also be served in a terrine.

554. Vegetarian partridge pie
PASTICCIO DI PERNICI (PSEUDO)

Follow the recipe for pheasant pie. Before putting through a food mill add:

    4 hard-boiled egg yolks
    a small glass of Marsala wine

555. Curried game pie
PASTICCIO DI CACCIA AL CURRIE

Ingredients:

    4 oz butter
    ⅓ oz curry
    14 oz ricotta
    black truffles
    4 oz onion
    ½ cup dry red wine

Make a flan case and fill with the following mixture: lightly fry the onion in butter and add the ricotta, a little caramelized sugar, salt, spices, a glass of wine, and the curry. Simmer until the mixture acquires a fairly thick consistency.

Put through a food mill, mix in the truffle cubes, pour into a mold and serve cold.

556. Potato pie
PASTICCIO DI PATATE

Chop **2 onions**, put into a cold oven-proof dish, peel and thinly **slice 6 boiled potatoes**, place these over the onions, and add:

> ½ oz butter
>
> 10 walnuts
>
> salt
>
> pepper

Fill the dish two-thirds full by adding **a glass of white wine**. Cover with **pastry crust** (recipe 534) and cook in the oven.

• • • • • • • • • • • •

557. Vegetable gelatin
GALANTINA VEGETARIANA

Note: Today few gelatin products are vegetarian. However, groceries sometimes carry Kosher gelatins, which are vegetarian.

Cut **1 lb fresh crustless bread** into cubes, soak half in **milk** and the other half in **red wine**, and add:

> 8 oz diced mozzarella

Mix with:

> 4 beaten eggs
>
> finely-diced black truffles
>
> skinned pistachio nuts
>
> powdered spices
>
> salt
>
> pepper

Fold into a napkin and sew in the shape of a chicken. Put in a saucepan:

> 4 pints water
>
> onions
>
> carrots
>
> celery
>
> a bouquet garni
>
> salt
>
> pepper
>
> 2 pints of dry white wine

Boil everything together for an hour and use the cooking liquid to make the gelatin. Serve cold, sliced and garnished with the gelatin.

558. Cheese schiacciata (a flat bread)
SCHIACCIATA AL FORMAGGIO

Beat **2 eggs** and mix together with:

> 1 pint of milk
>
> 4 oz grated Parmesan cheese
>
> 1 tablespoon of flour
>
> cayenne pepper (if you wish)

Put a layer of **shortcrust pastry** into a greased baking tin (recipe 541), cover with the liquid, and bake in the oven topped with small pats of butter.

559. Egg schiacciata
SCHIACCIATA ALL'UOVO

Follow the above recipe, replacing the cheese with:

> 3 chopped hard-boiled eggs

Sprinkle with small pats of **butter** and bake in the oven.

560. Schiacciata 'alla pizzaiola' (a flat bread topped with a tomato, garlic, and oregano stew)
SCHIACCIATA ALLA PIZZAIUOLA

Follow recipe 541 for **pastry**. Roll out the pastry, place a layer in a greased baking tin, and cover with a layer of **mozzarella, scamorza, fresh provolone**, or **any other soft cheese**. Sprinkle with:

> **pieces of peeled, seedless tomatoes**
> **chopped garlic**
> **chopped onion**

Bake for approx. 30 minutes in the oven.

561. Ricotta schiacciata
SCHIACCIATA DI RICOTTA

Make a **shortcrust pastry** (recipe 541) and cover with the following mixture, after it has been put through a food mill:

> **1 lb ricotta**
> **a small, chopped, lightly fried onion**
> **½ cup wine**
> **salt**
> **pepper**

Top with small pats of **butter** and bake in the oven until golden brown.

562. Schiacciata of truffled eggs
SCHIACCIATA D'UOVA TARTUFATE

Make the **shortcrust pastry** described in recipe 541, line a greased cake tin, and pinch the sides of the pastry to form a case. Fill with:

> **6 chopped, hardboiled eggs** covered with
> **a pint of béchamel** (recipes 652–653)

Sprinkle a handful of **chopped black truffles** and a few pats of **butter** over the dish and cook in the oven until golden brown.

563. Schiacciata 'al subisso' (a flat bread with 'deluge' sauce)
SCHIACCIATA AL SUBISSO

Make the **shortcrust pastry**, as described in recipe 541, and top with the following mixture:

> **1 pint subisso sauce** (recipe 686)
> **4 beaten eggs**
> **10 ground walnuts**

Top with small knobs of **butter** and bake in the oven until golden brown.

564. Schiacciata with cauliflower and mozzarella
SCHIACCIATA DI CAVOLFIORE ALLA MOZZARELLA

Follow recipe 541 for **shortcrust pastry**. Boil the **cauliflower** and place half on the pastry crust, cover with a layer of **sliced mozzarella**, add the remaining cauliflower, sprinkle with cheese, and top with pats of **butter**. Bake in the oven until golden brown.

565. Schiacciata with mushrooms
SCHIACCIATA DI FUNGHI

Follow recipe 541 and top with the following mixture: a layer of **béchamel** then a layer of **chopped, sautéed mushrooms**, and finally another layer of béchamel. Put a few pats of **butter** on top and bake in the oven until golden brown.

566. Schiacciata with eggplants
SCHIACCIATA DI MELANZANE

Slice and fry **5 eggplants** and make a fairly thick **tomato sauce**. Put a layer of **pasta** in a cake tin, as in recipe 560, and fill with the following mixture: a layer of fried eggplant and then one of tomato sauce, sprinkled with **Parmesan cheese**. Repeat for a few layers, ending with the tomato sauce and Parmesan topping. Bake in the oven until golden brown.

567. Filled bread rolls, Sicilian style
PANINI RIPIENI ALLA SICILIANA

Round bread rolls are used for this recipe. Scrape off the outside crust and remove the center "cork." Take out the soft spongy bread and fill the roll as follows:

- **4 oz diced fresh cheese**
- **4 oz diced Gouda (or Edam) cheese**
- **8 oz condensed milk**
- **a spoonful of flour**

Put back the "cork," moisten the rolls, roll first in **flour** and then in **beaten egg** and **bread crumbs** and fry. Pieces of peeled tomato or truffles can be added.

568. Filled rolls Swedish style
PANINI IMBOTTITI ALLA SVEDESE

Use **small, round rolls**, removing the round piece that functions as a "cork." Remove the soft spongy inside part and fill with the following mixture: lightly fry an **onion** in 2 oz butter and when golden brown moisten with **wine**. Mash in:

- **10 oz ricotta**
- **1 tbsp curry powder**
- **a good pinch of salt**
- **diced, black truffles** if you want a richer version

Moisten the filled rolls, roll in **flour**, toss in **beaten egg**, and fry.

569. Vegetable pie
TORTA DI VERDURA

Make the **pastry** in recipe 537, roll out two layers of dough approx. ⅛ inch thick. Lay one layer over the bottom of the cake tin. For the filling mash together:

- **12 oz ricotta**
- **2 oz butter**

Stir over low heat until it melts, then mix in:

- **1 lb boiled chopped spinach**
- **½ lb boiled chopped fennel**
- **4 canned artichokes**

Add:

- salt
- 1 oz pine nuts
- 2 oz raisins
- spices

Pour the mixture over the pastry, top with a pastry crust and bake in the oven.

570. Ricotta pie with artichokes
TORTA DI RICOTTA CON CARCIOFI

Make some **flaky pastry** (recipe 538) and shape into a turban. Bake and then fill with the following.

In butter, sauté:

- **6 well-cleaned, sliced artichokes**

Add a little liquid if necessary. In a separate pan, combine:

- 1 lb ricotta
- 2 oz butter
- salt
- pepper

Stir over low heat, put through a food mill, and mix in with the sautéed artichokes. Pour the mixture into the 'turban' and serve.

571. Ricotta pie with eggs
TORTA DI RICOTTA ALL'UOVO

Make a pastry with:

- 10 oz flour
- 4 oz butter
- a pinch of salt
- as much water as is needed

Roll out the pastry and line a greased cake tin. Fill with the following mixture:

- 12 oz ricotta
- ½ pint milk in which 1 oz corn flour (or any other cooking starch) has been dissolved
- 4 beaten eggs
- a good pinch of salt

Mix briskly, pour over the pie, and bake in the oven, after sprinkling with small pats of **butter**.

572. Deviled pie
TORTA INDIAVOLATA

Make **pastry** as in recipe 570 and fill with the following mixture:

- 14 oz ricotta
- a pinch of salt
- 1 finely chopped onion
- a good pinch of cayenne pepper
- chopped parsley and herbs
- nutmeg
- 3 ground cloves
- 2 chopped garlic cloves

Mix the ingredients together and place on the pastry, brush with **egg yolk**, and bake in the oven until golden brown.

573. Green pie
TORTA VERDE

Ingredients:

- 12 oz flour
- 5 oz butter
- ½ cup milk

3 eggs
10 oz spinach
2 oz Parmesan cheese

Make **pastry** as in recipe 571 and fill with the following mixture: **boiled spinach** that has been put through a food mill and blended with **1 tbsp flour** and the milk, the beaten eggs, a pinch of salt and grated Parmesan. Beat the ingredients well together and, after pouring on to the pastry, top with pats of **butter** and bake in the oven.

574. Egg tortelli with cream
TORTELLI D'UOVO ALLA CREMA

Make shortcrust pastry with:
10 oz flour
5 oz butter
a pinch of salt
just enough water to make the pastry easy to handle

Do not knead excessively. Grease 12 ovenproof custard cups and put a layer of pastry over the bottoms and sides of these (approx. ¼ inch thick). Then bake and fill with the following mixture:
6 chopped, hard-boiled eggs
a little cream
English sauce (recipe 589)

575. Ricotta tortelli
TORTELLI DI RICOTTA

Make **shortcrust pastry** as above and fill with:
ricotta that has been sautéed in **butter**
onion
salt
wine

Mix in **grated Parmesan cheese**, cover with a layer of **pastry** and brush with **egg yolk** before baking in the oven.

576. D. E. A. S. pizza (Duke Enrico Alliata of Salaparuta pizza)
PIZZA D. E. A. S.

Ingredients:
6 oz extrafine flour
8 oz scamorza cheese
2 oz Parmesan cheese
6 eggs
1 ½ pints milk
8 oz tomatoes

Boil the milk with a pinch of salt and throw in the flour, stirring continuously until it thickens. Remove from the heat and when cool mix in the beaten eggs and Parmesan. Pour into a greased cake tin and arrange fresh caciocavallo cheese slices and peeled tomato over the bottom. Sprinkle with:
bread crumbs
oregano
pepper
pats of butter

Bake in the oven.

577. The Queen's tortellini
TORTELLINI REGINA

Take **12 oz ricotta** or any other fresh, non-fermented cheese like mozzarella, primosale or scamorza, finely chopped. Mix with the following to make a cold filling:

4 oz grated Parmesan

2 egg yolks

finely chopped herbs

nutmeg

salt

Make a dough with:

10 oz flour

the whites of 2 eggs

2 oz butter

water as needed

Roll out the pasta ¼ inch thick and fill the tortellini with the above stuffing. Cut into whatever shape you wish, seal the edges and cook in boiling water, like macaroni. Drain and serve with a **Hollandaise sauce** (recipe 658).

578. Savory buns
GALLETTE PESANTI O RAVAZZATE

Make **brioche pastry** (see recipe 580) and cut into rounds with a big cup. Spoon in some **chicken stuffing** (recipe 707). Cover with another round of pastry, leave to rise, brush with **egg yolk**, and bake in the oven.

579. Gallette (savory buns French style)
GALLETTA FRANCESE

Ingredients:

2 lb flour

10 oz butter

a pinch of salt

2 eggs

Mix all the ingredients together, roll out the pastry (approx. ¼ inch thick) and cover the bottom

of a cake tin, putting a few pats of **butter** over this. Press the edges so they are nicely scalloped. Cook in the oven for 15 minutes. Put in a terrine:

½ pint heavy cream

2 eggs

a little salt

Beat briskly. Pour this over the 'galletta', sprinkle with butter, and put it back in the oven to bake a second time.

580. Filled brioche
BRIOSCIA FARCITA

Make the same pastry as for the **sweet brioche** (recipe 733), putting in a good pinch of **salt** instead of the sugar. Put half the pastry in a mold, fill with any **stuffing** of your choice, cover with the remaining pastry, leave to rise in a fairly warm, place and bake in a moderate oven for 45 minutes.

581. Brioche 'caciata' (filled with cheese and béchamel)
BRIOSCIA CACIATA

Make the **sweet brioche pastry** in recipe 733, putting in **salt** instead of sugar. When you line the mold with half the pastry, pour into the middle:

a béchamel

6 oz diced Gouda (or Edam) cheese

6 oz diced Gruyère

Cover with the remaining pastry. Leave to rise in a warm place and when it has risen nicely, bake in a hot oven.

582. Rustic pizza
PIZZA RUSTICA

Make a **brioche** as in recipe 733, putting in a pinch of **salt** instead of sugar. Put into a large tin. Inside the brioche, arrange:

> slices of fresh caciocavallo cheese
>
> chunks of peeled tomato
>
> oregano
>
> bread crumbs

After it has risen, pour on a little **oil** and bake in the oven for 45 minutes.

583. Vol-au-vent (a stuffed flaky pastry case)
SFOGLIA RIPIENA (VOL-AU-VENT)

Make **flaky pastry** (recipe 538) and line a cake tin (the pastry should be nearly 1 inch thick). Put a saucepan cover of the same size as the tin over this and cut off the extra pastry. Trace a circle a little over an inch from the edge, not quite through the thickness of the pastry. This allows you to open the pastry for filling. Brush with **egg yolk** and bake in a moderate oven. When the pastry has risen nicely and is golden brown, take out of the oven, remove the 'lid' you have cut out, and empty the pastry case out. Fill with **peas** in **béchamel**, **mushroom sauce**, or whatever else you wish. Serve hot.

584. Stuffed flaky pastry buns
SFOGLIATELLE FARCITE

Make **flaky pastry** (recipe 538) and cut into 3-inch discs. Bake in the oven and then fill with chicken stuffing (recipe 707), or any other filling of your choice.

585. Brioche with vegetarian chicken stuffing
BRIOSCINE FARCITE AL POLLO (PSEUDO)

Make the **brioche pastry** (recipe 581) and half fill some deep, narrow molds. Add half a spoonful of **chicken stuffing** or any other flavoring you wish (recipe 707) to these. Put more pastry on top, allowing at least an inch for the pastry to rise. Leave stand and bake in a moderate oven.

586. Sicilian delicacies
MANICARETTI SICULI

Make pastry with:

> 12 oz flour
>
> 5 oz butter
>
> as much water as is needed to make it into a nice pliable dough

This needs to be very lightly kneaded. Line the bottom and sides of oven-proof dishes or individual terrines with the pastry and bake in the oven. Remove, fill with **vegetarian chicken stuffing** (recipe 707), sprinkle with **chopped black truffles**, and heat in the oven before serving.

587. Mozzarella pie
CREMA DI MOZZARELLA IN TORTA

Make a pastry with:

> 10 oz flour
>
> 4 oz butter

a pinch of salt

enough water to make it into a nice soft dough that only needs light kneading

Roll it out fairly thinly (¼ inch) and line a cake tin or oven-proof dish. Slice the **mozzarella** and place in the pastry shell. Melt a **tablespoonful of flour** in **½ pint milk**, with a pinch of **salt**, and pour over the mozzarella. Bake in the oven topped with small knobs of butter.

588. Curried mozzarella pie
MOZZARELLA IN TORTA AL CURRIE

Ingredients:

14 oz Mozzarella

1 ¼ cup milk

12 oz flour

5 oz butter

1 egg

Make pastry with the flour and butter, adding a pinch of salt and water as needed to make a nice soft dough that only needs light kneading. Roll the pastry out ¼ inch thick and line a greased cake tin. Put sliced mozzarella over the bottom of the tin and cover with the milk in which **1 tsp curry** has been dissolved, as well as **1 tbsp flour** and the beaten egg. Bake in the oven after topping with pats of **butter**.

589. St Vito 'sfincione' (a rich and tasty savory pie)
SFINCIONE DI SAN VITO

Ingredients:

1 lb flour

3 eggs

2/3 cup oil

10 oz caciocavallo cheese

8 oz fresh cheese

4 eggplants

4 oz tomato concentrate

1 oz brewer's yeast

fennel seeds

parsley

spices

12 walnuts

Put the brewer's yeast into **½ cup milk** close to the fire or radiator for 30 minutes. Pile the flour into a heap and hollow out a well in the center. Throw in the yeast, ½ cup extra virgin olive oil, 2 whole eggs plus 1 white (keeping the yolk apart). Work all the ingredients together, adding a little tepid water if necessary to make it into a pliable but consistent dough.

Prepare the filling as follows: fry the eggplant cubes in hot oil and chop as if for meat. Dice the caciocavallo and the other cheese. Primosale is used in Sicily, but elsewhere provolone, raveggiolo, scamorza, etc. are used. Mix the cheese and minced eggplant together, adding the tomato concentrate, ground walnuts, fennel seeds, chopped parsley, lightly fried onion, spices, and pepper.

Grease a mold, cover the bottom with a round of paper, and lay half the dough over this, spreading out with your hands. Pour the stuffing mixture over this and cover with the remaining half of the dough, taking care to seal the edges carefully together. Leave the mold covered near a source of heat to allow the pastry to rise. Then brush with **egg yolk**, sprinkle with **Parmesan cheese**, and bake in the oven. This 'sfincione' is every bit as good as the version done with meat. It is in fact much lighter and more digestible.

590. 'Casatè' squares (with cheese)
LOSANGHETTE CASATE

Follow recipe 620 and when the milk becomes solid in consistency cut into square shapes, place in a oven-proof baking dish and sprinkle with:

Parmesan cheese

a few pats of butter

Bake in the oven until golden brown.

Savory fried dishes

591. Artichoke cutlets
CARCIOFI A COTOLETTE

Take **6 large artichokes**, clean well and slice, boil for a few minutes, sprinkle with **salt** and **pepper**, dip in **beaten egg**, coat with **bread crumbs**, and fry in hot oil.

592. Eggplant cutlets
MELANZANE A COTOLETTE

Cut some **eggplants** into slices after removing the peel, sprinkle with **salt** and leave for half an hour. Coat with **flour**, then dip in **egg**, cover with **bread crumbs**, and fry in hot oil.

593. D. E. A. S. fry (Duke Enrico Alliata of Salaparuta fry)
FRITTURA D. E. A. S.

Ingredients:
- 8 oz bread
- 3 oz Parmesan cheese
- 1 raw egg
- 3 hard-boiled eggs
- 1 lb zucchini
- 1 lb tomatoes

Soak the bread in **milk** until soft and squeeze dry. Mix with the grated Parmesan and the yolks of 3 hard-boiled eggs. Cut the hard-boiled egg whites lengthwise. Blanch the zucchini for a few minutes in boiling water (they must stay firm), drain, remove centers and fill them with the above mixture. Empty out the tomatoes (they should be about the the same size as the zucchini), removing the seeds, and fill with the mixture. Fry (in two separate pans) gently in butter until golden-brown. Fill the half egg whites with the remaining mixture, cover with **flour**, dip in **beaten egg**, roll in **bread crumbs**, and then fry. Serve together with the zucchini and tomatoes.

594. D. E. A. S. rolls
PAGNOTTINE D. E. A. S.

Take **6 round, freshly baked bread rolls**, grate the crusts, cut off the top of each roll, and remove the dough with your finger, leaving the rolls whole but empty inside. Fill them as follows. Filling:

6 oz Gouda or Edam cheese

8 oz Gruyère

8 oz pulp of peeled seedless
  tomatoes

chopped parsley

10 crushed walnuts, if you like

salt

pepper

Cut the cheese in ½-inch cubes and the tomatoes in small pieces, and mix together. Fill the rolls and close them up with the top of the rolls that you have removed, wet them in milk, sprinkle with **flour**, and dip in **beaten egg**. Fry in abundant oil.

595. Vegetarian meat rolls
PAGNOTTINE DI PSEUDO-CARNE

As in recipe 594, but use **vegetarian meat** (see recipe 708).

596. Vegetarian game rolls
PAGNOTTINE DI PSEUDO-CACCIA

Prepare as in recipe 594, but use a **vegetarian hare filling** (see recipe 545), partridge, foie gras, etc. (see relevant recipes).

597. Savory krapfen
KRAPFEN PICCANTI

Prepare as for **sweet Krapfen** (recipe 769) but use a pinch of **salt** instead of sugar and any **filling** of your choice instead of preserves (see pages 239 to 242).

598. Florentine 'bombette'
BOMBETTE ALLA FIORENTINA

Ingredients:

12 oz flour

1 pint water

4 oz butter

6 eggs (3 whole, 3 yolks)

Boil the water with the butter and a pinch of salt, add all the flour, stirring vigorously over a low heat for ten minutes, then pour into a bowl and allow to cool. When cold, stir in one yolk, add one stiffly beaten egg white, then another yolk, and using the same ladle, add another stiffly beaten white, and so on. Mix well and then toss spoonfuls into the frying pan. Any kind of **filling** can be used (see Fillings, pages 198–200), or scrambled eggs, etc.

599. Vegetarian fried cutlets
SGALOPPINE VEGETARIANE FRITTE

Ingredients:

1 oz dried mushrooms

1 ¼ oz walnuts

6 oz flour

6 oz butter

Leave the mushrooms in water for at least an hour, drain, squeeze out excess moisture, and chop up very fine. Shell and crush the walnuts, chop some **parsley** and keep separate. Melt the butter, mix in the flour with a pinch of salt and when well blended, remove from heat and stir in all the ingredients, mixing vigorously. When cool, make fritters, cover them with flour, dip in **beaten egg**, and fry in hot butter or oil.

600. Paris style ravioli
RAVIOLI ALLA PARIGINA

Take some **ravioli pasta** (see recipe 536), and roll out very thin. On the pasta dough place at equal distances little heaps of **vegetarian chicken stuffing** (see recipe 707). Cover with another layer of the dough. Use a pastry wheel to cut out the ravioli, and then fry or boil.

601. Savory bignés
SFINCE PICCANTI

Prepare as for Sicilian **bignés** (see recipe 794), but before cooking add:

> a pinch of salt
>
> pepper
>
> some cubes of cheese

602. Puff pastry half-moons
LUNETTE DI SFOGLIO PER CONTORNO

Knead together:

> 7 oz flour
>
> 2 egg yolks
>
> 2 oz butter
>
> enough hot water so that you can roll it out

Grease the rolled dough with butter and fold over three times. Roll out again, cut into half-moon shapes, and fry.

603. Curry balls
ARANCINE AL CURRIE

Make the **curry ball mixture** in recipe 13, but instead of onions use:

> 5 or 6 cubes of Gouda or Gruyère cheese

Roll balls 2 or 3 inches in diameter.

~~~~~~~~~~~~~~~

604. Bean croquettes
CROCCHETTE DI FAGIUOLI

Boil **beans** with a pinch of baking soda. Leave to cool, put through a food mill, add salt and pepper, and an equal amount of **thick béchamel**. Make the croquettes thumb-size. Dip in **flour**, **egg**, and **bread crumbs**

> Fry.

605. Ricotta 'bombette'
BOMBETTE DI RICOTTA

Mix together:

> 1 lb ricotta
>
> 4 oz flour
>
> 4 eggs
>
> 1 oz butter
>
> salt
>
> one grated lemon peel

With a spoon, drop the mixture into boiling oil. Fry on both sides and serve hot.

606. Ricotta 'panzanelle'
PANZANELLE DI RICOTTA

Take **12 slices of bread** from which you have removed the crust, and spread on the following mixture:

- 12 oz ricotta
- one finely chopped onion
- finely chopped parsley
- salt
- cayenne pepper

Mix well with a knife blade. Then spread one side of the bread with this mixture and fry the opposite side, spooning hot oil on the ricotta side as you cook.

607. Egg 'panzanelle'
PANZANELLE ALL'UOVO

Cut some **stale bread** in slices, remove the crust, dip in **milk** with a pinch of **salt**, and cover with **flour**. Dip in a mixture of:

- beaten egg
- chopped parsley
- salt
- pepper

Fry both sides in butter and serve with wal**nut sauce** (recipe 698) or other as preferred.

608. English mushroom cutlets
COTOLETTE DI FUNGHI ALL'INGLESE

Ingredients:

- 2 lb mushrooms
- 3 eggs
- 6 oz bread crumbs

Chop mushrooms finely and mix with 2 eggs, bread crumbs, salt, pepper, **nutmeg**, and very finely chopped **parsley**. Make flat fritters and dip in **flour**, then egg. Fry in butter or oil.

609. British cutlets
SGALOPPINE BRITANNICHE

Ingredients:

- 5 oz shelled walnuts
- 12 oz vermicelli
- tomato sauce as needed

Grate the walnuts and partly cook the vermicelli; mix with tomato sauce and form into a rectangular shape. Allow to cool and then cut in slices. Dip in:

- flour
- egg
- bread crumbs

Fry in oil.

610. Vegetarian chicken croquettes
CROCCHETTE DI POLLO (PSEUDO)

Take some **vegetarian chicken filling** (see recipe 711). Drop spoonfuls of this onto **flour**, roll with your hands into cylinder shapes, and dip in:

- flour
- beaten egg
- bread crumbs

Fry.

611. Dutch cutlets
COTOLETTE FRITTE ALL'OLANDESE

Follow recipe 444 for **vegetarian meat loaf**.

Divide into equal parts and flatten with your hands to form meat-like slices. Sprinkle lightly with **vinegar**, cover with **flour**, dip in **beaten egg** and then **bread crumbs**, and fry in oil.

612. Vegetarian meat ravioli
RAVIOLI DI PSEUDO-CARNE FRITTI

Take some **ravioli pasta** (see recipe 536), and roll out very thin. On the pasta dough place at equal distances little heaps of **vegetarian meat filling** (recipe 712). Fold over the other half to form pockets, and seal by cutting with a pastry wheel, then fry or boil and serve with whatever sauce you choose.

613. Potato balls
ARANCINE DI PATATE

Ingredients:

    4 lb potatoes
    4 oz Parmesan cheese
    2 eggs
    filling as wished

Peel the potatoes, then boil and mash them. Mix with the eggs, Parmesan, a good pinch of salt, and a sprinkling of **grated nutmeg**. Divide the mixture in as many parts as you wish. Make a hole in each piece, fill with the filling of your choice (see recipes 701–709), close up, and round into balls. Dip in **egg** and **bread crumbs**, and fry.

614. Fried skewers
SPIEDINI FRITTI

Cut out rectangular **slices of bread**, 2 by 1¼ inches thick. Make the same number of slices of **soft cheese** (provolone, scamorza, mozzarella, primosale, etc.) and chunks of **peeled tomatoes**, removing the seeds. Take the skewers (long cocktail sticks will do) and impale a slice of bread, then one of tomato, then one of cheese, then repeat and finish with a piece of bread. Cover in **béchamel**, dip in **flour**, then in **beaten egg**, and finally in **bread crumbs** before frying.

615. Milk fritters
FRITTI DI LATTE

Ingredients:

    2 pints milk
    8 oz potato or corn starch
    1 ½ oz butter
    4 oz Parmesan cheese
    2 egg yolks

In a sauce pan, melt the starch in the milk, add the salt, and heat, stirring all the time. When the batter has thickened, add the cheese and egg yolks, and continue to stir. Once combined, spread ½ inch thick on a buttered marble surface. When cold, cut into square shapes, cover in **flour**, dip in **egg whites** and **bread crumbs**, and fry.

616. Truffle squares
QUADRELLI TARTUFATI

Cut out squares of **stale bread**, after removing the crust. Cover one side with **béchamel** (see recipe 652), placing little pieces of **black truffles** on each, and then a slice of **Gruyère cheese**. Cover with another square of bread, also coated with béchamel. Dip in **egg batter** (see recipe 540), and fry. The squares can also be filled with other fillings (see recipes 701–709).

617. Montecassino crostini
CROSTINI DI MONTECASSINO

Remove the crusts and slice the **bread** in triangles. Cover with **slices of mozzarella**, and glue these together with a little **egg batter** (see recipe 649). Then dip in the same batter and fry in oil or butter.

618. Rice balls
ARANCINE DI RISO

Make a **thick risotto** (see recipe 155), and spread in a large square on a marble surface or wooden board, and allow to cool. Separately mix:

- **cubes of cheese** (Gouda, Swiss, Parmesan, etc.)
- **a little tomato sauce**
- **pepper**
- **chopped parsley**
- **some crushed walnuts**

Cut the risotto into 4-inch squares. Place one of these squares in the palm of your hand and press with three fingers of your other hand to make a concave dent in the square; put a spoonful of the cheese filling in the center and fold over with both hands to form a ball. Roll in **flour**, then **beaten egg** and **bread crumbs**. Deep fry in a pan, big enough for one ball at a time. Serve hot.

619. German style fried cauliflower
CAVOLFIORI FRITTI ALLA TEDESCA

Half cook the **cauliflower** in a steamer. Drain and soak in:

- vinegar
- salt
- pepper

Allow to soak well, then dip in **batter** (see next recipe), and fry.

620. Batter for immediate frying
PASTETTA PER FRIGGERE IMMEDIATO

Ingredients:
- 2 eggs
- 6 oz flour
- ½ tsp water

Beat the eggs with the flour until well mixed, and add water, salt, and pepper.

621. Eggplant croquettes
CROCCHETTE DI MELANZANE

Peel the **eggplants**, dice, and cook in a steamer. Grate an equal amount of **bread crumbs**, and add:

- a quarter as much grated cheese
- salt
- pepper
- chopped parsley
- 2 eggs

Mix together and make thumb-sized croquettes. Cover in flour, dip in **egg** and **bread crumbs**, and then fry.

622. Potato croquettes
CROCCHETTE DI PATATE

Peel **3 lb potatoes**, boil, and mash one by one, and add:

> **4 oz grated Parmesan cheese**
> **2 eggs**
> salt
> pepper
> chopped parsley

Make thumb-sized croquettes, cover in **flour**, dip in **egg**, and then fry.

623. Rice croquettes
CROCCHETTE DI RISO

Prepare a very **thick risotto Milanese** (see recipe 155) and make croquettes. Add:

> **4 oz cheese**
> chopped parsley
> pepper
> **12 crushed walnuts**

Cover in **flour**, dip in **egg** and then **bread crumbs**, and fry.

624. Broccoli with mozzarella
BROCCOLI ALLA MOZZARELLA

Take **2 equal-sized heads of broccoli**, and remove some of the stalks. Fill the openings in the broccoli with slices of **mozzarella** or other fresh cheese. Do the same with the other head of broccoli. Join the two together, like a loaf of bread, sprinkle with salt, and place together in a frying pan in equal portions of oil and butter. Cover the pan with a soup plate, and cook gently. When well braised on one side, turn over, add more oil and butter, and fry the other side. Then pour the fat out of the pan, holding the lid on firmly, and turn upside down, leaving the broccoli on the plate; add **lemon juice** and serve.

625. Mixed fry
FRITTURA MISTA

Slice **1 lb peeled potatoes** and sprinkle with salt. Peel **1 lb tomatoes**, cut in 4 to 6 pieces, remove the seeds, cover in **flour**, and dip in **egg** and then **bread crumbs**, adding some salt. Peel **2 or 3 eggplants**, cut into little fingers, and roll in flour, with some salt. Prepare some **squash fingers** too, and roll in flour. Fry everything, putting them side by side on the serving dish. You can add artichokes, chards, celery, or other vegetables; serve with **eggs** (see recipe 469) on the side.

626. Fried artichokes
CARCIOFI FRITTI

Remove the tough leaves and prickly parts, and then cut each **artichoke** into 8 pieces. Soak in **lemon** and **water**, then dip in **batter** (see recipe 539–540), and fry.

627. Fried carrots in batter
CAROTE FRITTE ALLA PASTETTA

Clean and scrape the **carrots** and cut in slices. Blanch briefly in boiling water, dip in **batter** (see recipe 540), and fry.

628. Fried celery
SEDANI FRITTI

As above, with celery.

629. Fried asparagus
ASPARAGI FRITTI

As above, with asparagus.

630. French fries
PATATE FRITTE ALL'INGLESE

Peel the **raw potatoes** and cut into finger shapes. Sprinkle with salt and leave to drain. Fry in abundant of oil and butter. Serve immediately.

631. Duchess biscuits
GALLETTINE DUCHESSA

Cook **12 potatoes** either in water or a steamer. Mash them, then mix in:

> **4 beaten eggs**
>
> **pepper**
>
> **salt**
>
> **chopped parsley**

Form little tangerine-sized balls. Press these into flat shapes like biscuits, fry in butter, and serve with **sauce** (see recipe 692).

632. Milanese cutlets
COTOLETTE ALLA MILANESE (PSEUDO)

Ingredients:

> **½ pint milk**
>
> **3 eggs**

> **12 oz flour**
>
> **10 walnuts**

Dissolve 4 oz of the flour in the milk, adding 1 beaten egg, a pinch of salt, the crushed walnuts, **parsley**, and **curry** (if you like the taste). Drop spoonfuls into hot butter in a frying pan, and turn over when they have solidified, without overcooking. Allow to cool on absorbent kitchen paper, cover in **flour**, dip in **egg** and **bread crumbs**, and fry (best in butter).

633. Cream cutlets
COTOLETTE ALLA CREMA

Prepare as in the previous recipe, but before dipping in flour, cover with a **thick béchamel** (see recipes 652–653).

634. Fried vegetarian meatballs
POLPETTINE FRITTE

Prepare as in recipe 52, but making the "meatballs" larger, and instead of boiling in broth, fry them. Serve garnished with **French fries** and **tomato ketchup**, if desired.

635. Salmi grenadines
GRANATINE AL SALMÌ

Fry **6 diced eggplants**, mince them and mix with:

> **12 crushed walnuts**
>
> **4 oz Parmesan**
>
> **3 eggs**

pepper

chopped parsley

enough bread crumbs to thicken

Serve with a good **salmi** (see recipe 699).

636. Winter grenadines
GRANATINE INVERNALI

As in recipe 635, but instead of eggplants use **dried mushrooms**.

637. Green vegetarian meatballs
POLPETTE VERDI

Strain **2 lb spinach**. Mix half with:

4 oz grated cheese

2 eggs

parsley

salt

pepper

enough bread crumbs to thicken

Make small balls and fry. Sauté the emaining spinach through a food mill and combine this with **béchamel** (see recipes 652–653) to pour over the meatballs.

638. Tasty tidbits
BOCCONCINI DI SOSTANZA

Make a **Corvo risotto** (see recipe 156) and when it is ready add:

cheese

12 crushed walnuts

chopped parsley

Make little balls, cover with **flour**, dip in **egg** and then **bread crumbs**. Fry, and serve with a **Hollandaise** or other sauce. Accompany with a vegetable side dish.

639. Basic chickpea fritters
PANELLE POPOLARI

Dissolve **8 oz chickpea flour** in **½ pint of water** and when well blended slowly add:

another 2 ½ pints water

salt

pepper

chopped herbs

Heat up, stirring continually, and when thick, spread the mixture in traditional square molds or in any ordinary plate. When cool, cut into squares or shape with your hands and fry in oil.

640. Choice chickpea fritters
PANELLE DI LUSSO

As above, but reduce the amount of water by ½ pint and substitute with:

½ pint cream

4 oz grated Parmesan cheese

Fry in butter.

641. Three-cheese milk croquettes
CROCCHETTE DI LATTE AI 3 FORMAGGI

Ingredients:

- 1 ½ pints milk
- 6 oz flour
- 4 oz butter
- 4 oz Parmesan cheese
- 2 oz Edam cheese
- 2 oz Gruyère cheese
- 2 egg yolks

Melt the butter and blend in the flour, with a pinch of salt and a pinch of grated nutmeg. Then pour in the milk slowly, stirring vigorously, and when well mixed and smooth add the two egg yolks. Allow to bind, and then remove from the heat and add grated cheese. Let cool, and when cold enough to handle make the croquettes. Cover these in **flour**, dip in **egg** and then **bread crumbs**, and fry.

642. Pope's tidbits
BOCCONI DI PAPA

Follow the above recipe, but add:

- 2 ½ oz shelled and crushed walnuts
- some chopped herbs

Make little balls the size of a large walnut. Flatten these like pancakes, and fry. Arrange on a platter, and pour on a **salmi** sauce (see recipe 699) with **chopped truffles**. Serve with mashed potatoes or some other side dish.

Sauces and fillings

643. Red butter sauce
ARROSSATO DI BURRO

Melt some **butter** in a saucepan and add **a spoonful or more of flour**, depending on how thick you want the sauce. When the flour turns reddish use it in the sauces you want, according to the individual recipes.

644. Clear butter sauce
ARROSSATO CHIARO

As in the previous recipe, but remove the sauce from the heat before it darkens.

645. Long-lasting red butter sauce
ARROSSATO PERMANENTE

Melt **1 lb butter** in a pan, and continue to add **flour** until it has been absorbed, so as to make a fairly liquid mixture. Cook over charcoal until it turns a golden color. Keep in an earthenware pot and use as needed. This will keep for up to six months.

646. Tomato sauce
SALSA DI POMODORO

Take **fully ripe tomatoes,** wash and crush them in a pan; add:

> **2 chopped onions for every 2 lb tomato**
> **one clove of garlic**
> **some basil leaves**

After simmering for about ¾ hour, pass through a fine food mill, and simmer again, to reduce the sauce. Add:

> **salt**
> **pepper**
> **equal amounts of butter** and **oil**

Make the sauce as dense as you want it. If the tomato is sour, add a pinch of baking soda and a little **sugar**.

647. 'Picchio-pacchio' sauce
SALSA PIK-PACCHIO

Cut **two large onions** into slivers and sauté lightly in 5 or 6 spoonfuls **olive oil.** When golden brown add **4 lb chopped ripe tomatoes,** after carefully removing the skin and all seeds. Add:

salt

pepper

1 clove of garlic

a pinch of saffron

some finely chopped parsley

basil

Cook until the sauce has thickened.

648. Sweet-and-sour 'picchio-pacchio'
PIK-PACCHIO AGRO DOLCE

As above, but add:

a good pinch of a standard spice mix

¾ oz sugar

a small glass of vinegar

Cook for ten minutes and use in cold dishes.

649. Spanish sauce
SALSA SPAGNOLA

In a pan, put:

a knob of butter

two spoonfuls of flour

Heat until it dissolves and then, stirring continually, add ½ pint homemade broth (see recipe 51) a little at a time. Now add:

an onion, chopped

a carrot, chopped

a clove

grated nutmeg

salt

pepper

Finally add another ½ pint broth and simmer gently.

650. Velouté sauce
SALSA VELLUTINA

As for Spanish sauce (see recipe 654), but add:

another pint of homemade broth (recipe 47)

two more onions, chopped

two more carrots, chopped

one clove

some celery, chopped

grated nutmeg

Simmer for an hour, strain and thicken with flour.

651. German sauce
SALSA ALEMANNA

Pour ½ pint velouté sauce (see previous recipe) into a pan with:

4 egg yolks

a little butter

some grated nutmeg

Heat and stir quickly, pouring in a glass of Marsala wine.

~~~~~~~~~~~~~~~~~~

652. Béchamel
SALSA BESCIAMELLA O SALSA DI LATTE SEMPLICE

Melt 1 tbsp butter with:

1 spoonful of flour

salt

white pepper

Gradually add ½ pint milk, stirring continually over a gentle heat.

653. Superior béchamel
SALSA BESCIAMELLA SUPERIORE

In a pan, put:
- **2 oz butter**
- **a spoonful of flour**

Heat gently, adding **½ pint milk** a little at a time. When this is done, remove from the heat and add:
- **a cupful of cream**
- **salt**
- **pepper**

654. Superior béchamel or 'mussolina'
SALSA ALLA CREMA O MUSSOLINA

Put in a pan:
- **5 oz butter**
- **1 tbsp flour**
- **salt**
- **pepper**
- **grated nutmeg**

Melt the butter, diluting with a little **water**. Thicken the mixture with **2 egg yolks**, remove from heat, and add:
- **a cupful of cream**
- **a spoonful of vinegar**

655. Brown sauce
SALSA BRUNA

In a small pan, mix:
- **1 oz flour**
- **4 oz butter**

Heat gently until the mixture begins to turn brown. Add water until you get the right consistency. Add pepper and salt to taste.

656. Curry sauce
SALSA DI CURRIE SEMPLICE

Make a **brown sauce**, and add **2 tsp curry powder** (see recipe 893)

657. Curry sauce and tomato
SALSA DI CURRIE E POMODORO

Cut a **tomato** into thin rings, fry in butter until golden brown, and add **curry powder**. Fry gently for 5 minutes, and then add:
- **4 oz tomato concentrate**
- **4 cloves**
- **6 coriander seeds**
- **3 bay leaves**
- **1 sage leaf**
- **3 crushed garlic cloves**

Mix and boil, adding **water**. Pass through a food mill and use later, after reheating.

658. Hollandaise sauce
SALSA OLANDESE

Ingredients:
- **4 oz butter**
- **1 oz flour**
- **1 tsp vinegar**
- **1 pint milk**
- **3 egg yolks**
- **salt**
- **pepper**

Mix the butter with the flour, add the milk little by little, and boil for 5 minutes. Remove from the heat, stir in the yolks, and mix until the sauce thickens; add the vinegar, mix well, and serve.

659. Egg sauce
SALSA D'UOVA

Ingredients:
- 1 hard-boiled egg
- salt
- 2 oz butter
- cayenne pepper
- ½ pint milk
- 1 oz flour
- pepper

Melt the butter with the flour in a pan, add the milk, salt and spices. Mix well and boil for 5 minutes. Add the egg, chopped very finely, and serve.

660. Green Florentine sauce
SALSA VERDE FIORENTINA

Finely chop:
- a few capers
- a small onion
- a clove of garlic

Mash together with a knife and place in a gravyboat. Add:
- plenty of chopped parsley
- some oil
- a little sage

Mix together with a blend of two-thirds good-quality **olive oil** and one-third **lemon juice**.

661. White sauce
SALSA BIANCA

Ingredients:
- 4 oz butter
- 1 tbsp flour
- 1 egg yolk
- 1 tbsp vinegar
- salt
- pepper
- water as required

Make a **red sauce** (recipe 643) with flour and half the butter, mixing over a low flame. Pour water in gradually, stirring continually. Add the remaining butter, pour in the vinegar, remove from the heat, bind with the yolk, and serve.

662. Italian fricassee sauce
SALSA FRICASSEA ITALIANA

Heat **a spoonful of flour** with **a knob of butter** until it browns. Gradually add:
- ½ pint water
- salt
- pepper
- chopped parsley

Boil briefly, remove from heat, and add:
- 2 tbsp cream or fresh butter
- 2 egg yolks

Mix vigorously until the ingredients have amalgamated. Add **juice of ½ lemon** and serve.

663. Caper sauce
SALSA DI CAPPERI

Ingredients:

- 2 oz butter
- ½ tbsp flour
- 2 oz drained capers (preserved in vinegar)
- salt
- pepper
- vinegar

Heat half the butter with the flour and when it browns add the rest of the butter. Pour in **½ pint water** very slowly and when it boils add the capers, half of which should be very finely chopped and the remainder left whole. Add 1 tbsp of vinegar and serve when cool.

664. Sauce supreme
SALSA SUPREMA

Make a **homemade broth** (see recipe 51), and prepare a little **clear red sauce** (recipe 644), to be mixed with the homemade broth. Heat until the right consistency, and add:

- the juice of one lemon
- a knob of butter
- chopped parsley
- salt
- pepper

665. 'Bianchetto' sauce
SALSA BIANCHETTA

In a pan, melt:

- 1 egg-sized wedge of butter
- 1 tbsp of flour

Mix vigorously. Before the sauce turns red, add:

- ½ pint water
- salt
- pepper
- chopped onion
- a bunch of aromatic herbs

Cook for a few minutes, remove the herbs, and serve.

666. Cook's sauce
SALSA RISORSA DI CUOCO

Put **a knob of butter** in a bowl with:

- some chopped parsley
- salt
- pepper
- nutmeg
- some very finely chopped onion

Mix together with the **juice of one lemon** and add to the hot dish as you serve it.

667. Yellow Hollandaise sauce
SALSA OLANDESE GIALLA

Put in a cup:

- 5 oz butter
- 3 egg yolks
- a pinch of salt
- 1 tbsp good vinegar

Let it sit for 4 hours. Heat in a double boiler, stirring until the sauce thickens, and serve with any appropriate dish.

668. Black butter
BURRO NERO

Put some **butter** in a pan and brown (taking care not to burn it). Then add some **chopped parsley**, fry and pour over the dish. In the same pan heat a little **vinegar**, and pour that over as well.

669. Genoese sauce
SALSA GENOVESE

Take:
- 4 oz pine nuts
- 2 oz crushed capers
- an egg-sized piece of bread dipped in vinegar
- 1 hard-boiled egg yolk
- a fresh sprig of parsley
- 3 crushed olives in brine
- ½ clove garlic
- a pinch of salt
- pepper

Mash together, put through a food mill, and add:
- 2 oz oil
- the juice of one lemon

670. 'Salmoriglio' sauce
SALAMORIGLIO

Squeeze **4 lemons** and mix with the equivalent amount of **olive oil**. Add:
- 2 cloves of garlic, diced
- chopped parsley
- oregano
- salt
- pepper

671. Papal sauce
SALSA PAPALINA

Squeeze **2 oz capers** preserved in vinegar and add an equivalent amount of **pitted olives**. Chop finely and heat with **minced onion** in butter. When golden brown, sprinkle with **water** and simmer for a short while, then add:
- more butter
- a tsb of flour
- 1 tsp of vinegar

Blend together and leave to cool.

672. Single-egg mayonnaise
SALSA MAJONESE MONOVINA

Take **1 egg yolk** and place in a deep bowl; add:
- a pinch of salt
- 4 or 5 drops of good olive oil

Stir continually. As soon as these ingredients are well blended, add a few more drops of oil, continuing to stir. When this has amalgamated, repeat the whole process until it becomes as thick as dough. You can then add more oil, alternating this with drops of **lemon juice**. When you have as much as you require, stop and serve. With the yolk of one egg you can make almost 2 cups of mayonnaise.

673. Ordinary mayonnaise
SALSA MAJONESE COMUNE

Break **4 farm-fresh eggs** and put the yolks in a bowl. Blend together with a pinch of salt and continue to stir while adding alternately drops of **oil** and drops of **lemon juice**. When the consistency is right, continue adding oil and occasionally a few drops of lemon juice and vinegar. You can also add **chopped parsley, white pepper**, or little **capers**.

674. What to do when mayonnaise doesn't come out right
MODO DI RIPARARE LA MAJONESE NON RIUSCITA

Sometimes, either because of an egg that is not fresh or because too much oil has been added all at once, the mayonnaise separates and won't blend properly.

If that should happen, put another egg yolk in another bowl, begin again, and when you are sure you have the right consistency, instead of adding more oil, add the sauce that didn't come out, little by little, stirring continually.

675. Pepper sauce
SALSA DI PEPERONI

Take some **large bell peppers**, fry gently in oil and remove the outer skin.

In oil and butter, sauté a chopped **clove of garlic**, and add:

  the peppers
  some peeled tomatoes (after removing the
    seeds)

Add:

  salt
  pepper
  a few leaves of basil

Heat until the sauce has thickened and serve. **Cayenne pepper** will make this sauce even spicier.

676. Hot sauce
SALSA PICCANTE

In a sauce pan, put:

  a cupful of wine
  some thyme
  a bay leaf
  a clove of garlic
  onion
  mustard

Heat until the mixture reduces (about two-thirds of the original quantity). Add a **homemade broth** (see recipe 51) and pass through a food mill.

677. Orleans sauce
SALSA D'ORLÉANS

In a sauce pan, put:

  4 tbsp vinegar
  butter
  chopped onion
  pepper

Blend together and add a **butter sauce** (recipes 643–645) which you have prepared separately. When serving, add:

  4 chopped pickles
  a boiled carrot
  3 hard-boiled egg whites (chopped)
  1 tbsp of pickled capers

Heat briefly and serve.

678. Sweet-and-sour sauce
SALSA AGRO-DOLCE

Make a **clear butter sauce** (see recipe 644) and add the following mixture. Melt some **sugar** in boiling **water**, and then add **lemon juice**. Mix together, adding more lemon juice according to taste.

679. Cucumber sauce
SALSA DI CETRIOLO

Peel a **cucumber**, remove the seeds, cut in little pieces, sprinkle with salt, and leave to drain for half an hour, keeping the juice. Cook the chopped cucumber in a little water until is soft, and then pass it through a food mill. Add the **juice of one lemon** and mix with a **clear butter sauce** (recipe 644) until the mixture thickens. Remove from heat and serve, adding the uncooked juice you have kept aside.

680. Béarnaise sauce
SALSA BEARNESE

In a pan, cook:
   a chopped onion
   a glass of vinegar
   an equal amount of water or, even better,
      vegetable broth
Add:
   salt
   a bay leaf
   any aromatic herbs you may like
Boil for half an hour. Pass through a food mill or sieve and add:

   a good knob of butter
   2 egg yolks
   1 tsp of flour dissolved in a little cold water
Bind in a double boiler. This can also be served cold.

681. Onion sauce
SALSA DI CIPOLLE

Take **8 medium-sized onions**, cut in strips and cook in **½ pint water**. Pass through a food mill and add to the **butter sauce** (see recipe 644).

682. Peanut sauce
SALSA D'ARACHIDI

In a pan, melt:
   2 tsp of peanut butter
Gradually add **vegetable broth** until the sauce is smooth. Add:
   salt
   pepper
   ½ cup cream

683. Green mayonnaise sauce
SALSA MAJONESE VERDE

Take some **mayonnaise** (recipes 672–673) and add a **mint and parsley pesto**. Heat briefly and pass through a food mill.

684. Mushroom sauce
SALSA DI FUNGHI

Ingredients:
- 1 oz flour
- 1 oz butter
- ½ pint milk
- 6 oz mushrooms
- ½ spoonful salt
- white pepper
- nutmeg
- ½ cup cream

Clean and wash the mushrooms, boil in the milk, remove and pass through a food mill. Melt the butter and stir in the flour. As soon as it begins to brown, add the mushrooms and milk. Cook for 5 minutes with salt, pepper, and a little nutmeg. Remove from heat, mix in the cream and use as required.

685. Mustard sauce
SALSA DI SENAPE

Mix:
- 2 tsp mustard
- ½ pint béchamel (see recipe 652)

Add:
- 1 tsp of vinegar
- some cayenne pepper if desired

686. 'Subisso' (or deluge) sauce
SALSA SUBISSO

Ingredients:
- 3 onions
- 2 oz butter
- ½ cup cream
- ½ pint milk
- 1 oz flour
- salt
- white pepper

Slice the onions, boil slowly in a little water, and when well cooked pass through a food mill. Melt the butter with the flour over heat, add salt and pepper, and pour the milk in gradually. Stir until it boils and add the sieved onions and cream.

687. Sauce without butter
SALSA IN MANCANZA DI BURRO

If you have run out of butter put the following in a pan:
- 3 yolks of egg
- 6 tbsp oil
- salt
- pepper
- nutmeg

Heat in a double boiler, stirring continually to bind.

688. Cold sauce
SALSA FREDDA

Blanch a sprig of **herbs** in boiling water, and then mash and put through a food mill. Add:
- 2 hard-boiled egg yolks

Mix together, then add:
- 4 tbsp oil
- 2 tbsp of lemon
- 1 tbsp of mustard

Serve cold.

689. English sauce
SALSA INGLESE

Put some sliced **bread** in enough **milk** to make a liquid mixture; pass through a food mill, add:

- plenty of cayenne pepper
- a spoonful of curry
- some salt

Boil briefly. Add a **knob of butter** when serving.

690. Worcestershire sauce (English sauce)
WORCESTERSHIRE SAUCE (SALSA INGLESE)

Boil the following ingredients together:

- ½ pint water
- 1 ½ pints Marsala wine
- 2 tbsp vinegar
- a sprig of thyme
- 6 oz chopped onion
- 4 chopped hot red peppers
- ⅕ oz cinnamon
- cloves
- nutmeg
- ½ tsp salt

Color with **caramelized sugar**. Pass through a food mill and squeeze in a cloth. Keep in bottles.

691. 'Remolata' sauce
SALSA REMOLATA

In a small bowl, combine the following, finely chopped:

- 2 shallots
- some chervil or other herb
- a clove of garlic

- salt
- pepper

Slowly add:

- some mustard
- oil
- vinegar

Mix well but without heating.

692. 'Ravigotta' sauce
SALSA RAVIGOTTA

Chop finely:

- chervil
- sage
- parsley
- shallots
- garlic
- tender celery leaves
- basil
- capers

Add **a raw egg yolk** and **a little oil**, stirring vigorously and adding a little **vinegar** every now and then. Continue until you have a thick sauce. Add some **mustard** if you like. This sauce is uncooked.

693. Pepper sauce
SALSA AL PEPE

Heat some **vinegar** in an earthenware pot with:

- thyme
- bay leaf
- parsley
- a pinch of pepper

Separately, make a **butter sauce** (recipe 643) and

dilute with **salted water**. Add the vinegar and herbs and let boil for ¼ hour, then put through a food mill. Heat again before serving.

694. Tartar sauce
SALSA TARTARA

In a bowl, put the following, all finely chopped:

    2 onions
    chervil
    sage
    parsley

Add:

    mustard
    salt
    pepper
    a little vinegar

Mix together, adding the **oil** a little at a time. This sauce is uncooked.

695. Chopped herb sauce (hachée)
SALSA TRITATA (HACHÉE)

In a saucepan over medium heat with **a knob of butter**, place the following, all finely chopped:

    some parsley
    onion
    basil
    celery

Cook in a little water, then add:

    1 tsp of flour dissolved in **a cup of water**

When the mixture thickens add:

    some chopped gherkins
    salt

pepper

Allow to bind and serve.

696. Italian sauce
SALSA ITALIANA

Put **a glass of white wine** in a pan with:

    mushrooms
    onion
    chopped parsley
    a bunch of herbs

Heat until the mixture thickens, and add **1 tbsp of oil**. Boil a little more and dilute with **water**, adding with a little **starch** and **salt**; add **a knob of butter** and finish cooking.

697. Ketchup
KETSCHUP

Reduce **2 lb tomatoes** to pulp by putting through a food mill and cook with:

    1 oz sugar
    ¼ cupful vinegar
    ¼ tsp cinnamon
    ⅛ tsp powdered cloves
    ¼ tsp ground cumin
    a pinch of cayenne pepper

Cook until the mixture thickens and preserve in bottles after adding **⅛ tsp salicylic acid**.

698. Walnut sauce
SALSA DI NOCI

Crush the **walnuts** finely and stir in cream, adding a pinch of **salt** and **pepper**. Make some more of the sauce, but instead of cream, add:

> parsley
> basil
> crushed garlic

Put through a food mill and dilute with a little **water** and oil. This sauce is excellent on macaroni.

699. Salmi
SALMÌ

Make a **red butter sauce** (see recipe 643) and add:

> chopped onion
> carrots
> thyme
> marjoram
> nutmeg
> parsley and other herbs

Dilute with **vegetable broth** or **a glass of good dry wine**. Cook, put through a food mill, bind and color with **burned sugar** or **caramel**. Chopped **black truffles** are excellent with this sauce.

700. French mustard
MOSTARDA FRANCESE

Take:

> 1 oz English mustard powder
> a pinch of salt

> 4 cloves of garlic that have been boiled for 15 minutes
> a few leaves of crushed tarragon, sage or other aromatic herb

Dilute in enough **vinegar** to give the right consistency. Put through a sieve and use a few days later. Store in a closed jar.

701. Eggplant filling
FARCIA DI MELANZANE O DI SOSTANZA

Peel and dice **2 peeled eggplants** and fry, then chop finely and place in a pan with:

> 2 oz butter
> 6 crushed walnuts
> salt
> pepper
> nutmeg
> chopped onion

Sauté gently for 10 minutes. Remove from the heat and make a mixture with:

> 4 oz bread crumbs
> milk

Allow the bread to soak up the milk. Add this to the fried eggplants with **4 egg yolks** for extra flavor if you like. Stir well when cold, and use as a filling.

702. Mushroom filling
FARCIA DI FUNGHI

Gently fry in butter:

> some well-chopped mushrooms
> crushed garlic
> parsley
> onion

Flavor with:

pepper

salt

nutmeg

When well cooked stir in a little **flour**. Depending how you intend to use the filling, when it is cold you can add **Parmesan cheese**, **bread** soaked in water, or **egg yolk**.

703. Truffle filling
FARCIA DI FUNGHI

As in recipe 702, but add:

truffles

a glass of Marsala wine

704. Truffle and walnut filling
FARCIA DI NOCI TARTUFATA

As in the next recipe, but use a couple of **good minced truffles** instead of mushrooms.

705. Mushroom and walnut filling
FARCIA DI FUNGHI E NOCI

Gently fry **2 chopped onions** in butter. When golden brown, add **1 tbsp dried mushrooms** that have been soaked in water for an hour and chopped, plus:

12 crushed walnuts

2 bay leaves

nutmeg

pepper

parsley

salt

Cook briefly and remove from heat.

In a separate pan, soak:

4 oz bread

milk

Heat and stir until you get a paste. When cool, add the other filling. Remove the bay leaves and add **4 egg yolks**. Stir vigorously. Use as a filling.

706. Cheese filling
FARCIA AL FORMAGGIO

As in recipe 705, but omit the mushrooms and add **3 oz grated cheese** when the mixture cools.

707. Vegetarian chicken stuffing
FARCIA DI POLLO (PSEUDO)

Ingredients:

1 pint milk

4 oz butter

4 tbsp flour

3 eggplants

8 walnuts

3 egg yolks

onion

Melt the butter with the flour and a pinch of salt, continuing to stir. Add the milk little by little along with:

1 tbsp of very finely chopped onion

chopped parsley

pepper

Remove from heat as soon as this is amalgamated. Fry the peeled diced eggplant, then chop finely and add to the sauce with the crushed walnuts, and mix in the egg yolks. To make this even tastier you can add:

chopped truffles

2 oz grated Parmesan cheese

The ingredients must all be ready before you heat the milk.

708. Vegetarian filling
FARCIA DI PSEUDO-CARNE

Take **4 eggplants**, peel and dice, and fry in oil. Remove them and mash with a weight. Add:

4 oz grated Parmesan cheese

10 crushed walnuts

nutmeg

pepper

3 tbsp béchamel (see recipe 652–653)

2 egg yolks

709. Cream filling
FARCIA ALLA CREMA

Gently fry in butter **6 oz of diced bread** soaked in **milk**. When of an even consistency, remove from heat, flavor with:

salt

white pepper

½ cup of cream

3 egg yolks

2 oz grated Gruyère cheese

Use as a filling.

Desserts, cakes and sweets

DOLCI DI CUOCO

710. Homemade pudding
BODINO ALLA CASALINGA

If you have some **stale bread** left over, you can use it to make an excellent cake, as follows.

Preheat oven to 350°F.

Slice the dry bread as best as you can, and spread some **butter** on each slice. Put the bread in a shallow baking mold, in layers, covering each layer with a sprinkling of **sugar** and a few **dried currants** and some **grated lemon peel**.

Pour enough **milk** to cover the bread and let stand, about 10 minutes. Bake 35 to 45 minutes or until set.

711. Stale bread pudding
BODINO DI PAN DURO

Ingredients:

    12 oz stale bread
    5 eggs
    2 oz butter
    4 oz currants
    8 oz sugar

Put the dry bread in water to soak, about 10 minutes. Remove the crust, squeeze dry and pass though a food mill.

Beat the eggs with the sugar and mix with the bread, adding the currants and some **grated lemon peel**.

Grease a baking mold with butter and pour the mixture in, and then cook by placing the mold over boiling water. Stir occasionally until thickened. When the pudding sets, up to one hour, serve by turning the mold out onto a plate and covering with any **hot syrup** you choose or with **grape syrup** (recipe 881).

712. Rice pudding
BODINO DI RISO

Ingredients:

    12 oz rice
    8 oz sugar
    4 oz dried currants
    2 pints milk
    2 oz butter
    2 eggs

In a medium-sized, heavy-bottomed saucepan, heat the rice with the milk over medium heat, and cook, stirring continually until the rice is soft but still whole. If the milk is not enough, add water. Add the sugar, some **grated lemon**

peel, and the currants. When the milk is fully incorporated, remove from heat, stir in the beaten eggs, mix and pour into a greased mold. Cook over boiling water until the pudding sets. When serving, you can cover with any **hot syrup**.

713. Bran pudding (cold)
BODINO DI SEMOLA (GELATO)

Ingredients:

> 8 oz bran
> 1 qt milk
> 4 eggs
> 1 lb sugar

To make the pudding: Boil the milk with 9 oz of the sugar and some grated (or finely chopped) **lemon peel**. When the milk boils, pour in the bran, stirring continuously, adding water if necessary. Remove from the heat and add the 4 beaten eggs, blending carefully. Pour into a greased mold and cook over boiling water until the pudding sets.

To make the syrup: In another pan place the remaining sugar and cook in:

> ½ cup water
> 1 cup red wine
> lemon juice

Turn pudding out of the mold and serve covered with the syrup.

714. Pistachio pudding
BODINO DI PISTACCHIO

Ingredients:

> 8 oz bran
> 4 oz pistachio

> 1 oz sugar
> 4 eggs
> 2 handfuls spinach

Blanch the pistachios in boiling water, peel and chop finely. Boil the spinach (or other mild-tasting greens), drain, and put through a food mill. Boil some **vanilla** in 2 pints of the spinach water and pour in the bran mixed with the sugar. If necessary, add water. Remove from heat when the mixture is dense. When cool, add the 4 beaten eggs, the sieved greens, and the pistachios. Pour into a mold that you have greased with butter and cook over boiling water until the pudding sets. Turn out of the mold and serve **hot syrup**.

715. Almond biscuit pudding
BODINO DI BISCOTTO MANDORLATO

Ingredients:

> 12 oz bread crumbs
> 10 oz sugar
> 2 pints milk
> 1 lemon
> 4 eggs
> 4 oz butter
> 4 oz currants
> 4 oz shelled and peeled almonds
> 3 bitter almonds

Put bread crumbs in a pan, with half the butter and heat, stirring continually with a wooden spoon. When of a golden color, remove and place in a pan with the milk, beaten eggs, sugar, well cleaned currants and the crushed almonds. Stir for 5 minutes and pour into a greased mold lined with paper. Place the remaining butter on top and cook over boiling water until the pudding sets. Serve with a topping of **fruit syrup**.

716. Almond and stale bread pudding
BODINO DI PAN DURO MANDORLATO

Ingredients:

- 12 oz stale bread
- 6 oz shelled and peeled almonds plus 2 or 3 bitter almonds
- 8 oz sugar
- 4 oz dried currants
- 4 oz butter
- 4 eggs

Take the bread and place in water until it is well soaked. Remove the crusts and squeeze out excess water. Add the beaten eggs, well-cleaned currants, sugar, crushed almonds, and the **grated peel of two lemons**. Stir vigorously for 5 minutes and then put in a greased mold. Cook over boiling water until the pudding sets and cover with **½ cup cream** when you serve.

717. Chocolate stale bread pudding
BODINO DI PAN DURO AL CACAO

As in previous recipe, but instead of almonds use **2 oz cocoa**, and when you serve, pour on a **hot chocolate sauce** (see recipe 897).

718. Australian pudding
BODINO AUSTRALIANO

Ingredients:

- 9 oz flour
- 6 oz butter
- 6 oz sugar
- 5 oz sultanas
- 1 tsp baking soda

Mix the ingredients together after dissolving the baking soda in a little water. Place in a well-buttered mold and cook over boiling water until the pudding sets. Serve with a topping of **hot syrup**.

719. Baroness pudding
BODINO BARONESSA

Ingredients:

- 6 oz bread crumbs
- 6 oz dried currants
- 4 ½ oz butter
- 6 oz flour
- 6 oz sugar
- a glass of port
- 4 eggs
- grated nutmeg
- grated orange peel

Mix all the ingredients, place in a buttered mold, and cook over boiling water tightly covered until the pudding sets. Serve with a **hot syrup**.

720. Admiral pudding
BODINO AMMIRAGLIO

Ingredients:

- ½ lb potatoes

4 carrots
¾ cup sugar
½ lb sultanas
4 oz flour
½ lb candied fruit
4 oz butter

Boil the peeled potatoes and carrots, and put through a food mill. Add the flour and butter. Mix and add the remaining ingredients. Place in a buttered mold and cook over boiling water until the pudding sets. Serve with **lemon syrup**.

721. Amber pudding
BODINO AMBRATO

Ingredients:
1 lb boiled carrots
5 oz crumbled dry cookies
6 oz butter
5 oz dried currants
5 oz raisins
5 oz sugar
nutmeg
2 crushed cloves
a pinch of salt
2 eggs
enough milk to make a thick paste

Cook in a greased mold for 3 hours over boiling water and serve with **grape syrup** (recipe 881) or other hot syrup.

722. Bread and butter pudding
BODINO DI PANE E BURRO

Preheat oven to 350°F. Ingredients:
1 lb sliced bread

3 pints milk
10 oz confectioner's sugar
8 oz dried currants
grated peel of 2 lemons or **vanilla extract**
5 oz butter
5 eggs

Work the egg yolks in the sugar and add the milk slowly, stirring continuously. In an oven-proof dish spread a layer of thinly sliced bread spread with butter. Scatter the currants and grated lemon peel, and add another layer of bread, followed by currants, and so on until the bread is finished. Then cover with the milk and egg mixture. Bake in the oven 35 to 45 minutes or until set and serve in the oven dish. Before serving add a spoonful of brandy and light.

723. English Christmas pudding
BODINO DI NATALE INGLESE

In a heat-proof ceramic or earthenware bowl place:
1 lb flour
¼ lb sugar
10 oz raisins
7 oz dried currants
1 cup butter
6 oz bread crumbs
6 oz candied lemon peel
4 ½ oz orange marmalade
2 oz almonds
grated lemon
juice of one lemon
3 eggs
enough vintage wine to dampen

Remove the raisin seeds and peel the almonds

in hot water. Crush and chop the almonds as finely as possible, as well as the currants and orange peel. Mix all the ingredients together in the bowl, cover with a cloth and a lid, and let stand overnight. Next morning place the bowl in a pan of boiling water which must be covered. Boil for 8 hours, taking care to add water as it evaporates. Turn out onto a plate, pour on some **brandy**, and light a flame as you serve. The alcohol will evaporate before the flame goes out.

724. Fruit tart
TORTA DI FRUTTA

Preheat oven to 350°F.

Make some **shortcrust pastry** (see recipes 541–542), and roll out thinly to cover a buttered pie pan. Pierce the crust to prevent blisters from forming. Prepare the fruit as follows. Use pitted whole **apricots**, **peaches**, and **cherries**. Place the whole pears upright, complete with stems, but remove the cores. The **strawberries** and **raspberries** should also be whole, as the **grapes** and the **mandarin orange segments**. Garnish the tart as richly as possible, sprinkle with **sugar**, and bake in the oven for 30 to 45 minutes.

725. Meringue cake
TORTA DI MERENGA

Preheat oven to 350°F.

Make some **shortcrust pastry** (see recipes 541–542) and also some **vanilla cream** (recipe 868), using about 2 cups milk.

Take **6 oz sponge cake** and cut ¼ inch thick. Line a pie pan with a sheet of pastry. On this spread half the slices of sponge cake, squeeze some **lemon juice**. Form another layer with the remaining sponge cake, sprinkling with lemon juice. Whip **3 egg whites** until stiff and add **confectioner's sugar**, then cover the top of the cake. Bake in the oven and as soon as the meringue begins to harden, cover with oven paper to prevent it from burning during the remaining cooking time. Serve cold.

726. Neapolitan cake
TORTA NAPOLETANA RIPIENA

Preheat oven to 350°F.

Make a shortcrust pastry (see recipes 541–542) using:

½ lb flour
4 oz sugar
4 oz butter
2 egg yolks
1 egg white

Separately, prepare a cream with:

1 pint milk
2 tbsp starch
4 oz sugar
3 egg yolks
the grated peel of ½ orange or lemon

Add:

4 oz dried currents or sultanas
2 oz pine nuts

Mix well. Roll out 2 sheets of pastry. Put one in a buttered cake tin and cover with the above mixture. Seal with the other pastry sheet, pressing the edges together, and decorating with any left over bits. Brush the top with **egg yolk** and bake. Sprinkle with **sugar** when cold.

727. Pine nut cake
TORTA PIGNOLATA

Pre-heat oven to 350°F. Ingredients:

- 1 pint milk
- 4 oz semolina
- 2 oz sugar
- 2 oz pine nuts
- 1 oz butter
- 2 eggs
- shortcrust pastry as needed

Cook the semolina in the milk, and when done remove from heat and add the sugar, beaten eggs, butter, and chopped pine nuts. Place a layer of shortcrust pastry (see recipes 541–542) in a pan, ½ inch thick with an inch-high edge. Pour the mixture in and make a crisscross pattern of flaky pastry on top. Bake in the oven for 30–40 minutes. Serve cold with a sprinkling of **fine sugar**.

728. Apple tart
TORTA DI MELE

Make a **shortcrust pastry** (see recipes 541–547), roll very thin (⅛ inch), and place in a pie tin. Spread some **apple jelly** (see recipe 861) on the pastry crust, cover with a crisscross pattern of pastry, and bake in a 350°F oven for 25 minutes.

729. Apple tartlets
TARTINE DI MELE

Take some **flaky pastry** (recipe 538) or **shortcrust pastry** (541–542) and roll out very thin (⅛ inch) and line a cake pan. Cover with a mixture of:

- apple jam
- two-thirds as much red currant preserve

Cover with layer of pastry of the same thickness. Seal the edges with **egg white** and brush the top with **egg yolk**. Score the pastry lengthwise with the point of a knife and then again sideways to make a crisscross pattern. With the back of a large knife, make deep cuts in the pastry from side to side, to form squares of serving-size pieces. Place in a 350°F oven. After separating the squares, they can be served hot or cold.

730. 'Frangipane'
FRANGIPANE

In a pan, put:

- 3 eggs
- 2 tbsp flour

Mix well, and add:

- 1 pint milk

Heat for 15 minutes, stirring continuously. Add:

- confectioner's sugar
- chopped orange blossom
- overcooked vermicelli, reduced to a pulp

Use to make a filling for cakes and tarts.

731. Almond 'Frangipane'
FRANGIPANE MANDORLATO

Take some **almonds** (with a few bitter ones), bland in boiling water for a few minutes and peel. Crush to a paste and mix with an **equal amount of sugar**. Mix in equal parts with **frangipane** (see recipe 730). Use as a filling for pastries.

732. Tuscan 'Frangipane'
FRANGIPANE TOSCANO

Ingredients:

> 6 oz potato flour
> 6 oz sugar
> 4 oz butter
> 6 eggs
> ½ tbsp cream of tartar
> 1 tsp baking soda
> grated lemon peel

Work the egg yolks with the sugar, and slowly add the flour, stirring continually. Add the melted butter, stiffly beaten egg whites, and last of all the cream of tartar and baking soda. Put in a 2-inch high baking tin greased with butter and cook in a 350°F oven.

733. Sweet buns
BRIOSCIA DOLCE

Ingredients:

> ½ cup extra-fine flour
> 6 oz butter
> 2 tbsp yeast
> 2 tbsp sugar
> 8 eggs

In ½ cup milk, melt the yeast and leave in a warm place (near the stove) for about ½ hour. Mix the flour with the sugar, salt, and 3 egg yolks, adding the melted butter and yeast. Add the remaining eggs one by one, stirring vigorously. Pour into a large mold, or a number of small ones, greased with butter. Allow to rise and then bake in a 350°F oven.

734. Rum babà
BABÀ

Make the same dough as for **sweet buns** (recipe 733), but a little less dense. Add:

> 3 tbsp confectioner's sugar
> 2 tbsp Marsala, Malaga or rum
> 3 tbsp each of seedless currants,
>   sultanas, and candied orange peel (all
>   finely minced)
> a little saffron dissolved in water

Pour into one large or several small molds, filling each about one-third full; allow time for the mixture to rise, and bake in a 350°F oven. Serve with a generous helping of **syrup**.

~~~~~~~~~~~~~~~~~~~

735. Savarin
SAVARINO

In a bowl with a little **milk** put **2 tbsp yeast**, and after ½ hour add:

> 3 eggs
> ⅔ cup sugar
> 1 ¼ cup melted butter
> 2 lb flour
> a pinch of salt

Mix everything with enough **cream** to obtain a smooth batter. Take a ring mold, grease with butter, and sprinkle with **peeled crushed almonds**. Fill the mold three-quarters full with the batter, and leave to rise in a warm place. When it has risen, bake in the oven as for the sweet bun recipe (733). Douse with **syrup** after removing from the oven.

736. Apple Charlotte
CIARLOTTA DI MELE

Ingredients:
- 1 ¼ lb apples
- ¾ cup sugar
- 1 ½ cup butter
- square bread slices

Slice the apples and place in a pan you have melted a little butter with the sugar and a little **cinnamon**; cook, remove from heat, and use as follows. Cut the bread in slices and dip in the melted butter. Use these slices to line the bottom and the sides of a smooth mold, taking care that no part is left uncovered. Add the apples with their syrup and cover with more slices of bread dipped in butter. Cook in a slow oven until it browns. Turn out onto a plate, pour on **1 tbsp of brandy** and ignite. The alcohol will evaporate. Serve hot.

737. Strudel
STRUDEL

Ingredients:
- 1 ½ lb apples
- 1 ¼ cup flour
- ¼ lb currants
- ½ cup butter
- ½ cup sugar
- 1 grated lemon
- ¼ oz powdered cinnamon
- 2 crushed cloves
- 1 pint milk
- 2 eggs

Mix the flour with the warm milk, eggs, and a third of the butter. When it is well mixed, let stand for ¼ hour. Roll out about ⅛ inch thick, and arrange the apples on top (these must be peeled and cut in thin slices) in a greased baking tin; add the well-rinsed currants, a sprinkling of sugar, cinnamon, cloves, and **grated lemon peel**. Pour on the remaining butter, keeping a little to brush the top of the strudel. Roll the dough and bake in the oven. Serve hot.

738. Watermelon gelatin mold
GELO DI MELLONE

Ingredients:
- juice of two watermelons
- 1 ⅓ cups sugar
- ½ cup cornstarch

Cut the watermelons in pieces, remove peel and seeds, and pass through a food mill. Dissolve the starch in a little of the juice and add to the rest of the juice. Add the sugar and **a stick of cinnamon**, then heat, over low flame, stirring continuously. When the liquid boils and thickens to the right density, remove from the heat. Take out the cinnamon stick. Pour into molds, and at the center of each mold put:
- chips of bitter chocolate
- candied pumpkin peel

When the mixture has set, turn the molds out onto **grape leaves**, sprinkle with a little **powdered cinnamon**, and garnish with **4 or 5 fresh jasmine flowers**.

739. Strawberry gelatin mold
GELO DI FRAGOLE

Ingredients:

- 1 ¼ lb strawberries
- 1 ½ pint water
- 6 oz starch
- 1 lb sugar

Put the strawberries through a food mill and dilute with the water with starch. Add the sugar and continue as in the melon jelly recipe (number 538).

740. Angelic food
CIBO ANGELICO

Ingredients:

- 2 lb sliced bananas
- 4 peeled sliced oranges (remove the seeds)
- 1 sliced pineapple in syrup

Arrange these artistically on a dish, sprinkle with sugar, and pour on the pineapple juice with **½ cup cream.**

741. Baked bananas
BANANE AL FORNO

Bananas are highly nutritious and very easy to digest, which is why they are recommended for the sick or anyone of delicate constitution. The nutritional value of a banana is highest when it is fully ripe, and the best way to eat it is raw. There are, however, various ways to cook bananas, including baking. Cut off about ½ inch of each end of the **unpeeled bananas,** place the

unpeeled bananas in a tin, and bake for 15–20 minutes. The banana skins will turn crisp and split open. Serve hot with **grape or syrup.**

742. Mocha cake
TORTA MOKA

Ingredients:

- 1 ½ cup butter
- 4 egg yolks
- ¾ cup sugar
- 10 oz sponge cake
- ½ cup strong black espresso coffee

Amalgamate the sugar with the egg yolks for 10 minutes, then slowly add the softened butter and some of the coffee, stirring continuously. Cover the bottom of a broad shallow pan with slices of sponge cake, and cover the sides to a height of 1 inch. Put a quarter of the butter and egg mixture aside, and pour the remainder on the sponge, putting another layer of sponge cake on top, sprinkled with coffee. Let stand for a few hours and turn out onto a cake plate; cover with the rest of the butter and egg cream and garnish with **toasted coffee beans.**

743. Buttered apples
MELE AL BURRO

Preheat oven to 375°F.

Use a small, sharp knife to remove the central core of **6 apples;** the hole you make should not go all the way through to the bottom of the apple. Make a filling of **4 tbsp sugar,** and **a pinch of grated lemon zest.**

Grease a cake tin big enough to hold all 6 apples with plenty of **butter**. Put in the oven, adding sugar and butter twice during cooking.

744. Presnitz
PRESNITZ

Ingredients:

- 3 oz currants
- 3 oz shelled walnuts
- 1/3 cup sugar
- 2 oz bread
- 1 1/4 oz shelled almonds plus 3 bitter almonds
- 1 oz pine nuts
- 1 1/2 oz candied orange or lemon peel
- a pinch of mixed spices
- a pinch of salt
- 1/2 glass Marsala wine

Chop the pine nuts, walnuts, almonds, and candied fruit very fine. Add the bread after dipping it in the Marsala, and the currants. Wrap this mixture in **shortcrust pastry crust** (see recipes 541–542), and shape like a large doughnut. Brush with **egg yolk** and bake in a 350°F oven. When cold, sprinkle with:

- fine sugar
- cinnamon

745. Sicilian 'buccellato' (mincemeat)
BUCCELLATO SICULO

As for recipe 744, but add:

- 8 oz seedless Pantelleria raisins
- 8 oz dried figs chopped very fine

- a pinch of pepper
- 2 oz candied pumpkin cut in cubes
- some grated orange peel

746. Cherry soup
ZUPPA DI CILIEGIE

Cut some **bread** in small squares and fry in butter. Put some butter in a pan, melt, and gently fry **2 lb black cherries**, after removing the stalks and pits. Roll them in **flour**, return them to the pan, sprinkle with **sugar** to taste, add **2 pints water**, and cook. Pour into plates and add the pieces of fried bread.

747. Rita's cake
PASTA RITA

Use as much **flour**, **butter**, and **sugar** as the weight of **4 eggs**. Mix the flour with the butter, the yolks with the sugar, and whip the egg whites separately. Join all the ingredients, adding:

- 4 oz currants
- grated lemon peel

Pour into a smooth buttered mold and cook in a 350°F oven. When ready, sprinkle with **confectioner's sugar**.

748. English tea pastries
PASTINE INGLESI PER TÈ

Ingredients:

- 6 oz fine flour
- 6 oz potato flour
- 6 oz butter

2 egg whites
warm milk as required

On a pastry board make a little mound of the flours and sugar together. Make a cavity in the middle, pour in the egg whites and add little pieces of butter. Add the milk, mix into a paste and knead for about ½ hour. Roll out about ⅛ inch thick, and cut into disks with a glass. Prick with a toothpick or fork, and place on a buttered pan. Bake in a 350°F oven.

749. Candied watermelon
SPICCHIALETTO OD ANGURIA CANDITA

Cut a **watermelon** in large pieces and remove only the green skin, leaving the white. Remove as many seeds as you can, without breaking up the chunks of melon. Cover completely in **salt** and leave for 48 hours. Then rinse in cold water. Keep changing the water until it loses its salty taste. Then boil until the white flesh becomes soft and transparent, after which put it in cold water in the sun, making sure that all the white is well exposed. Let stand until little white specks appear. At this point remove from the water and place in the following hot syrup, for every pound of watermelon:

2 lb sugar
3 pints water
vanilla

When the water boils and the sugar has completely dissolved, remove from the heat and add the watermelon. Let stand for 24 hours, then remove the watermelon, and boil the liquid again, reducing it somewhat. Remove from the heat, replace the watermelon in the liquid, and leave

for another 24 hours. Repeat this process 4 times in all. This can be eaten immediately or, if you prefer it candied, you must let it dry in a well-ventilated place on a cane screen.

750. Bignés
BEGNETTE

In a pan, boil:

½ pint water
a little salt
4 tbsp of butter
an equal amount of sugar
grated lemon

When nearly boiling, remove from the heat and add:

6 oz flour

Stir to form a paste. Put back on the heat and stir rapidly, making sure it does not stick to the bottom of the pan, until the paste is smooth. It is ready when it stops sticking to your fingers, i.e. after about ten minutes. Leave to cool for a few minutes, break in an **egg** and work it in, stirring vigorously. Then break in another egg and repeat until you have used 5 in all plus 1 egg white. Keep stirring until it comes off the spoon easily. Finally, add the last stiffly beaten egg white. Allow to stand for 2 hours. Take spoonfuls of the mixture the size of a walnut and drop into a frying pan, one by one. You can also make these bignés in the oven, dropping the spoonfuls into a buttered dish and brushing the top with egg yolk. When cooked, cut open one side of the bigné and fill as you please, with **sweet or savory filling**, e.g. cream, whipped cream, jam, scrambled eggs, béchamel, or other.

751. Lady's kisses
BACI DI DAMA

Ingredients:
- ½ cup butter
- ½ cup flour
- ½ cup of sugar
- a drop of vanilla extract
- 2 oz peeled chopped almonds
- 1 egg
- 2 bitter almonds

Make a smooth paste and roll it out. Use a glass to cut out rounds and bake in the oven. When done, join the pieces together two by two, filling with the following mixture:
- 4 oz good-quality chocolate, melted
- 1 oz peeled chopped almonds and hazelnuts

752. Peach tarts
CROSTATA DI PESCHE

Cover the bottom of a cake tin or oven-proof dish with slices of **buttered bread**. Take some ripe **peaches** (the flesh should come away easily from the pits), cut in half, and without peeling, put them on the bread, skin side down, like so many little boats. Fill the centers with **sugar** and **a knob of butter**. Put the tart in a 350°F oven and bake. During baking, sprinkle sugar on the peaches twice. Also excellent made with apples.

753. Plum tarts
CROSTATA DI PRUGNE

As recipe 752, but use **red plums**.

754. Apricot tarts
CROSTATA DI ALBICOCCHE

As recipe 752, but use **apricots**.

755. Almond bread
PANE MANDORLATO

Ingredients:
- ½ cup potato flour
- ¾ cup sugar
- ½ cup butter
- 6 oz almonds
- 3 bitter almonds
- grated lemon peel

Peel the almonds in hot water, dry them and crush with one-third of the sugar. Mix **3 egg yolks** for 15 minutes with the rest of the sugar, add the remaining ingredients, and continue to stir, adding stiffly beaten egg white last of all. When the mixture is blended, pour into a mold lined with wax paper and bake in a 350°F oven.

756. Stuffed bread
PAN RIPIENO

Ingredients:
- 1 cup sugar
- ¾ cup flour
- 6 eggs

Stir the yolks with the sugar for 30 minutes, add the stiffly beaten whites, and pour in the flour, stirring continuously. Bake in a 350°F oven in a tin greased with butter and sprinkled with flour. Cut in half, spread with **jam**, and coat with sugar (see recipes 864–865).

757. D. E. A. S. bread (Duke Enrico Alliata of Salaparuta bread)

PAN D. E. A. S.

Ingredients:

- ½ cup butter
- ¾ cup sugar
- ¾ cup flour
- 8 oz raisins
- 8 oz dried currants
- 8 oz candied squash (see recipe 809)
- 6 oz almonds
- 2 bitter almonds
- 3 eggs
- a glass of Marsala wine

Peel and crush the almonds, clean the sultanas, remove pips from raisins, crush the candied squash, and mix everything together with the stiffly beaten egg whites, and the yolks, with the sugar. Pour in a buttered mold and bake at 350°F.

758. D. E. A. S. rice bread (Duke Enrico Alliata of Salaparuta rice bread)

PAN DI RISO D. E. A. S.

Make the same **batter** as in recipe 772, place in a buttered mold, and let rise in a warm place.

When well risen, cook over boiling water for about 3 hours. Serve with **grape syrup** (recipe 881) or any other syrup of your choice.

759. Citrus flavored bread

PAN CEDRATO

Ingredients:

- 1 cup flour
- 1 heaping tsp baking powder
- 1 cup powdered sugar
- 9 oz butter
- 4 oz dried currants
- 3 eggs
- grated peel of 2 lemons

Mix the flour in a bowl with the baking powder, and add the melted butter; whip the egg whites until stiff, adding the sugar and grated lemon. Stir rapidly, pour into a greased tube mold not more than two-thirds full, and bake in a 350°F oven for 45 minutes.

760. Sardinian bignés (also called 'zeppole')

SFINGE SARDEGNOLE O ZEPPOLE

Ingredients:

- 10 oz semolina
- 10 oz boiled potatoes put through a ricer
- ½ cup milk
- 2 eggs
- a little saffron
- ½ oz fresh yeast

Dissolve the yeast in a cup of milk and leave near

a source of heat for ½ hour. Crush a little saffron and dissolve in warm water. Mix together with the semolina and potato, and let rise in a warm place. When the mixture has fully risen, drop equal-sized spoonfuls into hot oil. Serve warm with a topping of **honey** or **hot syrup**, or sprinkle with **sugar** and **cinnamon**.

761. Pearly rice
RISO PERLATO

Choose the best quality **large-grained rice**, wash, and place in an oven-proof dish greased with butter. Add **2 cups of milk** for every cup of rice, and **½ cup of sugar** and **1 oz butter** for every 3 cups of rice. Place in a 350°F oven, cover with a metal lid and cook until all the liquid has been absorbed.

762. Tuscan 'mostarda' fritters
FRITTURA ALLA MOSTARDA TOSCANA

Make the following paste:

- **1 lb flour**
- **1 ½ oz butter**
- **enough milk to make a thick paste**

Stir and leave for 45 minutes; roll out ⅛ of an inch thick, cut out rounds with a glass, and on half of these spread some **"mostarda"** (see recipe 700), covering with the other rounds and wetting the edges with **egg white** to seal. Fry, sprinkle with:

- powdered sugar
- cinnamon

Serve cold.

763. Iris
IRIS

Make some **Duke of Salaparuta rolls** (see recipe 594), but fill with any **cream** you like. When fried, sprinkle with **sugar** and **cinnamon**.

764. Apples in batter
MELE IN PASTETTA

Take some big round **apples**, peel and remove the cores with a potato peeler. Cut in round slices, dip in **batter** (see recipes 539–540), and fry. Sprinkle with **sugar** and **aniseed** or **honey**.

765. Fried peaches
PESCHE IN FRITTURA

Use **peaches** which are not too ripe, cut them into segments, dip in **batter** (see recipes 539–540), and fry. Sprinkle with **sugar** and serve hot.

766. Kitchenmaid's fritters
LOSANGHETTE ALLA SGUATTERA

Ingredients:

- **6 oz semolina**
- **1 ¼ pints milk**
- **2 eggs**
- **4 oz sugar**
- **2 oz butter**

Boil the milk with the butter and sugar and pour in the semolina, stirring continuously. Add some **scraped lemon peel**, and when the mixture has thickened, break in the 2 eggs, stir vigorously, and spread ½ inch thick on a marble surface greased with butter. When the mixture cools, cut into square shapes, cover in **beaten egg**, roll in **bread crumbs**, and then fry. Serve warm with a topping of **grape syrup** (recipe 881) or **honey**.

767. Rice fritters
FRITTELLE DI RISO

Ingredients:
- 2 pints milk
- ½ lb rice
- ½ lb flour
- 4 oz sultanas
- 1 ½ oz yeast
- 2 oz butter
- 1 oz chopped pine nuts
- 6 egg yolks
- 2 egg whites
- 3 oz sugar
- grated lemon peel

Take the yeast and dissolve it in a small cup of milk, and let stand in a warm place for half an hour. Mix with 3 oz of flour and cook the rice with half the milk until the mixture is thick (if necessary, add more milk). Stirring continually, sprinkle the sugar in, remove from the heat, and when lukewarm add the yeast. Knead the paste, adding more milk if necessary. Leave in a basin in a warm place to allow time for the yeast to rise, and then drop spoonfuls into a frying pan. Serve hot, with a topping of **apples** or **grape syrup**.

768. Pancakes
PANCHECCHE

Ingredients:
- 1 pint milk
- 2 eggs
- 1 cup flour
- jam

Blend the flour in a bowl with the milk, adding a little at a time to avoid lumps, then add the eggs, after beating them well. Melt **a knob of butter** in a frying pan and pour in a cupful of the pancake batter. When cooked on one side, turn with the help of a spatula. With practice, pancakes can be flipped by raising the skillet quickly with a slight turn of the wrist. Put the fried pancakes in a plate and roll them with a jam filling. Sprinkle with **sugar** and with a hot spatula burn the sugar on the top to give a caramel effect. Pancakes can also be filled with marzipan, "cassata' cream, blancmange, etc.

769. Sweet krapfen
KRAPFEN DOLCI

Ingredients:
- ¾ lb fine flour
- 3 oz butter
- 2 oz yeast
- 2 whole eggs
- 2 egg yolks
- a pinch of saffron
- 4 oz sugar

In **a small cup of warm milk,** dissolve the yeast and saffron and leave in a warm place for ½ hour. Mix the remainder of the ingredients to a smooth paste. If this paste is too soft, add a little flour until it can be rolled to a ½ inch thickness. Using a glass or metal cutter, cut out 2-inch rounds. With three fingers make a hollow in each and fill with **3 or 4 bitter cherries** or other fruit preserves. Wet the edges and stick the other half of the pastry rounds on top. Leave to rise in a warm place, then fry. Serve warm with a sprinkling of sugar.

770. Neapolitan pastry
DOLCE DI NAPOLI

Ingredients:
- ¾ cup flour
- ¾ cup sugar
- 6 oz almonds
- 3 bitter almonds
- 6 eggs

Peel the almonds in hot water and leave to dry in a warm place. Split open one-third of the almonds and crush the other two-thirds. Beat the egg whites with the sugar for 15 minutes over a dying charcoal fire. Then add the flour and egg yolks. Pour into a buttered mold sprinkled with a mixture of 1 tsp sugar and 1 tsp flour. Bake in a 350°F oven and then cut in slices. Take **2 cups of vanilla cream** (see recipe 868) and while still hot spread on the cake slices, replacing them in the mold as they were before. Coat with a **sugar glaze** (see recipes 864–867), placing the remaining half-almonds on top, and complete with a sprinkling of crushed almonds.

771. Cream 'bombette'
BOMBETTE ALLA CREMA

Make the same batter as for **Florentine bombette** (see recipe 598), but filling with a **cream** of your choice (see "Creams"). Sprinkle with **sugar** and serve cold.

772. St Joseph's cream puffs
SFINGE DI S. GIUSEPPE

Make the same batter as for **Florentine bombette** (recipe 598), but drop larger quantities into the pan, using a soup spoon. Without cutting, fill with **ricotta cream** (recipe 874). Spread the cream on the top and add strips of **candied orange**.

773. Sicilian cassata
CASSATA ALLA SICILIANA

In a cone-shaped mold about 2 inches high and 12 to 14 inches wide (or any other dish of this size), place a number of squares of **sponge cakes** (2 inches square, 1 inch thick) around the sides, overlapping so they adhere well. Cover the bottom, making sure that all the pieces adhere, then fill with **ricotta cream** (see recipe 874), and cover more with slices of sponge cake. Turn out onto a plate and brush with a **sugar glaze coating** (recipes 864–867). Decorate with **candied fruit** and strips of **candied squash**.

774. Cream fritters
CREMA FRITTA

Prepare as for **milk fritters** (recipe 615), but

omitting the Parmesan and salt, and using:

    4 oz sugar
    some grated lemon

Fry in butter and oil or, better still, butter only.

775. Vanilla tidbits
BOCCONCINI ALLA VANIGLIA

Ingredients:

    1 qt milk
    5 oz semolina
    2 oz butter
    3 oz vanilla flavored powdered sugar
    6 eggs
    chopped candied squash
    orange peel

Boil the milk with the butter and sugar, and sprinkle in the semolina, stirring continuously. When the mixture thickens, remove from heat, add 2 eggs, and stir; continuing to stir, add the stiffly beaten egg whites and the 4 yolks. Drop spoonfuls into a frying pan and fry. Serve with a sprinkling of vanilla sugar. Vanilla tidbits are even more delicate if cooked in sweetened boiling milk and served with the milk after thickening with **starch** and **egg yolk**.

776. German bread
PAN GERMANICO

Ingredients:

    1 lb extra fine flour
    ¾ cup butter
    ¾ cup powdered sugar
    6 eggs
    1 cup milk

    vanilla
    1 tbsp baking powder

Stir the sugar, egg yolks and butter for 20 minutes, and then add the flour and milk, followed by the stiffly beaten egg whites. Pour the mixture immediately into a buttered mold and bake in a 350°F oven.

777. Genoese cake
PASTA DI GENOVA

Ingredients:

    ½ cup flour
    ⅔ cup potato flour
    12 eggs
    1 cup sugar
    ¾ cup butter
    grated peel of 1 lemon

Mix the yolks with the sugar and butter, and gradually add the two different flours and the grated lemon. Stir for 25 minutes and then add 7 of the stiffly beaten egg whites. Pour into a buttered mold and bake in a 350°F oven.

778. St Lucy's rice ('cuccìa')
RISO DI S. LUCIA (CUCCÌA)

Ingredients:

    2 ½ qt milk
    6 oz rice
    4 tbsp cornstarch
    ¾ cup sugar
    peel of 1 lemon
    chocolate or other flavoring

Dissolve the starch and sugar in cold milk, heat, and pour in the rice, stirring continuously until cooked. Grate the lemon peel and turn out onto a plate, and leave to cool. Scatter with chocolate flakes, squares of candied pumpkin, orange peel, etc., as you like.

779. Corn bread rolls
PANETTI DI MAIS

Ingredients:
- ¾ lb corn flour
- ½ cup wheat flour
- 4 oz seedless raisins
- 4 tbsp sugar
- 1 oz yeast
- 4 tbsp milk
- 3 oz butter

Using 2 oz of the flour dissolved in milk with the yeast, make a batter and leave to rise in a warm place. In the meantime mix the two flours with warm water, and blend all ingredients together (except the raisins); knead the mixture for 30 minutes, then add the raisins. Make small balls of dough of the same size and flatten slightly. With a knife-point scratch a square-shape on each. Leave to rise in a warm place and bake in a 350°F oven.

780. 'Straccetti' (rags)
STRACCETTI

Ingredients:
- 10 oz flour
- 1 oz butter
- 2 eggs
- 1 oz sugar

Mix the ingredients together, dampening and adding flour as necessary to make a fairly solid dough, which you must knead well and then let stand for half an hour. Roll out to a thickness of about ⅛ inch and cut into square shapes an inch long. Fry, and when cool sprinkle with **sugar** and **cinnamon**, or coat with **honey**.

781. Neapolitan 'pastiera' (Easter cake)
PASTIERA DI NAPOLI

Boil **1 cup wheat** that has been soaked in water for 12 hours, and when cooked, strain and place in a pan with:
- 2 ½ oz sugar

Heat slowly until the sugar has all been absorbed. Remove from the heat and mix with:
- 2 pints vanilla cream (recipe 868)
- stiffly beaten egg whites
- 2 oz diced candied zuccata
- 2 oz candied citron
- 2 oz diced candied orange peel
- a few drops of orange or lemon blossom flavoring

Make a layer of **shortcrust pastry** (see recipes 541–542), roll out in two sheets. Place one on the bottom of a cake tin, pour the mixture in, and cover with the remaining pastry, making a criss-cross pattern on top. Bake in a 350°F oven.

782. Italian cake
FOCACCIA ITALIANA

Ingredients:
- 1 cup flour
- ¼ cup sugar

⅓ cup extra virgin olive oil

1 tbsp yeast

1 ½ oz butter

6 eggs

½ tsp aniseed

½ cup muscatel or other sweet wine

½ cup orange blossom water

This recipe requires at least 2 days.

Day 1: leave to macerate in wine. Dissolve the yeast in a cup of warm water with a lump of sugar and leave near the stove to rise.

Day 2, morning: mix the yeast with half the flour, and make a loaf, covering with the remaining flour. After 6 hours add 3 eggs, 2 tbsp butter, 3 tbsp sugar, 3 tbsp wine, and the remaining flour. Leave to rise for 3 hours. Then add 5 eggs, 5 tbsp sugar, 5 tbsp each of oil and wine, and leave to rise again. When well risen, add the remaining ingredients. If the dough is too soft, add more flour. Make a large flat cake, place on a buttered dish, and allow to rise again. Coat with egg yolk and bake in a 350°F oven.

783. Sponge cake
PAN DI SPAGNA

Ingredients:

¾ cup fine sugar

3 tbsp extra fine flour

1 oz powdered starch

6 eggs

Mix the egg yolks with the sugar, then add the flour and after kneading for ½ hour pour in 2 tbsp of beaten egg white. Continue until you have added all the whites. Put in a square tin lined with wax paper and bake immediately.

784. German cake
FOCACCIA TEDESCA

Ingredients:

2 oz candied fruit

½ cup sugar

⅔ cup bread crumbs

¼ cup dried currants

4 eggs

grated peel of 1 lemon

Mix the egg yolks with the sugar for 15 minutes, then add the bread crumbs, raisins, and chopped candied fruit, and finally the stiffly beaten egg whites. Mix together, pour into a greased tin, and bake in a 350°F oven.

785. Tuscan sweet bread
PAN DOLCE TOSCANO

Ingredients:

1 lb flour

⅔ cup butter

⅔ cup sugar

⅔ cup raisins

5 eggs

1 tbsp cream of tartar

2 tbsp baking soda

½ cup candied fruit

grated peel of 1 lemon

1 ½ cup milk

Mix the butter with 3 whole eggs, the sugar, and 2 egg yolks, adding the flour and milk gradually, then the remaining ingredients, except those in powder. Stir for 30 minutes, adding flour if too runny. Add the baking soda and cream of tartar, pour in a greased mold, and bake immediately.

786. Bologna bread
PANE DI BOLOGNA

Ingredients:

- 1 lb flour
- ¾ cup powdered sugar
- 8 oz butter
- 4 oz raisins
- 2 oz chopped pine nuts
- 3 tbsp candied lime peel
- 2 tsp cream of tartar
- ¼ tsp baking soda
- 3 eggs
- ½ cup milk

Mix the sugar, flour, cream of tartar and baking soda together and make a mound on the pastry board. Make a well in the center and add the butter, eggs, and milk. Mix together with the pine nuts and pieces of candied fruit. Knead the dough for a while and then divide in two loaves. Coat with egg yolk, and bake at 350°F

787. Sicilian 'pasta reale' (marzipan)
PASTA REALE SICILIANA

Peel **2 lb almonds** in boiling water with **4 bitter almonds**. Crush well, dampening with a little **cinnamon water** (obtained by boiling cinnamon in water). When the almond paste is smooth cook with **2 lb sugar**, stirring continuously. When the paste thickens and the sugar has dissolved, remove from the heat. When cool enough to handle, scrape up in spoonfuls, making whatever shapes you like, and place a wafer on top. Coat the top with a **sugar glaze** (see recipes 864–867) and bake briefly in a 350°F oven. You can also fill with any fruit preserve of your choice. If you are artistic you can shape these almond sweets in the traditional shapes known as Martorana fruits.

"Martorana" comes from the name of the nuns in Palermo who were famous for their delicious and finely decorated marzipan.

788. Jellied quince
CONSERVA DI COTOGNE

Ingredients:

- 9 lb quinces
- 6 lb sugar

Boil the quinces and remove from the water when they begin to break open. Remove the skin and cores, and put through a food mill.

Heat again with the sugar, and keep stirring until the mixture begins to stick to the spoon when you pick it up. Put in molds and leave to dry for several days before removing.

789. Ginette
GINETTE

Mix:

- 1 lb fine flour
- ½ lb sugar
- 5 oz melted butter

Add as many **egg yolks** as are necessary to make a firm paste, and leave to stand in a warm place for 2 hours. Make little tarts and bake in a 350°F oven. Fill each with a **fruit preserve** of your choice and serve cold. You can fill them with **strawberries**—if they are in season—sprinkle with **sugar** and cover with **cream**.

790. Sicilian quince jellies
COTOGNATA SICILIANA

Peel and cut in small pieces:
> 6 ½ lb quinces

Boil for 15 minutes in:
> ½ pint water
> juice of ½ lemon

When well cooked, put through a food mill and cook again with **6 ½ lb sugar**, stirring constantly. When the mixture begins to thicken and comes off the spoon in sheets, put in low molds greased with butter. Turn out of the mold after a few days.

791. English marzipan
MARZAPANE INGLESE

Peel **20 oz almonds** in cold water along with **3 or 4 bitter almonds** and leave in cold water for 24 hours. Then dry and crush, dampening with **orange blossom water**. Make a syrup with:
> 2 ½ cups sugar
> ½ pint water

Boil until it spins a thread of syrup at least ½ inch long. Mix the almond paste in and return to heat, stirring continuously until the mixture is solid enough to handle. Sprinkle some fine sugar on a sheet of paper and roll the paste to ¼ inch thickness in the sugar. Cut into any shapes you like. Coat with a **sugar glaze** (recipes 864–867)

792. Pastry sandwiches
LIBRETTE DOLCI

Ingredients:
> ⅔ cup sugar
> 3 oz extra fine flour
> 1 ½ oz butter
> 4 egg yolks
> 3 egg whites
> grated peel of ½ lemon

Amalgamate the yolks with the sugar for 20 minutes, then add the flour and mix for another 20 minutes. Finally add the melted butter and stiffly beaten egg whites. Place on a tin and bake in a 350°F oven. When ready, cut in slices and spread each with a **fruit preserve** or **jam**, then close them like sandwiches.

793. Neapolitan sweet pizza
PIZZA DOLCE DI NAPOLI

Make a flaky pastry with:
> 9 oz flour
> 5 oz sugar
> 2 egg yolks
> 1 egg white

For the filling you need:
> 7 oz ricotta
> 3 oz almonds and 2 bitter almonds
> 3 oz sugar
> 2 egg yolks
> 1 egg white
> 2 ½ pints milk
> 1 oz flour
> grated lemon

Make a cream with the milk, flour, one egg yolk,

and the sugar. Then add the other whole egg, the ricotta, and the crushed almonds (having peeled them in hot water). Mix together briskly and use as a filling between two layers of the pastry. Coat with egg yolk and bake in a 350°F oven. Instead of egg you can sprinkle with:

- fine sugar
- cinnamon
- grated lemon

794. Sicilian bignés
SFINGE ALLA SICILIANA

Use **yeast batter** (see recipe 539) to make the bigné, dropping spoonfuls in boiling oil and moving it with your finger. You can also make ball shapes. Serve with a sprinkling of **sugar** or brushed with **honey**.

795. Duchess biscuits
GALLETTA DUCHESSA

As for recipe 579, but instead of salt, pepper, and parsley add:

- a small glass of cream
- 4 oz sugar

Immediately after cooking, sprinkle with **fine sugar** and **cinnamon**.

796. Crumble cake
DOLCE SFARINANTE

Ingredients:

- ½ lb sugar
- ½ lb butter
- 5 oz rice flour
- 5 oz powdered starch
- 2 ½ oz potato flour
- 4 eggs
- 2 tbsp lemon juice
- 1 tsp baking soda
- vanilla

Melt the butter, remove from heat, and stirring constantly, add the egg yolks one by one; add the sugar, and then the lemon juice. Finally, blend in the different flours and the stiffly beaten egg whites, and lastly the baking soda. Pour in a greased tin and bake in a 350°F oven.

797. D. E. A. S. tartlets (Duke Enrico Alliata of Salaparuta tartlets)
TARTINE D. E. A. S.

Make some flaky pastry with:

- 10 oz extra fine flour
- 5 oz butter
- 1 oz sugar
- a little grated lemon peel

Add enough water to make the dough manageable. Roll out to about ¼ inch thick and arrange in molds or little oven-proof dishes. Bake in the oven, remove when half-done, and fill with the following mixture:

- 3 oz peeled crushed almonds
- 4 oz sugar
- 3 bitter almonds
- 4 egg yolks

Bake at 350°F and then sprinkle with **sugar**.

798. Apple waffles
OFFELLE DI MELE

Ingredients:

- 1 ½ oz candied fruit
- 4 oz sugar
- 1 lb apples
- 1 tsp powdered cinnamon
- 1 ½ lb flour
- 4 oz butter
- 1 egg

Peel and slice the apples as thin as possible and cook in 2 cups of water, adding more if necessary, until the apples become a mush. Then add the sugar and finally the chopped candied fruit and cinnamon. Remove from heat when the mixture thickens. Make a flaky pastry with the flour, butter, and as little water as possible, just enough to allow you to roll the dough about ¼ of an inch thick and cut into disks. Put the apple mixture on the disks, and cover with another disk, using egg white to seal. Make crisscross patterns with a pastry wheel and coat with egg yolk. Bake in a 350°F oven and sprinkle with sugar.

799. Pistachio waffles
OFFELLE DI PISTACCHIO

As for recipe 798, but use the following mixture:

- 1 ¼ cups candied pumpkin rind
- 4 oz pistachios (peeled in hot water)

The pumpkin and pistachios must be well chopped and mixed.

800. 'Four-fourths' pistachio cake
QUATTRO QUARTI DI PISTACCHIO
ALLA SICILIANA

Ingredients:

- 5 eggs
- flour and sugar (each equal in quantity to the eggs)
- 1 cup pistachios
- 6 oz (blanched and sieved) spinach
- ¾ cup butter
- 1 tsp each of baking soda
- 1 tsp cream of tartar

Blend the yolks with the sugar for 15 minutes and then add the melted butter and flour, continuing to stir and gradually adding ¾ of the pistachios (peeled and diced). Add the sieved spinach, the stiffly beaten egg whites, and last of all the baking soda and cream of tartar. Bake at 350°F in a buttered mold that has been lined with wax paper. When done, remove from the mold and cover with a **sugar glaze** (recipes 864–867). Sprinkle with the remaining chopped pistachios, and put in the oven briefly to dry out.

801. Almond crunch
CROCCANTE DI MANDORLE

Ingredients:

- 6 oz almonds
- 4 oz sugar

Peel the almonds in hot water, dry, and split. Cut in 3 or 4 slivers, place in a dry frying pan to toast. Separately dissolve the sugar in a pan and when it liquefies, pour in the almonds and stir over a low flame. When the mixture begins to darken, pour into small greased tart tins. Press with a lemon to flatten. When cool, remove from the tins and fill the centers with **whipped cream**.

802. Almond buns
FOCACCE MANDORLATE

Ingredients:
- **6 oz sugar**
- **6 oz almonds**
- **2 ½ oz potato flour**
- **3 eggs**
- **2 small oranges**

Mix the egg yolks with the sugar for 15 minutes, adding the flour, and then the almonds (which have been peeled in hot water and crushed with 1 tbsp sugar). Add the juice of the oranges, and the grated peel of one. Lastly, add the stiffly beaten egg whites, pour into molds (you can use paper muffin cups), and cook in a moderate oven. Add a **sugar glaze** (see recipes 867–867), and leave the mixture to dry in a 350°F oven.

803. Ravioli in wine
FRITTO DI-VINO

Make **ravioli pasta** (see recipe 536). Roll out about to the thickness of a coin and spoon on the following paste, which you need to prepare beforehand. In **1 pint red wine**, dissolve:
- **3 oz starch**
- **6 oz sugar**

Cook for at least ½ hour, stirring continually. Make the ravioli, turning the edges over and pinching them closed with your fingers. Fry and sprinkle with **sugar**. Serve hot.

804. Egg white puffs
UOVA ALLA NEVE

In a pan, boil:
- **1 qt milk**
- **6 oz sugar**
- **vanilla**

Break **7 eggs** and separate the yolks. Beat the whites until stiff, adding **1 oz powdered sugar**. Take spoonfuls of the egg white and drop into the boiling milk, turning over once. Remove and drain in a sieve. After cooking all the whites, remove the milk from the heat, strain, and add the liquid that has drained off the egg white balls. Put the milk in a saucepan over a low flame and thicken with the egg yolks. Before it boils pour over the whites, in a serving dish. Sprinkle with **grated chocolate**. Serve cold.

805. Belgian fried apples
MELE FRITTE ALLA BELGA

Peel the **apples**, slice ½ inch thick, remove cores, dip in **egg** and **cognac**, coat with **flour**, and fry in **butter**. Sprinkle with **sugar** and serve hot.

806. Chilean delicacies
MANICARETTI CILENI

Make the **pastry** described in recipe 542. Roll out ¼ an inch thick, line some small tart tins with the dough, and bake in a 350°F oven. When ready, spread with **blancmange** (recipe 849), and sprinkle with **grated chocolate**.

807. Milk 'panzarotte'
PANZAROTTE DI LATTE

Make the **pastry** described in recipe 536. Knead thoroughly and roll to a thickness of a coin. Place spoonfuls of **blancmange** (recipe 849) on the pastry crust about 3 inches from one another and cover with another layer of pastry. Cut with a pastry wheel. Fry and sprinkle with **fine sugar**.

808. Fried egg surprise
UOVA IN SORPRESA

Put some **whipped cream** in a small frying pan. Spread the cream out and put **2 half-apricots** on top. Pour some **syrup** on like melted butter. When you serve, bring the pan to the table so that the apricots will be taken for two fried eggs.

809. Candied squash ('zuccata')
ZUCCATA

For this recipe you need **white squash** or **long zucchini** or even the **white rind of watermelons**. Prepare as in recipe 749. It is very useful to have some of this on hand to decorate cakes and other sweet dishes.

810. 'Panzarotte' with jam
PANZAROTTE CON CONSERVA

Make a **shortcrust pastry** (see recipes 541–542), roll out ½ an inch thick, spoon on some **jam** or **ricotta cream** (recipe 874), fold over, and cut around each filling with a pastry wheel. Bake in a 350°F oven and sprinkle with **sugar**.

811. Mountaineer's 'buccellati'
BUCCELLATI MONTANARI

Make a pastry with:
- **10 oz flour**
- **4 oz butter and oil** (half and half—better still if you use all butter)
- **2 oz sugar**
- **4 egg yolks**
- **as much water as you need to make a thick paste**

Separately prepare the following filling:
- **1 lb dried figs**
- **4 oz almonds**
- **1 ¾ cups seedless raisins**

Mince everything together with some **candied orange peel**. Add:
- **a good pinch of pepper**
- **4 ground cloves**
- **a glass of Marsala wine**
- **5 oz candied 'zuccata' in little pieces** if you want the filling even richer

Fill the pastry and form shapes (fish, doughnuts, etc.). Cover with a **sugar glaze** (recipes 864–867), and bake in a 350°F oven.

812. Hazelnut bomb
BOMBA DI NOCCIUOLE

Ingredients:

 1 cup sugar
 2/3 cup rice flour
 5 oz butter
 3 oz peeled hazelnuts
 3 oz peeled almonds
 3 bitter almonds
 4 whole eggs
 1 egg yolk

Peel the almonds and nuts in hot water, dry, crush finely, and mix with the flour. Beat the egg whites, adding some sugar, and when well blended, add the nut and flour mixture together with the egg yolks and melted butter. Blend these ingredients thoroughly, place in a greased tube mold, and bake in a 350°F oven. Make **sugar glaze** (recipes 864–867) and place toasted hazelnuts on top. Put in a hot oven to dry out.

813. Wafers
CIALDONI

Ingredients:

 3 oz flour
 1 oz sugar
 2 tbsp soft butter
 7 tbsp cold water

Slowly dissolve the sugar and flour in the water, and then add the butter. Pour ½ tbsp of the batter in a hot wafer iron, close the iron, and put both sides of the wafer over the fire. Trim off the edges, open the iron, peel off one side and roll it around a cane tube before it cools. Fill with **cream** or freshly made **whipped cream**.

814. Tea cakes
PASTINE DA TÈ

Ingredients:

 1 cup extra fine flour
 ½ cup potato flour
 ½ cup sugar
 ¼ lb butter
 1 egg white
 milk as required

Mix the flour and sugar and form a mound on the pastry board. Form a cavity in the center and put the egg white and melted butter in. Mix adding enough milk to make a fairly soft pastry dough. Roll out as thinly as possible, cut rounds with a glass, prick holes with a toothpick, and bake in a 350°F oven on a buttered cookie sheet.

815. Almond cakes
AMARETTI

Ingredients:

 5 oz almonds
 10 oz powdered sugar
 1 oz bitter almonds
 2 egg whites

Peel the almonds, dry them, and chop up finely. Beat the egg whites with the sugar for 15 minutes, add the almonds, and make little walnut-sized balls. Flatten these, place on a buttered cookie sheet, sprinkle with flour, and cook in a 350°F oven.

816. Cocoa almond cakes
AMARETTI AL CACAO

Same as recipe 815, but adding **12 oz cocoa**.

817. Novara cookies
BISCOTTINI DI NOVARA

Beat together:

2 egg yolks

6 whole eggs

1 lb sugar

Then add:

1 lb flour

Pour spoonfuls of the mixture onto a buttered baking sheet, making finger shapes. Sprinkle with **sugar** and bake in a 400°F oven.

818. Custard
BERLINGOZZO DOLCE (CUSTARD)

In **1 pint milk**, dissolve:

2 tbsp cornstarch

2/3 cup sugar

a little vanilla

Stir into a smooth cream over a low heat. Beat **6 eggs** and mix with the cream. Pour into a buttered mold sprinkled with crushed sweets and place the mold in boiling water.

819. Mocha gelatin mold
GELÈA DI MOKA

Same as **cream jelly** (recipe 821), but without lemon; in place of the milk use **1 cup of strong black espresso**.

820. Blackcurrant gelatin mold
GELÈA DI RIBES

Ingredients:

1 lb blackcurrants

3/4 cup sugar

1 oz gelatin

1 cup water

vanilla extract

Same method as for sour cherries. (Note: Today few gelatin products are vegetarian. However, groceries sometimes carry Kosher gelatins, which are vegetarian.)

821. Cream gelatin mold
GELÈA DI PANNA

Ingredients:

6 oz sugar

8 oz whipped cream

1 oz gelatin

2 cups milk

3 lemons

Cut the lemons peel and squeeze it on the sugar. Leave the gelatin strips to soften in water, then drain and mix with the sugar and the milk over a low flame. This done, leave it to cool, and mix with the cream. Pour into a mold and freeze. To turn the jelly out of the mold, place for a moment in boiling water, and turn over. (See note above about vegetarian gelatin.)

822. Orange gelatin mold
GELÈA D'ARANCE

Ingredients:

4 oranges

2 oz gelatin strips (or powder)

1 cup sugar

1 ¼ cups water

1 lemon

Leave the gelatin in water to soften. Peel the oranges and squeeze the peel onto the sugar, then boil it in half the water with the juice of the oranges, and strain. Remove the gelatin strips from the water and boil with other half of the water. When it has dissolved, add to the syrup. Put in a mold and put in the refrigerator to set. (See note in recipe 821 about vegetarian gelatin.)

823. Sour cherry gelatin mold
GELÈA D'AMARENA

Ingredients:
- 1 lb sour cherries
- 1 cup sugar
- 1 ½ oz gelatin
- 2 cups water

Squeeze the cherries, crushing a few pits, and leave to macerate for 2 hours. Then squeeze the juice through a clean cloth. Heat and dissolve the sugar for 10 minutes in half the water and squeeze through the cloth again. Remove the gelatin strips from the water where they have been softening and dissolve in the remaining water over a low flame. Put all the ingredients together, pour in a mold, and put in the refrigerator to set. (See note in recipe 821 about vegetarian gelatin.)

824. Tangerine gelatin mold
GELÈA DI MANDARINO

Same recipe as for **orange gelatin mold** (recipe 822), but use:
- 10 tangerines

Leave the peel whole, removing the flesh through a hole cut in the top. Pour the gelatin into the empty skins and leave to set in the refrigerator. When serving, replace the tops of the tangerines so that they look like fresh fruits.

Ice cream and parfaits

GELATI E SORBETTI DI CUOCO

825. Apricot parfait
PERFETTO DI ALBICOCCHE

Ingredients:

- 1 pint cream
- 1 lb sugar
- 1 lb fresh or tinned apricots

Heat half the cream in a double boiler and when hot add the sugar, stirring until it dissolves. Remove from heat, and when cool add the rest of the cream, and put in the refrigerator to set. Peel and crush the apricots, and mix with the refrigerated cream. Stir quickly for 5 minutes, placing the container in a bucket of ice.

826. Banana parfait
PERFETTO DI BANANA

Ingredients:

- 8 bananas
- 1 pint cream
- 1 cup sugar

Peel and crush the bananas. Pour one-half the cream into a saucepan and heat over a low flame. When hot, add the sugar, mixing until well dissolved. Remove from heat, and when cool add the mashed bananas, making a smooth paste, then add the remaining cream. Pour into a mold and freeze.

827. Tangerine parfait
PERFETTO DI MANDERINI

Ingredients:

- 1 pint cream
- 1 lb sugar
- juice of 12 tangerines
- grated peel of 2 tangerines

Heat half the cream in a double boiler. When hot add the sugar, mixing until it dissolves. Remove from heat, and when cool add the tangerine juice and grated peel along with the remaining cream, stirring continually. Place in the freezer.

828. Lemon parfait
PERFETTO DI LIMONE

Ingredients:

- 1 pint cream

1 lb sugar

juice of 3 lemons

juice of 1 orange

grated peel of 3 lemons

Mix the sugar, lemon juice and grated peel and the orange juice and leave for one hour in a cold place. Partially freeze the cream, then add the lemon juice and sugar, which must be completely dissolved. Stir well and freeze.

829. Orange parfait
PERFETTO DI ARANCE

Ingredients:

1 pint cream

1 lb sugar

juice of 6 oranges

1 grated orange peel

Heat half the cream in a double boiler, and when hot add the sugar, stirring steadily until it dissolves.

Remove from heat. Add juice and orange peel, with the rest of the cream, mixing carefully. Freeze.

830. Peach parfait
PERFETTO DI PESCHE

Ingredients:

1 pint cream

1 lb sugar

1 lb ripe peaches (canned peaches can be used)

Slice the peaches and heat them in the sugar, making a syrup. Cool, pour in the cream, mix well and freeze.

831. Pineapple parfait
PERFETTO DI ANANAS

Ingredients:

1 pint cream

1 lb sugar

juice of 1 lemon

1 ripe pineapple (or canned)

Heat half the cream in a double boiler with half the sugar. Mix until the sugar melts, and remove from the heat. When cold, add the peeled pineapple diced into small chunks, and add the remainder of the sugar and cream along with the lemon juice. Mix vigorously, and then freeze.

832. Strawberry parfait
PERFETTO DI FRAGOLE

Ingredients:

1 pint cream

1 lb sugar

1 ¾ lb strawberries

Same as for apricots, recipe 825.

833. Watermelon parfait
PERFETTO DI MELLONE

Ingredients:

1 lb of watermelon pulp, without rind or seeds

Dice and prepare as for banana parfait, recipe 826.

834. Toasted almond parfait
PERFETTO DI MELLONE

Ingredients:

- 1 ½ pints cream
- 1 lb sugar
- 6 oz peeled almonds
- 1 tbsp caramel
- 1 tbsp vanilla sugar

Peel and toast the almonds, and then crush them. Steam half the cream with the sugar, stirring until it dissolves, and then add the remaining cream and the almonds. When cold, add the caramel and vanilla. Freeze.

~~~~~~~~~~

835. Hazelnut parfait
PERFETTO DI MELLONE

Follow above recipe.

836. Pistachio parfait
PERFETTO DI PISTACCHI

Ingredients:

- 1 ½ pints cream
- 1 lb sugar
- ½ lb spinach
- a drop of almond extract
- 1 heaping tbsp vanilla sugar
- ½ lb peeled pistachios

Wash the spinach and boil vigorously for 10 minutes. Drain well, and then squeeze and press the spinach. Peel the pistachios and reduce to paste. Continue as for toasted almond parfait, recipe 834.

837. Fresh coconut parfait
PERFETTO DI COCCO FRESCO

Ingredients:

- 1 ½ pints cream
- 1 lb sugar
- 1 tsp vanilla extract
- grated coconut

Cook half the cream in a double boiler, adding the sugar and stirring until it dissolves. Remove from heat, and when cold add the remaining cream, vanilla, and coconut. Freeze.

838. Walnut parfait
PERFETTO DI NOCI

Ingredients:

- 1 ½ pints cream
- 1 lb sugar
- 10 oz peeled walnuts
- 1 tsp caramel
- 1 tbsp vanilla sugar

Same as for toasted almond parfait (see recipe 834).

839. Mocha or chocolate parfait
PERFETTO DI MOKA O DI CIOCCOLATA

Ingredients:

- 1 pint cream
- 3 oz finely ground coffee
- 1 lb sugar

Make 2 cups strong espresso coffee and put aside. Cook half the cream in a double boiler and dissolve the sugar in it. Remove from heat and add the rest of the cream and the coffee. Freeze in the usual way. For chocolate parfait, instead of coffee use 2 cups of chocolate and reduce the sugar to 12 oz.

840. Chocolate cream
CREMA DI CIOCCOLATA

Ingredients:

- 1 qt milk
- 8 oz fine chocolate
- 6 oz sugar
- 4 tsp potato starch

Grate the chocolate and heat with the sugar and milk in a pan where you have dissolved the potato starch. Stir over a gentle heat until it thickens and pour into pudding cups. Allow to cool, then freeze.

841. Toffee ice cream
GELATO TORRONCINO

Ingredients:

- 1 qt milk
- 10 oz sugar
- 5 oz almond cakes
  (see recipe 815)
- 6 egg yolks
- 4 oz candied zuccata

Put the sugar, egg yolks, and a little **vanilla** in a pan and stir for 10 minutes. Then add the milk little by little and heat gently, stirring continually, until you get a smooth cream. Cool and make the parfait, but first add the candied zuccata in small pieces and the crushed almond cakes.

842. Roman punch
PONCIO ALLA ROMANA

Ingredients:

- 3 oranges
- 1 lb sugar
- 2 lemons
- 2 pints water
- 2 egg whites
- vanilla as needed

Heat 10 oz of the sugar for 5 minutes with two-thirds of the water, adding:

- a little grated orange
- lemon peel

Remove from heat, add the juice of the oranges and lemons, filter, and pour into the ice-cream machine. Cook the rest of the sugar with the remaining water until it spins a thread when you take a drop between two fingers. Pour over the stiffly beaten egg whites, and stir to make a smooth paste. Blend with the other mixture you have prepared, and then freeze.

843. Tea ice cream
PONCIO ALLA ROMANA

Ingredients:

- 1 oz tea
- 12 oz whipped cream
- 5 oz sugar
- 4 egg yolks
- 1/2 pint water
- 4 gelatin

Steep the tea in boiling water, and keep it hot (but not boiling) for 30 minutes. Separately beat the yolks for 15 minutes with the sugar, and then slowly pour the tea in, through a cheesecloth. Continue to heat until the mixture binds. Add the gelatin and allow to cool. Add the whipped cream, and freeze. (See note in recipe 821 about vegetarian gelatin.)

Marmalades, Jams, Jellies and Candied Fruit

MARMELLATE, CONSERVE E GELATINE

844. Tangerine marmalade
MARMELLATA DI MANDERINI

Boil **tangerines** until they are tender enough to be pierced easily with a fork. Drain them, then pour in fresh water and let sit for two days, changing the water twice a day. When they are ready, cut the fruit into quarters, take out all the seeds and slice into wafer-thin slices. Weigh and add an **equal quantity of sugar**, then place the tangerines and sugar in a saucepan and boil until you can spin a ½-inch thread from a drop of the syrup. Remove from the flame but allow to macerate in the saucepan for a day, then boil for another 15 minutes and put in sterilized jars.

845. Citron marmalade
MARMELLATA DI CEDRI

Follow recipe 848.

846. Lime marmalade
MARMELLATA DI LIMETTE

Follow the recipes for oranges (850 and 851), and during cooking add the **juice of one lemon** for every pound of fruit.

847. Bergamot marmalade
MARMELLATA DI BERGAMOTTI

Follow the recipe for tangerines, 844.

848. Green lemon marmalade
MARMELLATA DI LIMONI VERDELLI

Follow the recipe for orange marmalade (850), choosing **lemons** which have not yet ripened. Add the **juice of one ripe lemon** for each pound of fruit while cooking.

849. 'Manjar blanco' (milk jam)
MARMELLATA DI LIMONI VERDELLI

For every **quart of fresh milk**, add **1 lb sugar** and cook the liquid over a low flame. Stir occasionally, always in the same direction and with the same wooden spoon until it thickens (about four hours of cooking). This can be preserved like marmalade and is even more flavorful and nourishing. "Panzarote" (see recipe 807) and other sweets can be made with this filling.

850. Bitter orange marmalade
MARMELLATA DI ARANCE AMARE

Take **6 bitter oranges** and boil until well cooked (when they can be pierced easily with a fork). Drain and place in cold water for 2 days, changing the water twice a day. Cut in half, take out the seeds and slice in wafer-thin slices. Weigh the fruit and add **1 ½ lb sugar** for every pound of oranges. Cook over a low flame without water. When a drop of the syrup spins a ½-inch thread, cooking is complete. Leave for 24 hours, then boil for another 15 minutes and store in sterilized jars.

851. Sweet orange marmalade
MARMELLATA D'ARANCE DOLCI

Take **6 oranges** and puncture with a fork. Place in water at room temperature for 2 days, changing the water twice a day. Then cut the oranges in half and finally in ½-inch slices, and take out the seeds. Place in a saucepan on low heat, adding:

an equal quantity of sugar

a sliced lemon

Stir continually. When a drop of the syrup spins a ½-inch thread, they are ready. Leave for a day and then boil another 15 minutes and preserve in sterilized jars.

852. Apricot jam
MARMELLATA D'ALBICOCCHE

Remove the pits and cut the fruit in half. Weigh and place in a saucepan with an **equal quantity of sugar**. When a drop of the syrup spins a thread ½-inch long, turn off the flame and allow the fruit to sit for 24 hours. Boil 15 minutes more and store in sterilized jars.

853. Pear jam
CONSERVA DI PERE

Choose unbruised and **fully ripe pears**, then cut in half and remove the skins, cores and stems. Leave to steep in their own juice for 24 hours, alternating the pears with layers of **sugar** (9 oz for every pound of raw fruit). Then place the saucepan over the flame, stirring carefully so as not to break the fruit pieces. Boil until syrup spins a ½-inch thread and add **grated lemon rind**.

854. Blueberry jam
CONSERVA DI MORE

Measure **half the quantity of sugar** in relation to the amount of uncooked fruit. Cook for an hour, stirring and pressing with a wooden spoon. Preserve in sterilized jars.

855. Strawberry and currant jam
CONSERVA DI FRAGOLE CORINZIANA

Ingredients:
- **2 lb strawberries**
- **3 lb dried currants**
- **3 lb sugar**

Clean the fruit well, add the sugar and currants and cook for 20 minutes.

856. Pistachio preserves
CONSERVA DI PISTACCHIO

Shell and peel the **pistachios** in boiling water, then chop and weigh. Combine with an **equal quantity of chopped 'zuccata'** (candied squash, see recipe 809).

857. Candied orange rind
CONSERVA DI ARANCE

Put the **candied orange rind** in a chopper with equal quantities of **zuccata** (recipe 809).

858. Candied citron rind
CONSERVA DI CEDRO

Follow above recipe.

859. Candied tangerine rind
CONSERVA DI MANDERINO

Follow recipe 857.

860. Sterilized grape syrup
SCIROPPO D'UVA STERILE

Press the **grapes** to obtain 3 quarts of must and boil this until it has evaporated to half the quantity. Let drip through a cheesecloth filter until it is transparent, then add **2 lb of sugar** and put back on the fire until the syrup spins a ½-inch thread when drawn from a ball between your fingers.

861. Apple jelly
GELATINA DI MELE

Take **6 lb of apples**, red ones if possible, and wash them without peeling or cutting. Break them open and take out the cores then place in a saucepan with enough water to cover and boil for 1 hour. If they should dry up, add enough water to stir easily. Allow them to drain in a strainer overnight and add:
- **1 lb sugar for every cup of liquid**
- **a few drops of lemon juice**

Boil the syrup for 45 minutes, skimming off the foam that forms on the top.

862. Neapolitan medlars in gelatin
AZZERUOLE IN GELATINA

Choose large fruits and remove the pits by slicing off the tops with the tip of a knife, leaving the remaining fruit whole. Blanch in hot water until they can be peeled, then prepare a syrup with **2 lb sugar** to **3 cups water**. When this has come to a boil, throw in the fruit and cook for 10 minutes. Remove from the flame and leave for 24 hours, then boil again until the syrup thickens.

863. Tuscan 'mostarda'
MOSTARDA TOSCANA

Ingredients:

7 lb sweet grapes
3 ½ lb apples
1 lb pears
4 tbsp mustard powder
a pinch of grated lemon peel
6 oz candied citron
1 glass of sweet wine

Press the grapes and squeeze through a cheese-cloth. Peel and slice the apples and pears. Place them over a low flame in a saucepan with the wine and when this has evaporated, add the must. When the liquid is dense, add the finely diced candied citron and stir in the mustard powder dissolved in hot wine. Preserve in sterilized jars.

Frostings, Creams, Glazes and Syrups

CREME, SCIROPPI E VELATE

864. Uncooked sugar glaze
VELATA DI ZUCCHERO A FREDDO

Ingredients:

- 1 oz sugar
- 1 egg white
- 1 tsp lemon juice

Beat all the ingredients together and when they have reached a syrup-like consistency, pour over the cake and allow to harden in contact with the air.

865. White sugar frosting
VELATA DI ZUCCHERO BIANCA COTTA

In a pan, combine:

- 9 oz sugar
- ½ cup water

Bring sugar and water to a boil and when it sticks to your fingers without making a thread (or when the water has evaporated and no more steam rises from the pan), remove from the fire and stir in **1 tsp of lemon juice**. Spread rapidly on the cake before it hardens.

866. Pink and green sugar frosting
VELATA DI ZUCCHERO ROSA E VERDE COTTA

Follow the above recipe, using **food coloring** to add the color.

• • • • • • • • • • • •

867. Brown sugar frosting
VELATA DI ZUCCHERO BRUNA COTTA

In a pan, combine:

- 2 oz grated chocolate
- 3 tbsp water

Melt the chocolate, then add:

- 4 oz powdered sugar

Cook over a slow flame, stirring continually. When you can take a drop between your fingers and spin a ½-inch thread, remove from the flame and allow to cool by placing the pan in water and stirring. When it begins to form an opaque crust, spread on the cake, and place in the oven for 2 or 3 minutes.

868. Milk and vanilla cream
CREMA DI LATTE ALLA VANIGLIA

In **1 quart milk** dissolve **3 oz cornstarch**; beat in:
- **4 egg yolks**
- **5 oz sugar**
- **1 tsp vanilla**

Place on a very low flame and stir continually until it has reached the desired consistency.

869. Chocolate cream
CREMA ALLA CIOCCOLATA

Follow the above recipe, but instead of vanilla, add a **grated chocolate bar**.

870. Uncooked coffee cream filling
CREMA AL CAFFÈ A FREDDO

Combine:
- **4 egg yolks**
- **5 oz sugar**

Beat for 15 minutes, then add:
- **9 oz butter** which has been softened

Continue stirring and pour in **a cup of strong black coffee** a little at a time. This is excellent as a cream filling in pastries, or spread on cookies, cakes, etc. and can be garnished with whole coffee beans, chocolate chips or other.

871. Almond and hazelnut cream
CREMA DI MANDORLE O DI NOCCIUOLE

Follow the above recipe, omitting the coffee and adding **4 oz toasted crushed almonds** or **hazelnuts**.

872. Cream of citron
CREMA CEDRATA

Follow recipe 868, omitting the vanilla and scraping the **rind of two citrons** or, if not available, substitute with three lemons.

873. Cream of curacao
CREMA AL CURACAO

Follow recipe 868, omitting the vanilla and scraping in **the peel of two bitter oranges** or **3 sweet oranges**.

874. Ricotta cream filling for cannoli, Sicilian cassate, etc.
CREMA DI RICOTTA PER CANNOLI, CASSATE, ECC.

In **1 cup cold milk** dissolve:
- **1 tbsp cornstarch**

Then add:
- **9 oz powdered sugar**

Place on a low flame until it coagulates. Remove from the fire and add:
- **12 oz fresh ricotta**

Stir briskly and put through a fine food mill. Season with **cinnamon** (it is best to soak a stick of cinnamon in the milk as it cooks) or **chocolate** (adding 3 oz of grated or powdered chocolate to the milk) or with **vanilla** or **strong black coffee** (1 espresso cupful) or with **citron** (scraping the peels of two lemons) or **pistachios** (shelled, crushed and added at the end). To make the cannoli shells, see recipe 544, and recipe 773 for the cassata. This filling can also be used in the traditional San Giuseppe pastries (recipe 772).

875. Sugar syrup
SCIROPPO NEUTRO

In **1 cup water**, dissolve:

3 lb sugar

Stir continually. In a separate dish, beat together:

1 egg white

½ cup of water

Pour this into the sugar syrup gradually until the foam comes to the surface. Filter through a cheesecloth and cook briefly, then preserve in jars.

876. Cherry syrup
SCIROPPO DI CILIEGIE

Remove the seeds from **cherries** that are not overripe, crush and leave to soak in their own juice for 24 hours. Then put through a food mill and, finally, allow to drip through a cheesecloth filter bag until the juice is transparent. Then measure and add:

2 lb sugar for every 2 ½ cups liquid

Place over a low flame and bring to a boil, skimming off the foam. Remove from the fire and allow to cool, then bottle.

877. Redcurrant syrup
SCIROPPO DI RIBES

Crush **currants** and allow them to ferment by macerating in their own juice for a few days, stirring them twice a day. The fermentation is complete when the fruit will no longer float to the surface. Filter through a cheesecloth, then measure the liquid. For every quart of juice, add:

3 lb sugar

Place over a low flame, stirring continually. Boil for 2 or 3 minutes skimming off the foam, then let cool and bottle.

878. Blueberry or black mulberry syrup
SCIROPPO DI MORE O CELSE NERE

In a pan, combine:

2 lb blueberries or black mulberries

2 lb confectioner's sugar

Place over a medium flame without crushing the fruit, stir frequently. When the sugar has dissolved, boil briefly, then pour into a strainer and drain off the juice which can be bottled.

879. Orange and lemon syrup
SCIROPPO D'ARANCE E LIMONI

Combine:

1 pint of sugar syrup (recipe 875)

the rinds of 6 oranges

the rinds of 3 lemons

Let soak for 24 hours, then add:

the juice from the oranges and lemons

1 qt water

Allow to drip through a cheesecloth filter. Put **3 lb sugar** in a saucepan with the liquid, place on the fire and let dissolve while stirring continually. Boil to the desired consistency, and then bottle.

880. Barley syrup
ORZATA

Ingredients:

7 oz pearl barley

4 oz almonds

3 bitter almonds

3 qt water

1 ¾ lb sugar

Boil the barley in the water and when it has reduced to one-half the original quantity, remove from the fire. Crush the almonds and add to the cooled liquid, then filter, add the sugar and boil for 20 minutes. Bottle as soon as it has cooled.

881. Grape syrup (sapa)
SCIROPPO D'UVA (SAPA)

Make a must of the **grapes** by crushing the ripe fruit, then filter through a cheesecloth and let boil for several hours until it has evaporated to one-third of the original quantity. Allow to cool and bottle.

882. Black cherry syrup
SCIROPPO D'AMARENE

Remove the stems from the **cherries** and crush, taking out the pits. Allow the fruit to macerate for 48 hours together with the 10 pits, crushed to a fine pulp. Then press and filter through a cheesecloth. Put this clear liquid in a pot with:

4 ½ lb sugar for each 3 pints of juice

Boil for five minutes, skimming off the foam, and bottle when cool.

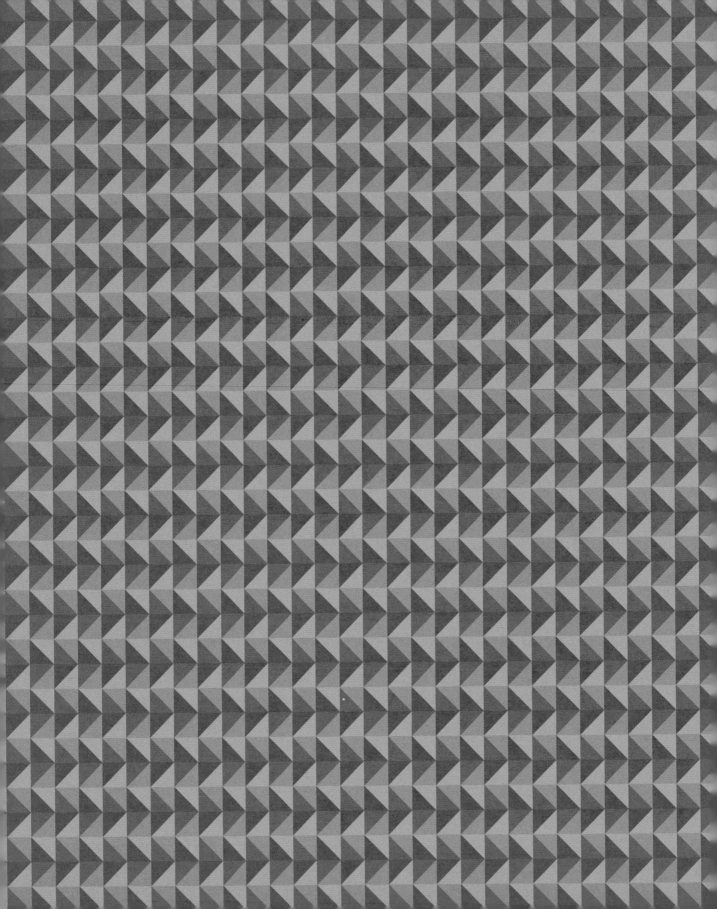

Miscellaneous

883. Pickled green olives (to be eaten within a month of picking)

OLIVE BIANCHE NUOVE

Choose large, unspotted **olives** which are not overripe, and break the pulp with a mortar or smooth stone, being careful not to smash the pit. Place them in water for 3 days, changing the water morning and evening, and the fourth day put them in **brine**. They can be eaten 4 to 6 days later, prepared in the following manner: remove the pits and place in fresh water for 30 minutes, then drain and season with:

> **fennel seed**
> **oregano**
> **garlic** or **parsley**

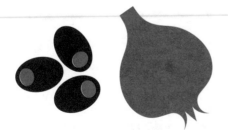

884. Pickled green olives in brine (can be kept for the entire year)

OLIVE BIANCHE IN SALAMOIA

For every **2 lb of choice green olives,** you will need:

> **2 lb ashes of burned wood** (not coal ashes)
> **3 oz salt**
> **⅓ cup water**

Mix the ashes with 1 quart water to make a mush in which to bury the olives, covering them with a weight (such as a board). Leave for 10 to 15 hours, and remove the olives when they have softened. Then place in fresh water for 4 or 5 days, changing the water morning and evening. Boil the salt in ⅓ cup water and when it has cooled, place the olives in this brine and preserve in an earthenware urn.

885. Pickled black olives

OLIVE NERE

Choose the variety that turns black on the tree and when very ripe, place them in a basket in alternate layers with **salt** and **rosemary**. Then cover with a weight (such as a heavy board). After 3 days remove the weight and turn the olives with a ladle to bring those underneath to the surface. Leave for another day and continue this operation until the olives have shed their bitter juices, then rinse off the salt and allow to dry in the open air, spread on a wooden surface. Then roll in **olive oil** and preserve in wide-mouthed containers, layered with a few sprigs of rosemary.

886. Baking powder (leavening agent)
BAKING-POWDER (MONTANTE)

Chemical leavening agent. It is possible to obtain the same effect as yeast in only a few minutes (that is, to make dough rise) by using the commercial chemical baking powders sold in the stores. But this can also be made at home very inexpensively. Take **finely powdered cream of tartar** and mix with an equal quantity of **baking soda** and twice the quantity of **flour**. It can be preserved in a jar or tin container in a dry place. When these two ingredients come in contact with water or humidity, they produce carbonic gas, the same gas that is released by yeast in the (slower) process of fermentation. The bubbles produced by the gas also keep bread light and spongy.

887. Fats used in natural cooking
GRASSI PER LA CUCINA NATURISTA

There are many fats offered directly by Mother Nature without having to resort to the butchering of animals: the natural butter extracted from cow's milk is the best of fats; then fine extra virgin olive oil with an acidity level below 2 percent; finally, seed oils (peanut, sesame, cotton, etc.) and coconut oil. Margarines transformed into butter-like substances should be avoided.

888. Canned eggplants and walnuts
BATTUTO DI PSEUDO-CARNE IN CONSERVA

Fried eggplants with walnuts are extremely useful in vegetarian cooking as a surrogate for beef. Since eggplant is not always available fresh, it is handy to keep some on hand by canning it when in season. Peel the **eggplant** and cut in cubes, sprinkling with salt and allowing to shed its liquid while resting in a colander until the bitter juices have drained off. Fry the cubes in **olive oil** and when golden brown remove and drain on paper towel, then weigh and mash with **1/3 the quantity of peeled walnuts**. Place in airtight glass jars, pressing the contents down well so that no air pockets remain. After sealing, sterilize the jars by placing on a rack in boiling water for 15 minutes.

889. Caramelized sugar to use as a coloring agent
CARAMELLO PER COLORIRE

Butter a saucepan and add **9 oz unrefined or raw sugar**, mix slowly over a low flame until it becomes dark, but take care not to let scorch.

Add a small quantity of **water** and cook until the sugar is dissolved.

890. Gelatin
GELATINA NEUTRA

Today few gelatin products are vegetarian. However, groceries sometimes carry Kosher gelatin products, which are vegetarian.

Non-vegetarian gelatin is extracted from the tendons and bones (especially the feet) of dead animals, not only those that have been butchered, after these parts have been treated by a process of boiling and purification.

To prepare gelatin, follow the instructions on the packaging, which will usually instruct you to disolve the gelatin in broth or water.

891. Sweet gelatin
GELATINA DI SOSTANZA DOLCE

Follow the instructions on the gelatin packaging, using **sweetened water** instead of salted water or broth.

892. Curdled milk
LATTE CAGLIATO

In an earthenware container, put:

1 qt milk

Add:

the juice of 3 lemons

Then squeeze the liquid through a cheesecloth. Stir and allow to rest at 60°F for 12 hours. Then butter a napkin and pour in the curdled milk, tie the four corners into a sack and hang until the liquid has dripped through. Place this liquid between two dishes with a weight on top. When it has solidified, serve in slices with sugar, jam or whatever you prefer, or with salt. It is very nourishing.

893. Curry
CURRIE

This is an Indian spice which serves to season minestre, sauces, soups. It is sold already packaged, but a close approximation can be easily prepared at home by mixing the following, all well dried and powdered:

3/5 sweet red pepper
1/5 cayenne
1/5 saffron

The quantity of cayenne can be varied according to taste, and likewise that of the saffron.

894. Steamer
MARMITTA A VAPORE

In order for vegetables and greens to preserve all their flavor and minerals, a steamer is useful. There are different types available in the stores, but it is easy to construct one of your own. The bottom of the inner pan should have colander-size holes and be 2 to 3 inches above the bottom of the larger pan, thereby forming a boiler chamber between the two in which the water is placed. When it boils only the steam should come in contact with the food placed in the upper vessel. It must also have a tightly-fitting lid.

895. Vegetable gelatin
GELATINA VEGETALE

Another basic substance provided by nature in the vegetable world is the gelatin contained in seaweed. This can be extracted by boiling the seaweed in water for one hour. **Agar Agar** is a vegetarian gelatin substitute produced from a variety of seaweed vegetation, and is now widely available in grocery stores.

896. Means of preserving citrus and other thick-skinned fruits: oranges, lemons, limes, citrons, prickly pears, apples, winter pears, etc.
MODO DI CONSERVARE GLI AGRUMI
ED ALTRA FRUTTA A BUCCIA DURA

Take very fine sand and dry it out, if possible in an oven. After allowing to cool, spread the sand in a waterproof container, then place the fruit on top (taking care that the fruit is not touching), with the stem turned downwards. Cover with more sand and place other layers of fruit if you wish. If the sand has not been adequately dried, the fruit will not be preserved properly. The process will greatly increase the life of these citrus fruits.

897. Hot chocolate
CIOCCOLATA CALDA

Shave **chocolate bars** in **water or milk** (1 cup water or milk to every 2 oz chocolate), melting over the flame.

Raw

PART 3

Food

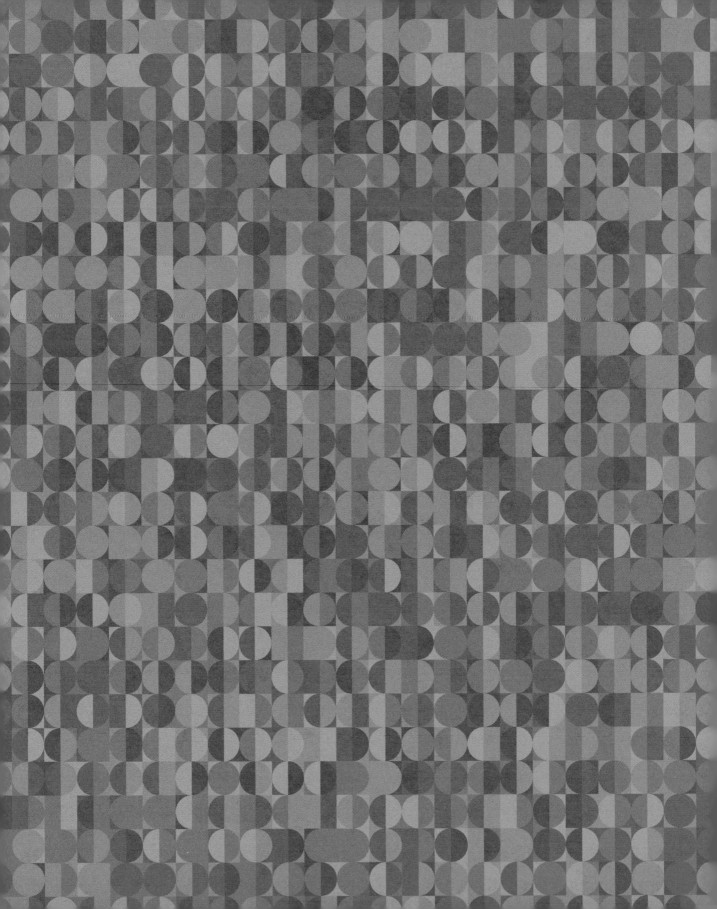

Raw food diets

NATURISMO CRUDO

Preliminary considerations

We have dwelt at length on the subject of vegetarianism, providing recipes for all those who wish to make the effort, certainly beneficial to them, of eliminating meat from their lives. Nonetheless, some of our readers may still be tied to old habits, including that vicious cycle of: cooking, cooks, kitchen help, pots and pans, courses, formal dinners, all things which are a waste of money and energy that could much more profitably be invested in activities contributing to the evolutionary advancement of mankind. But there is something even better if we wish to free ourselves not only of the burden of kitchen work, cooking and feasting, but also of the strain on our organism in requiring it to transform and assimilate cooked foods and animal products, not only meats: and that is a dietary regime based on everything offered by nature, unaltered by cooking.

It is certain that, along with the destruction of vitamins, cooking seriously alters the acids, minerals, and all of the energy-producing elements present in raw food. Such elements, as confirmed by scientific research, are not only

useful to our organism but necessary for our health.

For example, sugar that is found in its unaltered state in fruit, milk and in certain roots, if combined with acids and minerals is of great nutritional and energetic value, easily metabolized by our body. However, when it is cooked or neutralized by industrial processes, it becomes inert material that cannot be transformed by our bodies. Our organism expends great effort to invert and metabolize refined or cooked sugars. Our body often lacks the resources and the energy to carry out this exhausting process of restoration, especially with the passing of years, and thus these neutralized sugars pass into our blood without having been inverted, causing diabetes and other serious deficits. We have seen that the raw tomato acts as a dissolvent and a diuretic; it is energizing, digestive and refreshing. However, when cooked it becomes exactly the opposite, functioning as an irritant to the intestines and urinary tract, causing indigestion and generally losing all its energizing effects. These mysterious processes, only some of which have recently been discovered by science, are far more complex, and by personal observation we can have some idea of their extent: when we see, for example, that fish live in perfect harmony with their environment in an aquarium when the water is continually renewed with fresh sea or spring water, but that they begin to suffer and die within 24 hours if the water stagnates, despite our attempts to provide those substances contained in running water with dietary supplements. There exists, therefore, a vital element in the living products of the earth. The prevention of all illness by stimulating the body's natural defenses is awe-inspiring.

If we live in harmony with nature, undisturbed by irrational eating habits, our body is perfectly resistant to most external attacks. If we distract the natural defenses of our organism by forcing it to engage in laborious digestion and continual detoxification, we are making it susceptible to attacks from disease. Additionally, if the body is unable to free itself of all the toxins taken in, this causes a slow but progressive accumulation of poisons in our system and decreases our ability to eliminate these with the passing of years. If we are able to combat some of these alimentary errors in our youth, they can be fatal, instead, in later life.

With a raw food diet, one achieves a veritable liberation from illness. We know that our organism requires proteins, carbohydrates, minerals, fats, cellulose and vital elements such as vitamins. All this is given to us by nature in vegetables, fruits, nuts and seeds, milk and eggs, and is combined so wisely that any modification man may wish to make can only have negative effects. If we leave to nature the task of elaborating

these substances, we must only understand how to make proper use of them. Here as well nature gives us the indication, through our natural cravings and by alternating her products with the seasons.

It must be borne in mind that we need no more than 1 or 2 oz of protein daily, and that quantity can be provided by 4 oz of nuts or a cup of milk or 1 egg. Next come carbohydrates and fats. These can be consumed in greater quantities in the winter when our body needs more calories, and especially by eating olive oil and butter. All the rest, minerals, cellulose and vitamins of all kinds can be found in nuts, in uncooked leafy greens, in root vegetables and in fruit. In my opinion, even the chopping and modification of these products should be avoided. If you observe the goat, the rabbit, the gazelle, they refuse to eat even the tenderest sprouts if these have been touched by man.

Vegetables as well as fruit bought at the market should be washed in running water. Nuts should be shelled at the moment in which we eat them, and providing we have good teeth, we should avoid mechanical chopping or grinding.

For those who still place importance on the ritual of the meal, on the various courses and their aesthetic aspect, as well as those whose teeth are no longer able to chew nuts, we offer some basic recipes in this section that offer the possibility of a great many variations. The interesting and essential information is that a handful of nuts or cereals or legumes soaked in water and a few pounds of assorted green vegetables and fruit is all we need, and this is also the most rational and healthy of diets.

In order to prepare raw food menus it is first of all necessary that all of the kitchen utensils and equipment as well as the vegetables themselves be extremely clean; they must be washed in fresh running water. It is also necessary to have a juicer, a grater, a grinder and a mortar.

Specific properties of some vegetables

Almonds are a complete food because they contain carbohydrates, proteins, fats, minerals, and a great quantity of vitamins; if they are skinned in cool water (never in hot water because this destroys many of their nourishing elements) and finely ground, they have a remarkable refreshing effect for those who suffer from stomach ailments. Prunes, fresh or dried, soaked in cold water, are laxative and useful for those who suffer from constipation. The daily intake may be regulated according to one's needs. They also have a refreshing effect and can be eaten in large quantities to achieve the desired results with no harmful side effects, as in the case of medicines. Garlic, in addition to containing a great many vital elements, when taken raw is a powerful disinfectant of the digestive tract. Carrots, like onions, have beneficial effects that have not yet been adequately studied, due to the quantity of minerals and vitamins they contain. Parsley is useful in regulating the circulation and metabolism.

Fruit containing high levels of sugar is energetic and refreshing, and therefore when we are tired or physically exhausted, we should eat dates, raisins, bananas, dried figs, etc. followed by a drink made of almond or coconut extract. All the organic acids found in fruit are precious to our body.

All leafy vegetables, such as spinach, lettuce, endive, and root vegetables, contain minerals and sodium. Thus it is advisable to use only limited doses of salt, and to eliminate it completely whenever possible since it has been shown that a quantity exceeding our daily requirements is harmful. If we eat nuts, there is no need of cereals, but these can be added to our meals if we allow them to soak in water until they become soft. They must then be rinsed in clear water, ground and flavored with grated roots, chopped vegetables, garlic, onion, oil and lemon, which will provide an extremely rich source of energy to help sustain us during the most exhausting physical labor.

For intellectual exertion a few nuts will serve to replace the energy we have consumed. It is a mistake to worry about germs that may be found in raw vegetables because these do not penetrate the tissue of living plants but remain on the exterior. Thus they can be easily eliminated by careful washing. Besides which, if we are accustomed to eating raw vegetables and do not create, by eating meat, an unhealthy environment in which germs can multiply, we build up a natural immunity to such germs.

Principle values of raw vegetables

Proteins are necessary for the regeneration of tissue, bones, hair.

Legumes and green vegetables: peas, beans, chickpeas, wheat, oats, rice.

Seeds and nuts: walnuts, hazelnuts, almonds, peanuts, chocolate, cumin, pistachios, pine nuts.

Mushrooms: black truffles, white truffles and mushrooms.

Cereals and dried legumes. foods which produce energy and provide calories and vital strength.

Raw cereals: oats, rice, rye and wheat, chestnuts, sweet potatoes, beets, dried figs, dates, raisins, honey, whole cane sugar, carob, bananas and similar produce. Olive oil, butter, peanut oil, sesame oil, coconut oil.

Foods rich in minerals and vitamins: these function to repair the body's tissues and metabolism.

Leafy vegetables: all raw salad greens: peas, lettuce, endive, watercress.

Vegetables: squash, cucumber, cauliflower, cabbage, turnips, artichokes, asparagus, tomatoes, parsnips, radishes.

Fresh fruit: grapes, apples, pears, cherries, apricots, peaches, prunes, figs, strawberries, blueberries, red currants, raspberries, coconut, pineapple, watermelon, melon, oranges, tangerines, and citrus fruits in general.

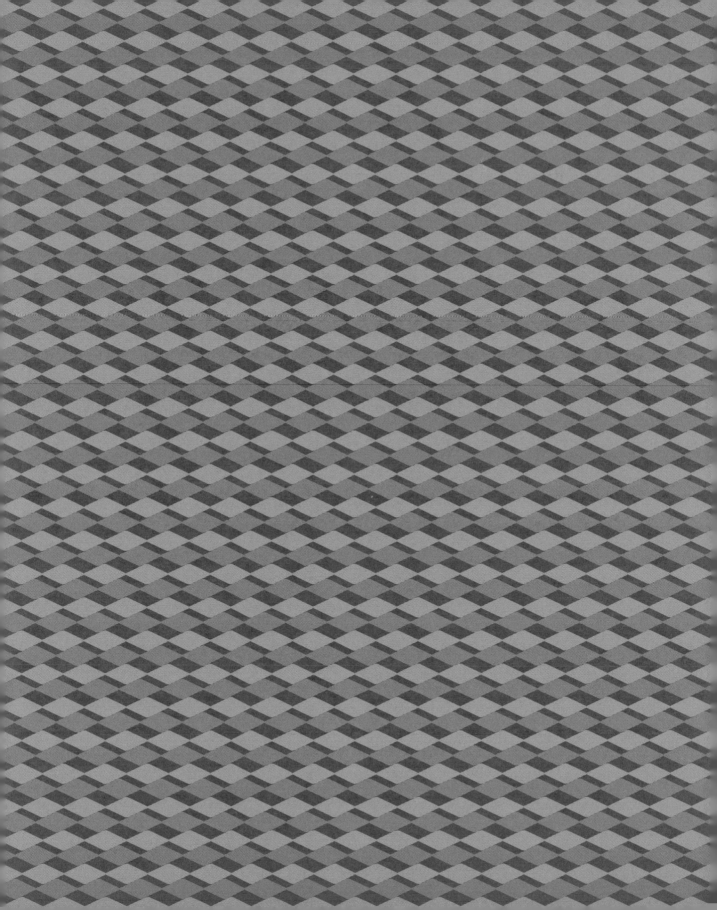

Raw broths and minestre

BRODI E MINESTRE CRUDISTI

898. A complete meal
ALIMENTO COMPLETO

For people who suffer from stomach ailments or those who are of weak constitution. The following recipe serves one person, and can be eaten morning and evening if you are sick.

Start by preparing almond milk: In a bowl, cover **20 almonds** in water and soak for 12 hours. After soaking, strain the almonds and discard the soaking liquid. Grind or crush the almonds, place them in a cheesecloth bag, and soak in bowl containing about 1 cup of water. After a few minutes, wring the bag well, return to the water and repeat several times, until you have squeezed as much liquid from the almonds as you can.

Alternatively, you can use a blender or food processor: Simply add 1½ cups of water to the almonds and blend on high. Then pour the mixture through a cheese cloth.

To prepare the oats: In separate bowl, soak **1 tbsp rolled or steel cut oats** in **½ cup water**. After the oats have softened slightly, add

½ cup of almond milk to the bowl containing the oats and water.

To finish: Add a **1 ½ tbsp honey** or **grape syrup** to the mixture and add the **juice of ½ lemon**. Eat immediately. All the elements necessary for our well-being are contained in this one dish.

899. Summer soup
BRODO ESTIVO

Ingredients:
- **2 lb tomatoes**
- **2 cucumbers**
- **1 onion**
- **a few radishes**
- **parsley**
- **fresh herbs of your choice**

To start: Chop the above, and place the ingredients in a large bowl. Sprinkle the mixture with a pinch of salt, and let stand for at least 2 hours. After 2 hours, pass the mixture through a food press or blend in a food processor. Add the juice of one lemon and **a few drops of olive oil**.

To serve: Pour the mixture of pressed tomatoes and cucumber in individual serving bowls. If you wish, add **truffles** or chopped **raw mushrooms** or **ground nuts** in each serving dish. You can also place a few small slices of **cantaloupe** in each dish. These ingredients may be varied according to the season and to individual taste.

900. Winter soup
BRODO INVERNALE

Ingredients:

>   5 lb large squash, peeled
>   2 onions
>   5 lb carrots, peeled
>   turnips, peeled
>   1 lb leeks, trimmed
>   radishes
>   a clove of garlic
>   fresh herbs of your choice

To prepare the vegetables: Finely chop the above, and place the ingredients in a large bowl. Add:

>   1 tbsp tomato concentrate
>   the juice of two lemons

Mix and sprinkle the mixture with salt, and let stand at least 2 hours. After 2 hours, pass through a food press or blend in a food processor.

To serve: Pour the mixture into individual serving bowls. In each bowl, add:

>   crushed nuts or seeds
>   fresh minced parsley

If the quantity is scarce, lengthen with freshly squeezed orange juice or other citrus fruit.

901. Curry soup
BRODO AL CURRIE

Follow recipes 899 or 900, but add **1 tbsp curry powder** together with **salt** before leaving the vegetables to drain.

902. Almond soup
BRODO MANDORLATO

Follow recipes 899 and 900, but add **a cup of almond milk** to the dishes before serving. Prepare as follows: Crush **4 oz peeled almonds** (about ½ cup), place in a cheesecloth bag and let soak in **1 ½ cups of lukewarm water**. After a few minutes, wring the bag well, return to the water and repeat several times, until you have squeezed as much liquid from the almonds as you can.

Alternatively, you can use a blender or food processor: Simply add 1½ cups of water to the almonds and blend on high. Then pour the mixture through a cheesecloth.

903. Watermelon soup
BRODO D'ANGURIA

Slice:

>   1 lb tomatoes
>   1 small onions
>   1 clove garlic

Sprinkle with salt (if possible celery salt), and allow to drain in a colander for 2 hours. After 2 hours, put through a food press or blend in a food processor, together with **4 lb (underripe) watermelon pulp** (unless you prefer it very sweet in which case use riper watermelon). Combine the juices with:

1 tsp English mustard

a few drops of oil

the juice of 1 lemon

To serve, place the soup in individual serving bowls and garnish with **a handful of crushed nuts.**

904. Cucumber and watermelon soup
BRODO DI COCOMERO ED ANGURIA

Ingredients:

2 lb cucumbers

2 lb watermelon

1 lb onions

1 clove garlic

herbs

a few carrots

Finely chop the cucumbers, watermelon, onions, garlic, herbs, and carrots. Place in a colander and sprinkle with **salt** (preferably **celery salt**) and **grated nutmeg.** Allow to drain for 2 hours. After 2 hours, put the mixture through a food press or blend in a food processor and add **oil** and **lemon.**

To serve, place the soup in individual serving bowls and garnish with **a handful of crushed nuts.**

905. Cucumber juice soup
BRODO DI CETRIOLO

Peel and chop **cucumbers**, sprinkle with salt and allow to drain in a colander placed over a bowl to collect the juice, about 1 hour.

To the cucumber juice, add the **juice of ½ a lemon** and sprinkle with **olive oil.** Garnish with **parsley** and **chopped onion.**

The remaining cucumber can be served as a separate cold dish: Combine with **mayonnaise** and garnish with **grated nuts.**

906. Grapefruit juice soup
BRODO DI POMPELMI

Peel and slice **4 grapefruits** and **2 large onions.** Add:

a clove of garlic, chopped

celery leaves, chopped

Mix the grapefruit, onions, garlic, and celery leaves together, sprinkle with salt, and allow to drain through a sieve for 2 hours, retaining the juice in a large bowl.

After two hours, discard the onions, garlic, and celery leaves. Take the grapefruit slices and squeeze the remaining juice into the bowl. Combine with:

4 tsp rolled or steel cut oats, which have been soaked 12 hours in water

the juice of 1 lemon

4 tbsp olive oil

907. Almond minestra
MINESTRA DI MANDORLE

Peel **5 oz almonds** and place in lukewarm water, grind and put into **3 pints water** for 15 minutes. Add:

2 oz semolina

4 peeled, grated carrots

salt

celery

Leave for another 15 minutes, mixing from time to time. To serve, stir well, and pour into soup dishes, and finish by grating **celery root** on top of each bowl before serving.

908. Chestnut minestra
MINESTRA DI CASTAGNE

Slice:

> 2 lb tomatoes
>
> 3 oz onions
>
> 4 carrots
>
> 2 zucchini

Sprinkle with salt (if possible celery salt), leaving to drain in a colander for 2 hours. After 2 hours, put the tomatoes, onions, carrots, and zucchini through a food press or blend in a food processor and combine all the juice with:

> the juice of 2 lemons
>
> 4 tbsp olive oil
>
> ¼ lb raw peeled grated chestnuts

This can also be made with dried chestnuts that have been ground and soaked in water.

909. Corn soup
MINESTRA AL GRANONE (MAIS)

Slice:

> 2 lb tomatoes
>
> 1 cucumber
>
> 2 zucchini
>
> 3 onions

Sprinkle with:

> salt
>
> a small clove of garlic, chopped
>
> a pinch of oregano

Sprinkle with salt (if possible celery salt), leaving to drain in a colander for 2 hours, collecting the liquid in a large bowl. After 2 hours, pass the tomatoes, onions, carrots, and zucchini through a food press or blend in a food processor and mix with the juice.

To serve, cut the kernels from an ear of **corn** with a sharp knife, letting them fall into serving bowls (using one ear for each serving). Then cover with the soup.

This makes a delicious soup and is extremely nourishing if the corn has been harvested at the right moment.

910. Raw springtime minestra
MINESTRA PRIMAVERILE CRUDA

Ingredients:

> 2 lb oranges
>
> 5 oz tender peas
>
> 6 oz young and tender fava beans (shelled and skinned)
>
> 2 carrots, sliced or grated
>
> 1 small onion, diced
>
> 1 lemon
>
> olive oil

Squeeze the juice of the oranges into a large bowl, and then add the peas, fava beans, carrots, and onion. Add the juice of 1 lemon and a splash of olive oil. Serve from a central bowl.

911. Winter minestra
MINESTRA INVERNALE

Ingredients:

- 2 lb yellow squash or pumpkin, cut in slices and sprinkled with salt, and then soaked for at least 2 hours
- 1 lb onion, sliced
- 4 carrots, sliced or grated
- 1 stalk celery
- 1 clove garlic, peeled
- parsley
- 4 sliced oranges

Put all the vegetables through a food press or blend in a food processor and combine the juice with that gathered from the drained vegetables. Add:

- 1 tsp of English mustard powder
- a few tbsp of extra virgin olive oil

To serve, place 3 ground walnuts or other nuts of your choice in each serving bowl and pour the soup over the nuts.

912. Cantaloupe minestra
MINESTRA AL CANTALUPO

Ingredients:

- 2 lb tomatoes
- 7 oz onions
- 1 cucumber
- 1 clove garlic, chopped
- parsley, chopped

Wash and crush the tomatoes. Slice the onions and the cucumber. Combine in a large bowl. Add the chopped parsley and garlic, and sprinkle with salt and mix together. Transfer the mixture to a colander and allow it to drain for 2 hours, retaining the liquid. Then put through a press or food processor and join all the vegetable liquids together. If you wish, finish with 1/2 cup cream.

To serve, slice a cantaloupe and place slices in each serving bowl. Finish by pouring the vegetable juices over the canteloupe.

913. Beet minestra
MINESTRA DI BARBABIETOLE

Ingredients:

- 2 lb beets, peeled and sliced
- 4 carrots that have been washed and sliced
- 4 oz onions, sliced
- parsley
- 1 clove garlic, peeled
- oregano

Sprinkle these ingredients with salt and leave to drain in a colander for 2 hours. After 2 hours, pass the ingredients though a food press or blend in a food processor and season the minestra with lemon and oil.

To serve, pour the minestra into serving bowls and garnish with ground nuts.

914. Semolino minestra
MINESTRA AL SEMOLINO

Slice:

- 2 cucumbers
- 2 lb tomatoes
- 4 oz onions

Sprinkle these ingredients with salt (celery salt if you have it) and leave to drain in a colander, using a large bowl to collect the juices. After 2 hours, put the solid ingredients through a food press and combine this with the juices and:

olive oil

lemon juice

abundant parsley

Serve in individual serving bowls with **2 tbsp semolina** in each bowl. The semolina will soak up the juices and makes a delicious soup.

915. Spicy minestra
MINESTRA PICCANTE

Slice:

1 lb zucchini

2 cucumbers

4 carrots

4 oz onion

1 lb tomatoes

Slice and sprinkle the above with **salt** and **oregano**. Allow to drain in colander, using a large bowl to collect the juices. After 2 hours, put the solid ingredients through a food press or blend in a food processor and combine with the juice.

Dissolve **2 tsp English mustard powder** with the juice of **1 lemon** and some **minced garlic** and add to the broth. To serve, put a few **asparagus tips** and finely sliced **carrots** or **tender green peas** or **raw sliced truffles** in each bowl, and pour the soup over.

916. Corn soup, version 2
MINESTRA AL GRANONE

Take **6 ears of tender corn** and cut off the kernels with a sharp knife. Put in soup dishes and pour in:

raw tomato juice or orange juice

celery salt

extra virgin olive oil

917. Minestra with tomato extract
MINESTRA DI POMODORO CONCENTRATO

Take **4 oz tomato paste**, lengthened with **the juice of 4 or 5 oranges**, a bit of **lemon juice** and **salt**. Add:

ground walnuts or other raw nuts

cumin

sweet corn

You may also add **½ cup cream**.

918. Raw tomato minestra
MINESTRA AL POMODORO FRESCO

Clean **2 lb ripe tomatoes**, put them through a food mill and add:

3 grated carrots

chopped onion

garlic

finely chopped herbs

Season with **oil** or **cream**, a pinch of **salt** and a few **tender green peas** if they are in season.

919. Minestra with cereals and dried legumes
MINESTRA DI CEREALI E LEGUMI SECCHI

Choose whatever **cereal** or **legume** you like in the quantity of 1 oz per person, and soak in water with a pinch of baking soda. When the beans or grains are swollen and soft (they must soak for no less than 12 hours), remove and rinse in running water, then grind. Prepare a **raw vegetable broth** (recipes 899 or 900) and serve over the soaked and ground beans in soup plates, adding:

lemon juice

oil or cream

a grating of celery hearts or **finely chopped parsley**

920. Complete tomato minestra
MINESTRA DI POMODORO COMPLETA

Wash, peel and cut in half horizontally **2 lb fresh ripe tomatoes**; remove the seeds, and turn upside down to drain, collecting the juice. Chop the pulp and place in soup dishes, adding **chopped onion** and **parsley** to each dish. Pour in the tomato juice and sprinkle some **celery salt** on top, then add:

ground nuts

olive oil or cream

lemon

4 tbsp oat flakes which have been soaked for 6 hours

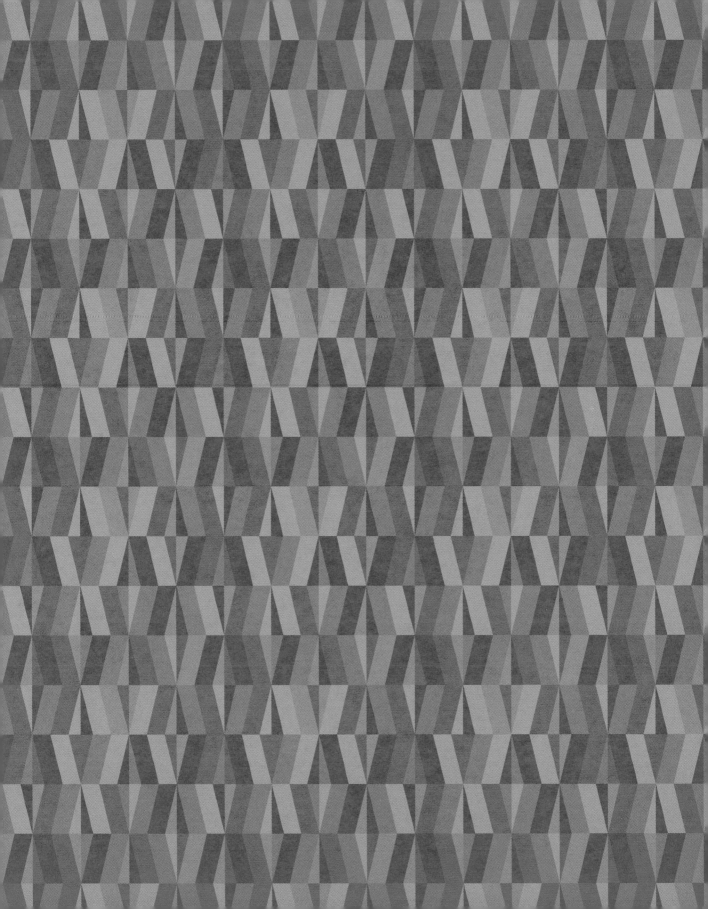

Raw courses

921. Asparagus tips with mayonnaise
PUNTE DI ASPARAGI ALLA MAJONESE

Cut off the tender tips of the asparagus, arrange in a serving dish and cover with **mayonnaise**. The asparagus can be sprinkled with **ground cumin** or any **crushed nuts** or **seeds**.

922. Tomatoes
POMIDORI AL

Remove the seeds from several large **tomatoes**. Slice and pour a dressing over them made of:

    oil
    lemon
    chopped parsley

Cream can also be used.

923. Mushrooms 'trifolati' (stewed with oil and garlic)
FUNGHI TRIFOLATI

Clean and thinly slice **1 lb mushrooms**. Chop **garlic** and put in **olive oil** with mushrooms that have been steamed in a double boiler at 100°F.

924. Raw mushrooms
FUNGHI NATURALI

Choose nice, big, meaty **mushrooms**. Slice thinly, wash well, and drain. Cover with **lemon juice**, **oil**, and **chopped parsley** or, if you prefer, **fresh cream**.

925. Truffles 'trifolati'
TARTUFI TRIFOLATI

Follow the recipe for mushrooms (recipe 923) but substitute truffles.

926. Artichokes with mayonnaise
CARCIOFI ALLA MAJONESE

Choose **tender artichokes**, remove all the tough and thorny leaves. Slice thinly, and soak in **water** and **lemon** to avoid discoloring. Drain, arrange in a serving dish, and cover with **mayonnaise**, sprinkling with **chopped parsley** or **other herbs**.

927. Spinach with mayonnaise
SPINACI ALLA MAJONESE

Chop **1 lb spinach,** rinse under running water, drain, chop finely, and cover with **mayonnaise** or **heavy cream** and **chopped truffles** or **other mushrooms.**

928. Cauliflowers and apples
CAVOLFIORI E MELE

Grate equal quantities of **cauliflowers** and **apples** and cover with a dressing of:

>   oil
>   lemon
>   herbs

Sprinkle with **sliced truffles** or **other mushrooms.**

929. Tomatoes with walnuts and onion
POMIDORI ALLE NOCI E CIPOLLA

Halve the **tomatoes** and dust with:

>   ground walnuts
>   chopped onion
>   parsley

Sprinkle with an **oil and lemon dressing** or **fresh cream** and serve.

930. Stuffed tomatoes with truffles
POMIDORI TARTUFATI RIPIENI

Slice **tomatoes** in half, remove the core and seeds, stuff with **chopped truffles.** Sprinkle with an **oil and lemon dressing** or **fresh cream** and serve.

931. Lemons
LIMONI

Peel and slice **lemons.** Sprinkle with **oil,** and dust with **chopped garlic** or **onion** and **parsley.**

932. Squash with tart apples
ZUCCA MELATA

Grate equal amounts of **raw squash** and **tart apples** (Granny Smith are good) in a small bowl. Add just enough **cream** to bind and stir.

933. White cabbage
CAVOLO CAPPUCCIO PROTEIZZATO

Finely chop the tender leaves of **1 head of cabbage.** Cover with **mayonnaise** and sprinkle with **crushed nuts.** Salt and pepper to taste.

934. Spicy tidbits
BOCCONCINI PICCANTI

Work the following ingredients into a paste:

>   **6 oz ground hazelnuts**
>   **½ clove crushed garlic**
>   **a pinch of salt**
>   **4 oz butter**
>   **1 tsp English mustard powder**

Make into small balls, add **lemon juice,** and serve the mixture with small **tomatoes, onions,** or **artichokes.**

935. Raw truffles
TARTUFI NATURALI

Whether black or white, both varieties are extremely rich in phosphorus and are a real source of energy. Wash well in fresh water, chop, and serve with a dressing of **oil**, **lemon**, and **parsley**, or with **chopped garlic** and **onion**.

936. Avocados
PALTAS O NOCI AVOGADRE PROTEIZZATE

Remove the stone and skin and cover with a dressing of:

    oil
    lemon
    parsley

937. Special lettuce
LATTUGA AL POMODORO PROTEIZZATA

Ingredients:

    chopped lettuce
    tomato juice
    celery
    chopped parsley
    onion
    garlic flavoring
    ground peanuts
    celery salt
    olive oil
    lemon

Mix the ingredients and sprinkle with **ground cumin** or **walnuts** before serving.

938. Turnips with an herb dressing
RAPE GUARNITE PROTEIZZATE

Grate **6 nice white rutabagas** or **turnips** and cover with a dressing of:

    2 onions cut into fine strips
    marjoram
    fresh garlic
    celery salt
    oil
    lemon

Garnish with **salad greens** and sprinkle with **cumin** or any other **ground nuts**.

939. Fennel with a nut dressing
FINOCCHI ARRICCHITI

Finely chop **fennel**, sprinkle with **ground almonds** and **walnuts** or any other nuts. Season with:

    celery salt or a small pinch of ordinary salt
    olive oil
    lemon

Garnish with tender young **beets** or **carrots** and **tomatoes**.

940. Coconuts
NOCI DI COCCO PROTEIZZATE

Remove the bark-like skin and cut into even-sized pieces. If you wish, cover with **fresh cream**.

941. Carrots
CAROTE PROTEIZZATE

Grate **12 carrots** and arrange on a serving dish with:

- 2 chopped onions
- fresh chopped garlic
- 8 ground walnuts

Cover with a dressing of:

- oil
- lemon juice
- celery salt

Garnish with **lettuce leaves, tomato slices, melon,** or **cucumber.**

942. Lettuce and beets
LATTUGA E BARBABIETOLA PROTEIZZATE

Ingredients:

- escarole or other curly-leaf lettuce
- thinly shredded tender beets
- chopped onion
- a finely chopped clove of garlic
- herbs
- olive oil
- celery salt
- lemon juice

Mix together and sprinkle with **ground cumin** or any other **ground nuts** to provide extra protein.

943. Triple fortified vegetarian salad
NUVOLATA TRIPLA SOSTANZIATA

Grate **1 lb tart apples** and line a salad bowl with a layer of these, then sprinkle with **cumin** and **ground walnuts**, and make a second layer with **6 grated carrots**. Cover with a **dressing of your choice** and dust with chopped, skinned **almonds,** or any other ground nuts. Just let the shredded fruit fall into the serving dish or salad bowl without tossing.

944. Cauliflower
CAVOLFIORI PROTEIZZATI

Finely chop **cauliflower** and cover with an **oil** and **lemon** dressing, or with **mayonnaise,** and sprinkle with **ground walnuts,** or **peanuts** or any other nuts.

945. Corn with mayonnaise
MAIS ALLA MAJONESE

Choose ears of **corn** that are still tender, or milky-yellow. Cut the kernels off the cob into a serving dish with a sharp knife. Cover with a **mayonnaise** (see recipes 672–674) and sprinkle with **parsley** or any other herb you choose.

946. Tender wheat in sauce
FRUMENTO TENERO SALSITO

Pick the **wheat grains** when they are still tender, remove the outside husk, and serve with a dressing of either **mayonnaise** (see recipes 672–674), **raw tomato sauce, oil** and **lemon** or **cream.**

947. Chickpeas with sauce
CECI OD ALTRI LEGUMI VERDI SALSITI

To prepare raw, these leguminous vegetables need to be picked while still tender, before fully ripening. Remove the outside skin or husk and serve with a **mayonnaise dressing**, or **raw tomato sauce**, **oil** and **lemon** or **cream**. You can also use canned chickpeas.

948. Artichokes
CARCIOFI

The **artichokes** should be picked while still very tender. Clean well, leaving only the edible part and rubbing with **half a lemon** so that they do not turn black. Open up the central leaves, season with a pinch of **celery salt**, and season with an **oil** and **lemon** dressing or with **mayonnaise** or **cream**.

949. Green fava beans and artichokes in sauce
FAVE VERDI E CARCIOFI SALSITI

Remove both the shells and inner skins from the **fava beans**. Finely slice the **tender artichoke hearts**. Arrange the vegetables in a serving dish and cover with a **mayonnaise sauce**, a **raw tomato sauce**, or an **oil**, **lemon** and **parsley** dressing.

950. Lemon salad
INSALATA DI LIMONI PROTEIZZATI

Peel and thinly slice some **nice firm lemons**. Arrange in a serving dish and cover with ground walnuts or any other crushed nuts you may have. Sprinkle with:

> **olive oil**
> **a little salt** (preferably celery salt)
> **chopped parsley**

951. Corn with tomato and cucumber
MAIS AL PROMODORO E CETRIOLO

Take **6 ears of corn** with kernels that are still milky-white. Remove them with a sharp knife (taking care not to cut too deeply). Arrange a mound of the kernels in a serving dish, cover with slices of **peeled tomatoes**, and season with a dressing of:

> **oil**
> **lemon**
> **celery salt** (or a pinch of ordinary salt)
> **a little chopped parsley**

A **vegetable mayonnaise** can be used as an alternative.

952. Scorzonera salad (scorzonera hispanica)
SCORZONERA IN INSALATA

Ingredients:

> **6 pieces of scorzonera**
> **1 large onion**
> **1 clove garlic**
> **herbs**

Carefully clean the scorzonera and grate, adding the chopped onion, garlic, and herbs. Serve with an **oil** and **lemon** dressing or with **mayonnaise**.

Garnish with slices of **tomato** or **cucumber** or any other fresh vegetables you choose.

953. Mixed salad
INSALATA MISTA

Use **3 large onions** and any other fresh vegetables you like (cucumbers, cabbage, turnips, radishes, carrots, etc.). Chop all the vegetables, and season with:

> celery salt
>
> oil
>
> lemon

Sprinkle with a handful of **cumin** or any other **ground nut** you choose.

954. Spinach salad
INSALATA DI SPINACI

Finely chop **spinach**, and mix with:

> chopped celery
>
> herbs
>
> onion
>
> fresh garlic

Season with a dressing of:

> oil
>
> lemon
>
> celery salt

Garnish with **2 shredded carrots** and **cumin seeds** or **ground walnuts**.

955. Natural olives
OLIVE EFFICIENTI

Some varieties of **olive** lose their bitter taste once they ripen. These olives can be eaten without being treated with caustic substances that may deprive them of their natural nutritional properties. These varieties are extremely popular in Sicily, where they are known as "passoloni acciurati." They are rich in vitamins, especially if seasoned with **olive oil** and **lemon juice**.

956. Chestnuts
CASTAGNE

Raw, peeled chestnuts, slowly chewed, are rich in protein and carbohydrates and constitute an excellent source of energy. However, if your teeth are not up to all that chewing, the chestnuts can be grated and served in vegetable broths, salads, or other raw vegetable dishes. Dried chestnuts can be ground and left to soak in broth until they are nice and tender.

957. Melon salad
POPONE ALL'INSALATA

Thinly slice a **melon** in about 1-inch pieces, arrange in a serving dish, and season with a dressing of:

> oil
>
> lemon
>
> chopped parsley
>
> a little garlic flavoring

Sprinkle any **ground nuts** you wish over this dish for extra protein.

958. Melon, dressed up
POPONE

Slice as in the previous recipe. Cover with **mayonnaise** and sprinkle with **chopped truffles** or **ground walnuts**. Garnish with a generous helping of **parsley** and serve.

959. Sour truffled apples
MELE ASPRE TARTUFATE

Finely slice the **apples**, cover with **oil** and **lemon**, and sprinkle with **chopped truffles** or **ground walnuts** or other nuts. Garnish with **parsley**.

960. Sour apples with carrots and chestnuts
MELE ASPRE CON CAROTE CASTAGNATE

Chop the **apples** and **carrots** and arrange in a serving dish with a dressing of:

> oil
>
> lemon
>
> parsley

Grate raw, peeled **chestnuts** and sprinkle over the vegetables.

961. Tomatoes with walnut stuffing
POMIDORI RIPIENI ALLE NOCI

Take **2 lb ripe tomatoes** of the same size, remove the core and seeds, and fill with the following mixture:

> **4 oz ground walnuts**
>
> **6 shredded carrots**
>
> **a fistful of rice** that has been soaked in

water for 4 hours and drained

> **fresh chopped garlic**
>
> **herbs**
>
> **celery sauce**
>
> **a pinch of salt**
>
> **cumin**

Arrange on a serving dish and season with a dressing of:

> oil
>
> lemon
>
> parsley

962. Tomatoes with chestnut stuffing
POMIDORI CASTAGNATI

Peel some nice, round **tomatoes**, remove the core and seeds, sprinkle with a little salt (preferably celery salt), and fill with carefully peeled, freshly ground **chestnuts**. Cover with a dressing of:

> oil
>
> lemon
>
> parsley
>
> 1 teaspoon of English mustard

963. Stuffed baby onions
CIPOLLINE RIPIENE

Choose some small, even-sized **onions**, peel, and scoop out the inside through the root end. Cover with a **mayonnaise sauce** or a dressing of:

> oil
>
> lemon
>
> parsley
>
> 1 teaspoon of English mustard

964. Orange salad
INSALATA DI ARANCE

Take:

- 6 oranges
- 8 ground walnuts or any other nuts
- 4 tbsp extra virgin olive oil
- 2 tbsp lemon juice
- a little salt
- ginger
- fresh garlic
- chopped onion

Finely slice the oranges and then halve the slices (leaving a few whole). Mix the halves with the other ingredients in a salad bowl and an hour before serving garnish with the whole slices. Sprinkle with **cumin** and **parsley** and serve.

Fresh dairy produce

LATTICINI CRUDI

Fresh milk, an indispensable and primordial source of nourishment when it is supplied straight from the dairy, is an excellent source of protein. This applies to all dairy products: milk, butter, and uncooked, unsalted, milk curds. Uncooked eggs are also a vital source of nourishment.

Fully grown adults, whose bones no longer need to strengthen, unlike those of children, require only limited amounts of these nutritional elements. Two ounces a day of protein derived from dairy produce are adequate for an adult's needs.

This dairy-derived protein should be taken together with the restorative nutritional elements in fruit and garden produce.

A cup of milk, a little cream, fresh, unsalted cheese or curds alternated with a raw egg a day are an excellent source of nourishment, although they should not be unduly indulged in.

965. Milk curds
CAGLIATA

Milk, before it is made into cheese, begins to curdle and the whey separates as a watery liquid from the curd after coagulation. The curd is delicious and healthy.

966. Fresh cream ('fiordilatte')
FIOR DI LATTE, PANNA O CREMA

If unpasteurized milk is left to stand, after 24 hours the fatty part, or cream, comes to the surface. Cream is a wonderful flavoring for sweet sauces, and indeed for all sauces.

967. Fresh butter
BURRO NATURALE FRESCO

Made from beaten cream, fresh butter is not sterilized and is an extremely delicate fat, fragrant and rich.

968. Heavy (double) cream cheeses
FORMAGGINI A DOPPIA PANNA

Made from milk curds and double cream, these have a high nutritional value when eaten raw.

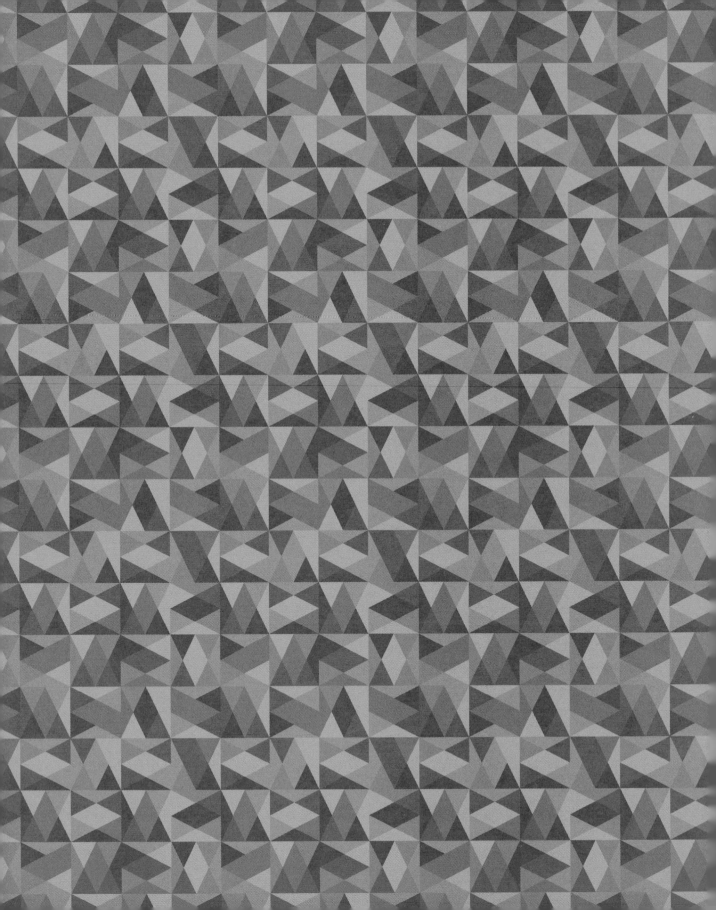

Raw sauces

969. Pink sauce
SALSA ROSSA

Make an ordinary **mayonnaise** (recipe 673) and mix in **a tablespoonful of tomato paste** or **fresh tomatoes** that have been put through a food mill or pulsed in a food processor.

970. Green sauce
SALSA VERDE

Make an ordinary **mayonnaise** (recipe 673) and add a paste made of **ground parsley**, **mint**, **garlic**, and **onion** that have been put through a food mill, or placed in a food processor. Whip the paste together with the mayonnaise and serve.

971. Tomato paste
CONCENTRATO DI POMODORO NEL VUOTO

When the tomato paste is vacuum prepared at a low temperature, it retains all the natural nutritional properties of raw tomatoes. If the concentrate has a thick consistency and is made with fully ripe tomatoes, it can be preserved in jars for the winter. You can also buy a excellent tomato paste in stores.

972. 'Salamoriglio'
SALAMORIGLIO

This is an olive oil, lemon, and oregano dressing. To prepare, beat the juice of **4 lemons** with:

  the same amount of olive oil
  fresh garlic
  chopped parsley
  a little oregano

This is excellent as a dressing for tender artichoke hearts, asparagus tips, fresh fava beans, shredded chestnuts, etc.

The sauce can be mixed with cream, but is, however, excellent on its own.

Raw bread and bread rolls

PANI E PAGNOTTE CRUDISTI

973. Raw bread
PANE RAW

Raw breads are made using a food dehydrator, or by letting a raw loaf stand at room temperature for 6 to 12 hours. Alliata anticipated the modern home food dehydrator, writing that it would be ideal for making raw breads. In describing the machine that would be required, he wrote that bread "cooked in a vacuum at a maximum temperature of 100°F will fully retain its nutritional properties … When small household ovens are put on the market at reasonable prices, allowing vacuum cooking at a low temperature, a number of cooked dishes can be made that fully preserve their nutritional value."

Any of the breads below can be prepared using the method Alliata suggests—essentially leaving raw bread dough to set for 6 to 12 hours, or until the loaf reaches the firmness you prefer—or by using a food dehydrator.

To use a dehydrator, prepare dough using one of the recipes below and form the dough into either loaves or slices. To form into slices, roll the dough out on a wooden board and shape it into squares with a knife. Turn on the dehydrator

and set it to 115°F. Then place the bread on the dehydrator tray, and insert it into the machine. Dehydrate for about 1 hour. Then flip the bread, and dehydrate for another 1½ hours. Then, flip the bread once again, and dehydrate for 30 to 40 minutes more, or until the bread has reached a firmness you like. You may find that you enjoy softer and thinner slices of raw bread than with conventional bread recipes.

For loaves, dehydrate at 145°F for 1 hour—then reduce the temperature to 110°F. Dehydrate for another 6 hours or so. Tastes best if eaten right out of dehydrator, but the bread should stay fresh for about 3 days.

974. Fig bread
PANE DI FICHI

Wash some **figs** well and put them through a food processor. Mix with as much **wholemeal rye flour** or **oats** or **banana flour** as needed to make the mixture into a pliable dough. Sprinkle flour over the outside and leave to rise in a moderately warm room (not over 100°F) for 6 to 12 hours.

975. Peanut and almond bread
PANE D'ARACHIDI MANDORLATO

You will need two-thirds the quantity required of **peanuts** and one-third of **ground almonds**. Mix with as much **banana flour** as is needed to make a dough (as above). Let stand for 6 to 12 hours.

976. Sugar-free bread for diabetics and weightwatchers
PANE ANAZUCCHERINO PER DIABETICI ED OBESI

Peel and grind **pine nuts** and **peanuts** and mix with as much **wholemeal rye flour** as is needed to give the mixture a dough-like consistency. Make into a ball and dust with the same flour and let sit for 6 to 12 hours.

977. Carob bread
PANE DI CARRUBE

Soak **2 lb carobs** in water for 2 hours, remove the seeds and the tough shells, and put through a food processor with:

- **12 oz dried figs**
- **8 oz pine nuts**

Work the ingredients into a dough, adding **grated lemon peel** and as much **rye flour** as is needed to give it the right consistency. Let sit for 6 to 12 hours.

978. Chestnut bread
PANE DI CASTAGNE

Shell and peel some raw **chestnuts** and finely grind them. Grind a third of the quantity of **dates** and mix together to make a nice pliable dough. Let stand for 6 to 12 hours.

~~~~~~~~~~~~~~~~~~~~~~~~~~~~~~

979. Almond and rice loaf
PAGNOTTA DI RISO MANDORLATO

Grind:

- **10 oz wholemeal rice flour**
- **8 oz hazelnuts or almonds**

Make the flour into a dough, adding:

- **4 tbsp honey**
- **grated orange or lemon peel**

Make into a ball, roll in a floured dish cloth, and keep it under a weight for 12 hours.

980. Cocoa loaf
PAGNOTTA DI RISO MANDORLATO

Grind **20 oz dried figs** or **dates** and mix with **4 oz cocoa powder**. Form a rounded loaf, flatten slightly and sprinkle with flour. Let stand for 6 to 12 hours. This loaf is a great source of energy and is very flavorful.

981. Date and walnut loaf
PAGNOTTA DI DATTERI E NOCI

You need **two-thirds dates** and **one-third walnuts**. Put the dates through a food processor and crush the walnuts. Mix with the flour of any **cereal** of your choice (banana flour is best). Mix the ingredients together to make into a nice consistency, flatten slightly, sprinkle with flour. Let stand for 6 to 12 hours.

Raw sweet dishes

DOLCERIE CRUDE

982. Marzipan or almond paste
MARZAPANE O PASTA REALE CRUDA

Ingredients:

- **1 lb sweet almonds**
- **2 or 3 bitter almonds**

Soak almonds in water for 12 hours until the skin peels off. Finely grind and moisten the almonds with **orange flower** or **jasmine water** (this is obtained by soaking the flowers in water for a few hours, or it can be easily purchased in a grocery).

When the nuts are well ground, mix together with **honey** to make the mixture easier to handle. Pastries and delicacies of all kinds can be made with this paste.

983. Marzipan with pistachio nuts
MARZAPANE AL PISTACCHIO

Make the **marzipan** as above and add **4 oz peeled, ground pistachio nuts** (which have been soaked in lukewarm water until they shed their skins). Mix in **2 oz spinach** or any other ground greens. These give the paste its green color, its mineral salts, and nutritional properties.

984. 'Buccellato crudista' (dried minced fruit rolled in almond paste)
BUCCELLATO CRUDISTA

Make the **marzipan** as in recipe 982, roll out the paste, and fill with the following dried fruit conserve:

- **12 oz dried figs**
- **4 oz raisins**
- **4 oz dates**
- **2 oz pine nuts**
- **powdered cinnamon**
- **orange peel**

Put the dried fruit through a food processor, or food mill, cover with the almond paste and make into a "tarallo" (a ring-shaped biscuit). Cover with a dusting of **cinnamon** and **icing sugar**.

985. Canapés with raw fillings
TARTINE CRUDISTE

Grind **8 oz almonds**, after soaking in fresh water for 12 hours. Make a paste with:

2 oz potato flour

a tablespoonful of orange or rose water

enough honey to make these into a fairly thick paste

Roll out the paste and line small terrines. Fill with the following mixture:

8 oz dried figs

6 oz pitted raisins

2 oz pine nuts

2 oz dates

5 walnuts

grated orange peel

Put all the ingredients through a food processor or food mill. Dust with **icing sugar** and powdered **cinnamon**.

986. Stuffed dates
DATTERI RIPIENI

Remove the pits and make a slit in the **date** on one side only. Fill with **marzipan** (recipe 982), arrange in a little paper basket, and brush with **honey**.

987. Coconut pudding
BODINO DI COCCO

Take the same quantity of **coconut pulp** and **choice dates**, put through a grinder, and make a paste. Make into any shape you please and cover with **grape syrup**.

988. Carob pudding
BODINO DI CARRUBE

Clean the **carobs** and remove the seeds and tough parts. Put through a food processor with a third the quantity of **pitted dates**, or choice dried **figs**, **grated lime** or **orange peel**, and a little **semolina** (if the mixture needs to be firmer in consistency). Leave to set in a floured mold for a few hours and serve with a generous helping of **honey**, **grape syrup** or **cream**.

989. Chestnut pudding
BODINO DI CASTAGNE

Shell and peel **1 lb chestnuts** and finely grind. Quickly pulse **1 lb dried prunes** in a food processor with **freshly grated orange peel**. Mix the ingredients together, adding extra **honey** if needed to make them into a nice, firm paste. Make the pudding into any form you please and cover with **cream**.

990. Pistachio pudding
BODINO DI PISTACCHI

Grind **two-thirds of almonds** and **one-third of peeled pistachio nuts** (which have been soaked in warm water until they shed their skins). Mix as much **chestnut flour** as required to give the mixture a firm consistency. Make into any form you please and leave for 3 to 4 hours. Serve with a generous helping of **grape syrup** or **honey** or **cream**.

991. Bitter orange pudding
BODINO D'ARANCE AMARE

Pulse the peel of **4 fresh bitter oranges** in a food processor and mix with:

- **1 lb choice dried figs**
- **4 oz raisins**
- **2 oz peeled almonds** (soaked in warm water until they shed their skins)
- **6 walnuts**

Mix all the ingredients together, adding a little **banana flour** if necessary to give the mixture a dough-like consistency. Leave for at least 2 hours and serve with a generous topping of **syrup** or **cream**.

992. Stuffed apples
MELE RIPIENE

Peel some nice big **apples** and rub with half a **lemon** to prevent them from discoloring. Remove the core and fill with **marzipan**. Arrange in a serving dish and cover with a **cream** and **honey** mix.

993. Pear compote
COMPOSTA DI PERE EFFICIENTI

Choose some nice ripe **pears**, peel, and cut into pieces, removing the core and arranging in a serving dish. Sprinkle with **honey** and **heavy cream** and dust with **chopped pistachio nuts**.

994. Winter compote
COMPOSTA INVERNALE

Choose some dried winter fruit: **peaches, apricots, prunes**, etc., and soak in just enough water for the fruit to absorb the water. Serve with a **cream** and **honey sauce** and a sprinkling of **chopped almonds**.

995. Uncooked chocolate
CIOCCOLATA CRUDA

Add **powdered sugar** and **cocoa powder** to almond paste (recipe 982) until it acquires a nice firm consistency. Make into small balls and roll in cocoa powder. These can be kept in tin foil and made into a variety of candies.

996. Cookies
BISCOTTI

These can be made with **wheat flour** or **corn flour**, adding **brown sugar** or **honey** to sweeten and bind. A food dehydrator is recommended at a temperature of not over 100°F.

Any recipe for ordinary cookies can be used for raw cookies as long as it does not contain yeast.

997. Cantaloupe with grape syrup
CANTALUPO ALLO SCIROPPO D'UVA

Slice a **cantaloupe** melon, arrange in a plate, and pour over it **a few tablespoonfuls of grape syrup**, and sprinkle with **ground walnuts** or any other crushed nuts.

998. Flat fig loaf with grape syrup
FOCACCIA DI FICHI ALLO SCIROPPO D'UVA

Wash some choice dried **figs** and put through a food processor with pieces of **unripe orange** or **lemon peel**. Make into a dough-like consistency with a third of the quantity of **ground almonds** or **walnuts**.

Shape into a thick flat loaf, sprinkle with flour, and pour over a generous helping of **grape syrup** or **honey**.

999. Oranges with a coconut and almond topping
ARANCE MANDORLATE AL MIELE

Peel and slice **6 oranges**, arrange in a dish with **a few walnuts**, and cover with **sliced banana**. Grate a generous amount of **coconut** and sprinkle over the oranges, then dust with peeled, chopped **almonds** and cover with **honey** and **cream**.

1000. Dried fruit compote
COMPOSTA DI FRUTTA SECCA

Get whatever dried fruit you can find in the store: **peaches, apricots, pears, prunes**, etc. Wash well and leave to macerate in enough fresh water for the fruit to absorb it all. Leave to soak for 24 hours. Before serving, add a little **brown sugar** or **honey** in the fruit juice. The compote can be eaten without adding sugar or served with **cream**.

1001. Fruit salad with a sweet mayonnaise
MACEDONIA DI FRUTTA ALLA MAJONESE DOLCE

Ingredients:
- **8 oz bananas**
- **8 oz pineapple**
- **8 oz apple**
- **8 oz pears**
- **6 oz almonds** or **pine nuts** (or any other nuts)

Chop the fruit, sprinkle with the ground nuts, and season with a sweet mayonnaise made from **honey** and **beaten egg yolks** and **lemon**.

1002. Spring fruit salad
MACEDONIA DI FRUTTA PRIMAVERILE

Follow recipe 1001, using **cherries, apricots, peaches**, and **pears**. Serve with a sprinkling of **honey** or any of our other **syrup** recipes.

1003. Winter fruit salad
MACEDONIA DI FRUTTA INVERNALE

Slice the **bananas, apples**, and **pitted orange segments**, add some carefully washed, pitted and dried **currants** or some ordinary black **raisins**, and a fistful of **pine nuts** or any other nuts, and serve with a sweet **mayonnaise** (see recipe 1001) or **grape syrup** concentrate, or with **honey** and **lemon juice**.

Drinks and herb teas

BIBITE E TISANE CRUDE

1004. Almond milk
LATTE DI MANDORLE O MANDORLATA

Peel **4 oz sweet almonds** that have been soaked for 12 hours in fresh water, grind and roll in a cheesecloth. Tie the cloth up and plunge into **½ pint water**. (Alternatively, you can use a cheesecloth bag.) Wring out well and repeat the process several times. The milk can be sweetened with **honey**. It is excellent for people with stomach complaints.

Alternatively, you can use a blender or food processor: Simply add 1½ cups of water to the almonds and blend on high. Then pour the mixture through a cheesecloth.

1005. Coconut milk
LATTE DI COCCO

Follow the recipe for almond milk, substituting shaved cononut.

1006. Tonics with juice
BIBITE EFFICIENTI ALLO SCIROPPO D'UVA

All fresh fruit juices are excellent tonics and, among these, grape juice, which contains all the vitamin properties of the grape, is highly recommended. Add soda water if you wish.

1007. Herb teas and tonic infusions
TISANE ED INFUSI EFFICIENTI

These can be made in a double boiler (under 100°F). So as to fully extract the vital properties of the herbs, these must be kept at a lower temperature for slightly longer. When prepared this way your herb teas and tonics will be more aromatic and healthy.

1008. Peanut butter
PINDAKAAS

A vegetarian staple, which Alliata includes as a beverage. In the first edition of this book, Alliata recommended a new variety—manufactured by the Dutch firm W.A.L. Nienhins—that had just arrived on the Italian market. It is sadly no longer available.

1009. Fresh olives
OLIVE RIPIENE EFFICIENTI

Choose **new olives** (see recipe 883), which have not been treated in any way and consequently retain all their food value. Serve with a **mayonnaise dressing** or with **chopped fresh garlic** and **parsley**, **oil**, and **lemon**.

List of recipes

718 Australian pudding
719 Baroness pudding
720 Admiral pudding
721 Amber pudding
722 Bread and butter pudding
723 English Christmas pudding
724 Fruit tart
725 Meringue cake
726 Neapolitan cake
727 Pine nut cake
728 Apple tart
729 Apple tartlets
730 'Frangipane'
731 Almond 'frangipane'
732 Tuscan 'frangipane'
733 Sweet buns
734 Rum babà
735 Savarin
736 Apple Charlotte
737 Strudel
738 Watermelon gelatin mold
739 Strawberry gelatin mold
740 Angelic food
741 Baked bananas
742 Mocha cake
743 Buttered apples
744 Presnitz
745 Sicilian 'buccellato' (mincemeat)
746 Cherry soup
747 Rita's cake
748 English tea pastries
749 Candied watermelon
750 Bignés
751 Lady's kisses
752 Peach tarts
753 Plum tarts
754 Apricot tarts
755 Almond bread
756 Stuffed bread
757 D. E. A. S. bread (Duke Enrico Alliata of Salaparuta bread)

758 D. E. A. S. rice bread (Duke Enrico Alliata of Salaparuta rice bread)
759 Citrus flavored bread
760 Sardinian bignés (also called 'zeppole')
761 Pearly rice
762 Tuscan 'mostarda' fritters
763 Iris
764 Apples in batter
765 Fried peaches
766 Kitchenmaid's fritters
767 Rice fritters
768 Pancakes
769 Sweet krapfen
770 Neapolitan pastry
771 Cream 'bombette'
772 St Joseph's cream puffs
773 Sicilian cassata
774 Cream fritters
775 Vanilla tidbits
776 German bread
777 Genoese cake
778 St Lucy's rice ('cuccìa')
779 Corn bread rolls
780 'Straccetti' (rags)
781 Neapolitan 'pastiera' (Easter cake)
782 Italian cake
783 Sponge cake
784 German cake
785 Tuscan sweet bread
786 Bologna bread
787 Sicilian 'pasta reale' (marzipan)
788 Jellied quince
789 Ginette
790 Sicilian quince jellies
791 English marzipan
792 Pastry sandwiches
793 Neapolitan sweet pizza
794 Sicilian bignés
795 Duchess biscuits
796 Crumble cake

797 D. E. A. S. tartlets (Duke Enrico Alliata of Salaparuta tartlets)
798 Apple waffles
799 Pistachio waffles
800 'Four-fourths' pistachio cake
801 Almond crunch
802 Almond buns
803 Ravioli in wine
804 Egg white puffs
805 Belgian fried apples
806 Chilean delicacies
807 Milk 'panzarotte'
808 Fried egg surprise
809 Candied squash ('zuccata')
810 'Panzarotte' with jam
811 Mountaineer's 'buccellati'
812 Hazelnut bomb
813 Wafers
814 Tea cakes
815 Almond cakes
816 Cocoa almond cakes
817 Novara cookies
818 Custard
819 Mocha gelatin mold
820 Blackcurrant gelatin mold
821 Cream gelatin mold
822 Orange gelatin mold
823 Sour cherry gelatin mold
824 Tangerine gelatin mold

ICE CREAM AND PARFAITS

825 Apricot parfait
826 Banana parfait
827 Tangerine parfait
828 Lemon parfait
829 Orange parfait
830 Peach parfait
831 Pineapple parfait
832 Strawberry parfait
833 Watermelon parfait
834 Toasted almond parfait

929 Tomatoes with walnuts
and onion
930 Stuffed tomatoes with truffles
931 Lemons
932 Squash with tart apples
933 White cabbage
934 Spicy tidbits
935 Raw truffles
936 Avocados
937 Special lettuce
938 Turnips with an herb dressing
939 Fennel with a nut dressing
940 Coconuts
941 Carrots
942 Lettuce and beets
943 Triple fortified
vegetarian salad
944 Cauliflower
945 Corn with mayonnaise
946 Tender wheat in sauce
947 Chickpeas with sauce
948 Artichokes
949 Green fava beans and
artichokes in sauce
950 Lemon salad
951 Corn with tomato
and cucumber
952 Scorzonera salad
(scorzonera hispanica)
953 Mixed salad
954 Spinach salad
955 Natural olives
956 Chestnuts
957 Melon salad
958 Melon, dressed up
959 Sour truffled apples
960 Sour apples with carrots
and chestnuts
961 Tomatoes with walnut stuffing
962 Tomatoes with
chestnut stuffing
963 Stuffed baby onions
964 Orange salad

FRESH DAIRY PRODUCE

965 Milk curds
966 Fresh cream ('fiordilatte')
967 Fresh butter
968 Heavy (double) cream cheeses

RAW SAUCES

969 Pink sauce
970 Green sauce
971 Tomato paste
972 'Salamoriglio'

**RAW BREAD AND
BREAD ROLLS**

973 Raw bread
974 Fig bread
975 Peanut and almond bread
976 Sugar-free bread for diabetics
and weightwatchers
977 Carob bread
978 Chestnut bread
979 Almond and rice loaf
980 Cocoa loaf
981 Date and walnut loaf

RAW SWEET DISHES

982 Marzipan or almond paste
983 Marzipan with pistachio nuts
984 'Buccellato crudista'
(dried minced fruit rolled
in almond paste)
985 Canapés with raw fillings
986 Stuffed dates
987 Coconut pudding
988 Carob pudding
989 Chestnut pudding
990 Pistachio pudding
991 Bitter orange pudding
992 Stuffed apples
993 Pear compote
994 Winter compote

995 Uncooked chocolate
996 Cookies
997 Cantaloupe with grape syrup
998 Flat fig loaf with grape syrup
999 Oranges with a coconut and
almond topping
1000 Dried fruit compote
1001 Fruit salad with a sweet
mayonnaise
1002 Spring fruit salad
1003 Winter fruit salad

DRINKS AND HERB TEAS

1004 Almond milk
1005 Coconut milk
1006 Tonics with juice
1007 Herb teas and tonic infusions
1008 Peanut butter
1009 Fresh olives

Index

Polenta from Lodi, 78
Potatoes, 81
Red Pudding, 100
Truffle Squares, 179
White Pudding, 100

H

Hazelnut(s)
  and Almond Cream, 246
  Bomb, 228
  Nut-Flavored Milk Disks, 136
  Parfait, 235
  Spicy Tidbits, 274
Herb(s). *See also specific herbs*
  Chopped, Sauce (Hachée), 197
  Dressing, Turnips with a, 275
  Eggs 'alla Marinara' (Sailor-
    Style) or in Green
    Sauce, 144
  Eggs with, 145
  Eggs with Sage, 143–44
  Empress Style, 143
  Omelet, 149
  'Ravigotta' Sauce, 196
  Salmi, 198
  'Salmoriglio,' 285
  Scallops, 139
  Teas and Tonic Infusions, 297

I

Ice cream and parfaits
  Apricot Parfait, 233
  Banana Parfait, 233
  Chocolate Cream, 236
  Fresh Coconut Parfait, 235
  Hazelnut Parfait, 235
  Lemon Parfait, 233–34
  Mocha or Chocolate
    Parfait, 235
  Orange Parfait, 234

Peach Parfait, 234
Pineapple Parfait, 234
Pistachio Parfait, 235
Roman Punch, 236
Strawberry Parfait, 234
Tangerine Parfait, 233
Tea Ice Cream, 236
Toasted Almond Parfait, 234–35
Toffee Ice Cream, 236
Walnut Parfait, 235
Watermelon Parfait, 234

J

Jam(s)
  Apricot, 240
  Blueberry, 240
  'Panzarotte' with, 227
  Pear, 240
  Strawberry and Currant, 241
Jellies
  Apple, 241
  Neapolitan Medlars in
    Gelatin, 241
  Sterilized Grape Syrup, 241

K

Ketchup, 197
Krapfen
  in Broth, 46–47
  Savory, 176
  Sweet, 217–18

L

Leek(s)
  'Duxellese' Minestra, 69–70
  Soup, 71
Legumes. *See also* Bean(s); Lentil(s)
  Dried, and Cereals, Minestra
    with, 270–71

Dutch Cutlets, 178–79
German Style Vegetarian
  Scallops, 137
Médaillons in Salmi, 138
Mock Meat Ravioli, 179
nutritional value, 25
Vegetarian Meat Loaf, 137
Vegetarian Steaks, 138
Lemon(s), 274
  Cream Gelatin Mold, 229
  Green, Marmalade, 239
  and Orange Syrup, 247–48
  Parfait, 233–34
  preserving, 254
  Roman Punch, 236
  Salad, 277
  'Salmoriglio,' 285
  'Salmoriglio' Sauce, 192
  Sandwiches, 36–37
Lentil(s)
  'alla Cantiniera,' 85
  Chilean, 68
  English Style Mock
    Meatballs, 139
  Imperial Purée, 51
  Italian-Style Broth, 44
  Mock Foie Gras, 163
  or Bean Purée, 50
  or Cream of Lentils Purée, 53
  with Pasta (Minestra), 65
  Pie, 163
  Purée with Tapioca, 49
  and Rice Minestra, 72
  Soup, Egyptian Style, 71
  Springtime Purée, 53
  Superior Vegetarian Broth, 44
Lettuce
  and Beets, 276
  and Egg Salad, 38, 148
  'Fidellini' and Mayonnaise, 37
  Pasha Chops (a Savory Rolled
    in Cabbage or Lettuce
    Leaves), 136–37

A NOTE ON THE TYPE

This book is set in Bembo, a typeface designed by Stanley Morison for the Monotype Corporation in 1929. It is based on letterforms created by Francesco Griffo for the Venetian printer Aldus Manutius around 1495.

Small headings are set in Neutraface, designed by Christian Schwartz for House Industries in 2002 and influenced by the modernist work of architect Richard Neutra.

The typeface used for chapter titles and recipe names is Salaparuta Script, designed by Melville House especially for this volume. It is an upright script inspired by Italian lettering from the 1920s and '30s.